• HALSGROVE DISCOVER SERIES ➤

ONE MAN'S MOOR

An exploration of aspects of Dartmoor

WILLIAM D. LETHBRIDGE

HALSGROVE

British Library Cataloguing-in-Publication Data
A CIP record for this title is available from the British Library

ISBN 1 84114 515 7
ISBN 978 1 84114 515 0

HALSGROVE
Halsgrove House
Lower Moor Way
Tiverton, Devon EX16 6SS
Tel: 01884 243242
Fax: 01884 243325
email: sales@halsgrove.com
website: www.halsgrove.com

Printed and bound by D'Auria Industrie Grafiche Spa, Italy

Author's Preface

I have trekked Dartmoor's acreage for just over thirty-five years. However, I have also over several of those years travelled around the world quite extensively, touring Iceland to view that country's exciting natural phenomenons, as well as its birdlife. I have trekked in the high Himalayas in Nepal, from the sub-tropics to snow level, been on safari in Africa, swam among literally millions of Carp in a pea green lake in a defunct volcano on the Samoan island of Upolu and had lunch with village elders under the roof of their community Fale, travelled to the depths of the Grand Canyon, toured western Russia, before perestroika, travelled the length of Canada by train, stopping off to snowmobile in the rocky Mountains and dog sleigh into the depth of pine forest. I have also visited Thailand, Malaysia, Singapore and the Maldives, Cuba, Ecuador and the Galapagos Islands, where good photo shots were impossible to miss.

One of my loves is the prehistoric sites around Europe, especially in Brittany, where I have visited and photographed almost every standing stone, stone row and tomb.

But no matter how far and wide my travels have taken me, Dartmoor calls as soon as I arrive home. If asked why, I reply it is because there is beauty everywhere, all over the world, but Dartmoor is so accessible, it is on my doorstep, it has a charm of colourful ruggedness. Up on the moor every day is different, often a corner is turned or a hill is climbed and the aspect that comes into view takes your breath away, like listening to a piece of music when, somewhere in its midst, its sheer beauty swallows your entire being until some intrusion brings you back down to earth.

It is Dartmoor's river valleys that are the most positive attractions. I never walk in a straight line but meander here and there with eyes peeled for whatever is there to see. Among the interesting items I have found and recorded is a stone row on the escarpment below Shell Top, a covered kistvaen on Giant's Hill, and a holed stone along with one or two mortar stones that were generally unknown to us. I decided to write this work in order to plough something back, a thank you if you like, for the pleasure the area has given to me.

William D. Lethbridge
Plympton, Devon
2006

Acknowledgements

First I must thank my wife for being so very supportive, in being there behind me during the eleven long years of research and writing. My thanks also go to my children who have enthusiastically encouraged when frustration and self-doubt has crept into my thoughts.

Reaching out to those individuals and organisations that have given their time freely and willingly to help in the project, I thank wholeheartedly, as they come to mind: Len and Triff Vincent; Mr and Mrs Hext of Newton Abbot; Colonel and Mrs Spencer; John Anscome; Mr and Mrs Dewdney; Horace Northam; Mr E.S. Lock (North Hessary Television Station); The BBC; Hugh Robinson (of the DPA); Mr F.G. Warne; Doug Pidgeon (Leat Man); William George Shillibeer (and thanks to Vera his wife for the coffee, cakes and jam and cream scones during my visits); Mr Taylor; Mr B. Palmer; the Legassick family; the William's family of Yeo Farm, Meavy and their neighbours the Thompson family; Mrs Elizabeth Beer née Ware; John Ware; Wilfred Ware; George and Margaret Dunne of Brisworthy; Mr and Mrs Cyril of Trowlesworthy; Frank Sercombe (Dartmoor China Clay); Jeff Hackney of Wadham College, Oxford University; James (Jim) Woolcombe; Colin Moore (South West Water Authority); Professor R.I. Page, Corpus Christi College, Cambridge University; Dr Sandy Gerrard; Shirley Blaylock (National Trust); Mark Pool, Torquay Reference Library; Mrs Virginia Brisco, St Albans, Herts; Eric Ash, former WBB Director; John Pike, former WBB Managing Director, for allowing me to peruse at leisure a mountain of WBB archives; John Silverlock for his information on Hemerdon China Clay Works; Heather Harvey, née Olver, for information on the family's time at Small Hanger; Terry Fry; John Lee; Cris Cleave, EEC; Robert Williams, for the occasional walk and measuring outings taken with me; Mrs Brenda Williams; Ted Tossell; Arthur Vanstone; George Prout; David and Violet Pummel; Phillis Harner, née Vincent; Tom Selleck; Libby Stuart, Duchy of Cornwall; Ann, Debbie and Alan at the Plymouth & West Devon Records Office. Wheel Martin China Clay Museum: Plymouth Local studies Library; Truro Record Office; Devon Record Office, Exeter; Record Office, London; *Evening Herald* and the *Western Morning News*; The Domesday Book (Devon); Rodney Castleden's *British History*. I am indebted to John my son-in-law, Alan Wills and Dave Dawson for putting me on the right road with my early computer efforts.

A special mention must be made towards the books of William Crossing and R.H. Worth for they gave me the inspiration to trek deep into the moor and seek out what was there to be seen and found. I must not forget Trixy, my youngest daughter's faithful little Jack Russell, and my own dear friend Toffee, for the pleasure of their company on many a walk, both now sadly deceased.

All colour photographs and illustrations are by the author.

Contents

Chapter 1   *The Railway to Princetown*   7

Chapter 2   *North Hessary Tor*   25

Chapter 3   *Old Tin Workings*   39

Chapter 4   *Water*   97

Chapter 5   *The Warrens*   133

Chapter 6   *China Clay*   165

The Sister Rivers of Southern Dartmoor

Every stage has a backcloth to enhance the drama created in front of it; the imposing jagged ruggedness mounting the hills above the beautiful Burrator reservoir, backdrops the river Meavy from almost all angles of its stage, the magnificent twin peaks of Leather Tor and Sharpitor, along with Sheepstor's impressive bulk, dominate where the Meavy tributaries converge into one. Each hold secrets of history around every corner, along every sparkling stream, for the inquisitive to ponder, where man has toiled, created and abandoned, allowing time to close in and shroud his labour with mystery. No other Dartmoor valley bears the scars of man's endeavour quite like the little sister of the Plym.

There are Stone Rows from a prehistoric age,
winding roads and lanes.
A vestige of a tramway,
and a bed for bygone trains.

Old dry stone walls survive, still standing,
others lay like debris on the ground;
vermin traps foil the weasel,
sparing rabbits in the pillow mounds.

Root crops were pulled and stored,
in the frost free potato caves;
and dead folk of Bronze Age times,
were interred in the cold granite graves.

Tinners' workings everywhere,
revealing misty glimpses of their past;
a long forgotten firing range, sits,
under the redundant television mast.

Great evergreens form the plantation,
where once spread a cluster of Farms;
chequered fields lay brown under branches,
killing dead, their once rustic charm

Creeps allow sheep to wander on the moor,
ancient crosses show the way;
leats now feed the reservoir,
that still quells a thirst, for the present day.

CHAPTER 1

The Railway to Princetown

Far fewer words would be required to write this chapter if Thomas Tyrwhitt had not arrived and settled within our midst. This gent leased well over two thousand acres of boulder-strewn moorland from his friend the Prince of Wales, choosing a plot to develop which hemmed the border of Walkhampton Common, with the 'keep-like' tor of South Hessary watching over it.

Thomas grew up within the cradle of the church, his father being a wealthy vicar helped his silver spoon to glisten and learning meant an Eton schooling, then on to Christchurch, Oxford, earning a Master of Arts and a Doctor at Law. Life introduced him to the very privileged, including the Prince of Wales, to whom he became Private Secretary.

The date was now 1785 and at the energetically young age of twenty-three, he moved away from the bosom of his family's Essex home to pursue deeply into an adventure on the barren emptiness of Dartmoor. Naming the acreage 'Tor Royal', he set about clearing its surface of rocks and boulders, utilising their usefulness to build the land's enclosing walls, leaving the sparse soil free to be turned, harrowed and seeded, transforming the waste into a sea of waving flax. Intentional vision or a natural expansion of a creation, cottages were built to house the labour, roads laid to here and there and an inn, the Plume of Feathers, where to drink and be merry, after a hard day's toil. The miracle on the moor was growing.

As his busy schedules raced by, tremendous strides in various directions of opportunity were made by Thomas; he was appointed Auditor to the Duchy of Cornwall, Lord Warden of the Stannaries, and became a Member of Parliament, representing three different seats in turn, including Okehampton and Plymouth. His influential standing persuaded the government to build a prison to house the French Prisoners of War, hitherto held in hulks in the Tamar estuary. The land surveyed for the project was two miles from the house of Tor Royal, just a stone's throw and a little more from the Plume of Feathers. Thomas laid the customary foundation stone when construction began during the

Dartmoor Prison.

Tramway stone sleepers.

very cold winds of March in 1806. For three years men tore the heart out of the Walkhampton Tors, quarrying and shaping the granite to build the prison that was to hold the enemy from the war. Barracks for the military guard, a corn mill, brewery and more housing sprang up. A fair and a market was granted to the area, which was by now named Prince's Town, in honour of Thomas's friend and patron, the Prince of Wales.

The Meavy weeps to the sea from a mire on a bitter windswept col, eluding the vast central basin of Dartmoor by no more than a few yards, trickling quietly through a reed bed, before seeping its way over and around the beautiful spreading bog moss near the brow of Devil's Bridge Hill. History tells a story where the Meavy is born:

> *Here many miles from home,*
> *to them in a hostile land,*
> *men trudged by, wearily hobbling, limping,*
> *war wounds festering, gangrene stinking.*
>
> *Defeated men of a dictator's army,*
> *filed past in ones and twos,*
> *the weak almost to their knees,*
> *whilst the strong in mind and limb, shoulder the amputees.*
>
> *Fifteen miles and more from Devil's Point*
> *and the distance was nearly done;*
> *from the rat infested Prison Hulks,*
> *the kettle drums and guns of battles they never won.*
>
> *Fourteen hundred feet higher than the sea,*
> *the cold moorland mist was down,*
> *and Thomas Tyrwhitt's new prison built to house them,*
> *and their memories to drown.*
>
> *They fought and lost in the rawness of war,*
> *Wellington to conquer their general.*
> *A small man, like Nelson, disfigured;*
> *to the British a tyrant a scoundrel.*

The stench of Trafalgar, burning flesh, the blood,
the guns, the screams, leaping flames of fire;
Nelson lay fatally wounded in Victory,
sending men wearily hobbling, limping,
gangrene stinking, past the weeping mire.

Later, American captives from the skirmishes with President Jefferson, after he closed US ports to all British warships in 1807, were to endure a sea journey over the Atlantic Ocean. Pioneers and settlers, most of European descent, made their way grudgingly past the same mire, to join the French in the grey granite hell hole of Dartmoor prison, hundreds never to see a future materialise in the great Land of Promise, dying before hostilities ceased and the peace treaties were signed in 1816.

Time for Thomas Tyrwhitt had gone by at its usual pace, never still for a moment, keeping a path for life fresh and clear, ready for him to accept that which came his way. He had vacated his parliamentary seat, been appointed to the prestigious post as Gentleman Usher of the Black Rod, and a sword had touched his shoulder to announce him a knight.

Tramway stone sleepers near Plymbridge.

The avenue of events for Prince's Town fell silent when the last of the internees were released to freedom, allowing a quiet decade to drift slowly by, leaving nothing but the rustic life of a declining rural populace to fill an ever-widening breach in Sir Thomas's expectations for his moorland domain. A multi-racial society under armed guard had gone, leaving the quiet atmosphere of the moor shattered with their passing.

But by now the forever industrious Sir Thomas had visions of a railway to connect Plymouth with Prince's Town. The idea conceived, it did not come to fruition until 1826 when the last stretch of line from King's Tor to Prince's Town was eventually laid, passing the Meavy head mire before reaching its destination just yards away, where the Devil's Elbow Inn (latterly the Railway Inn) stands.

Fresh enthusiasm pulsated through the area, harnessed horses oozing white lather of sweat, pulling drays laden with freight, provisions and huge pieces of granite cut and fashioned to suit the need of some new structural design for buildings many miles away.

Tramway bridge over the Yestor Brook.

After much land-owning wrangling and local bureaucratic activity Sir Thomas laid the first stone for his new railway enterprise after Parliament gave it its blessing. One hundred feet and more beneath the fields of Leigham a tunnel over six hundred yards in length was burrowed; bridges were built, embankments raised and cuttings deep and shallow excavated. Literally thousands of granite sleepers, along with a few of slate and limestone, were cut and laid to carry the rails that ran eventually from Sutton Harbour right up into the heart of the moor.

The line wound and climbed to fourteen hundred feet from beside the tidal waters of the Plym estuary, gradually elevating horse-drawn wagons high above the deciduous woodlands

Tyrwhitt's stables on Roborough Down.

The eleven-mile stone, now missing.

Tramway on Roborough Down.

The twelve-mile stone, beside the track at Yelverton.

of the beautiful lower Plym valley, twisting and winding serpent-like through stream-trickling, leaf-dappled combes. The whining screech of steel straining over steel echoed as the contour arcs were traversed, passing green fields and farmyards until the heath of Roborough Down was reached. Here a wonderful panorama progressively opened up into view: a little turn of the head to the right finds Shaugh Moor and the hump of Wigford Down, and far beyond, fading into the blue, is Shell Top. To the left of this lofty eminence stretches the seemingly never-ending Langcombe Ridge which converges with the great hill of Eylesbarrow, Raddick Hill and the rugged Meavy tors. The stone marking the eleven-mile point (now missing) is passed before the dominating skyline of the Walkham comes into view. Just a little farther on, Tyrwhitt's stables await the tired horses with rest, hay and clean bedding. With fresh pulling power, the harnessed wagons trundle on, shod hooves clip-clopping or splashing between the railway sleepers, while the line meanders over a terrain more suited to the wagon-master's task, giving licence for his wits to rest, before the thunder of exertion climbing, heaving, pounding and snorting around the curves of Yennadon and the quarried tors where the springs flow into the Walkham. Prince's Town is just a little while away; time for rest before the return journey down again.

The Plymouth & Dartmoor Tramway had arrived, but not without financial complications. The inadequate estimated cost resulted in fretting concern for the principal investor, Tyrwhitt, who had invested £1000 in the scheme. The building of the line now came to a halt for twelve long months, nearly three miles short of its designated terminus, until Mr Johnson, the line's contractor, brought relief to Thomas's sweating brow by injecting resources from his pocket to finish a truly wonderful enterprise. But, alas, ill fate was beginning to intervene in Sir Thomas Tyrwhitt's life of adventures.

The Massey Lopes estate could see the advantages of a tramway passing through its land, so much so, it gave the family the incentive to become the major shareholder in the project, entrusting the venture's route to their part-time surveyor, William Shillibeer, who was also the Headmaster at Walkhampton School. This extremely able man chose the contours of this railway masterpiece, not knowing it would hold intrigue for generations long after its struggling death-throes finally subsided and the short life it lived came to a sad and reluctant end.

In his seventieth year, Thomas an ailing old man, could see his market town (now known as Princetown) dying, and with it died his own creative instincts to battle on. For the first time in a highly successful and distinguished life he was meeting failure. There were no other doors to open and for him financial doom came before the mournful sound of life's tolling bell. Sir Thomas knocked on the door as Black Rod for the last time and sold his beloved Tor Royal to the highest bidder, leaving this disenchanted old bachelor to cross the English Channel to live in the warmer climate of Calais. Sadly his days lasted only twelve months more. Unlike other noted Westcountry people his reputation did not follow him into history and only a small monument to his memory can be found at Princetown, in the Church of St Michael, the place of worship that was built by the French and Americans during their time in his prison

Within a few generations the exploits of various industries and sheer total neglect have eaten away at the twenty-four-mile-long abandoned tramway, leaving little evidence of its once proud existence. But the lack of major structural features hardly detracts from the pleasures of a stroll along accessible sections of what remains of this little wonder. A number of milestones are passed, of which only eight now remain. Twelve inches across, they are cylindrical in shape and fashioned with an inclined top bearing inwards to the track neatly and lightly inscribed, counting down the miles to go.

High above the valley, the meandering bed traverses,
Sharp, around curves where tiny streamlets cry,
From the wooded hillside, steep, down into the Plym.

Around ranks of Granite Sets,
Aged oaks and beech protrude their weaving roots.
Moss and ivy clothe Cuttings, dank and musty,
Where rain, waters muddy pools

Symphonies of wind play in the trees;
Little Wrens sing out
from concealment among the waving leaves.

Clamber beneath pink rhododendron and storm-ravaged boughs,
Foxgloves for light grow tall;

Pennywort and fern grace a certain charm,
And lichen shrouds a wall.

Blackthorn and bracken shade the redundant way,
And rabbits use the banks to burrow.
Stunted shining bluebells carpet around,
And sets ripped out replaced by the furrow.

Walk between heather, and gorse bearing yellow flowers,
When the day is still.
Walk along the leats, through lingering scent of blossom in May,
When chaffinch show off their echoing trill.

Yennadon and the higher moor,
Dramatic views fading, deep into the sky.
Cattle graze, the skylarks sing,
Ravens black, croak, their presence on thermals high.

On a bend the Yes Tor Brook is spanned,
Where sets are built into the walls.
Above, quarries whisper in the wind, the ghost of yesterday.
On the wing a buzzard calls.

Tyrwhitt's dream came to an end,
The Plume of Feathers is still there.
Let's drink to the man who created the story:
The Tramway, left to die without care.

The future held no respect for Sir Thomas Tyrwhitt's creation and fifty years after his death it was abandoned, left to disintegrate and fall into the ruin we see today.

Financially embarrassed for the majority of its working life, the old tramway from Princetown to Yelverton was sold to the newly-formed Princetown Railway Company, its standard gauge track, bar a few deviations, coursed the same route. It linked with the South Devon & Tavistock Railway at Yelverton and for the first time a gateway from the moor to Plymouth and countrywide was open. For many people, previously cocooned in the heart of nowhere, the steam railway opened up new horizons. While some, wrapped in isolation, were content with life, others were eager to see what other places offered – a wish fulfilled to while time away in the city, to visit a friend or relation, and to get back in time to satisfy the hours one laboured.

High summer spread a warm glow on the muted celebrations when the line opened in 1883. The system was incomplete, with the line terminating at Horrabridge, and the intended station and siding at Yelverton yet to be built. The people of that hamlet apparently cared little to have a goods depot with its associated rolling stock in their midst, fearing its noisy presence would bring the tone of the area down. Nevertheless compromises were eventually reached and two years later steam drew breath from the flames and the train pulled out of Yelverton Station. The Princetown Company had got their railway, but, like the South Devon & Tavistock line, the strings were pulled by the mighty Great Western.

Princetown Station and its sidings lay beside the ever-running spring of Meavy Head. With the sun's rays spreading their warmth on a late summer's day, time rests lazily on the quiet, idyllic scene. Trucks are laden and coaches stand waiting. The engine taking water stands silent but for the occasional hiss of steam.

The Station Master, lapels held fast, so proudly standing,
Someone reading, another walking.
There's someone sitting, whistling,
Men laughing and ladies talking.

The points are set, the signal's down,
The Train is about to leave.
The flag is waved, the whistle's blown,
For a journey around the tors to weave.

Yet the scene is different in wind and rain,
When the mist is down, in ice and snow.
The Station Master wears a frown,
Because wheels won't turn and the train can't go.

Terribly severe winters on the moor,
Often laid the branchline low,
In 1891 a blizzard blew,
Holding passengers marooned in the freezing snow.

Yelverton Station. Waiting for the Down train.

Two days after the blizzard, not far from Routrundle, where now stands a lonely pine, a farmer and his dog out searching and digging for buried sheep heard calls for help and found the train to be all but covered by snow. The grateful passengers, six in all, and the train's crew, were eventually escorted to safety and comfort by the farmer to his home near Eggworthy. It was early March and for days the weather screamed across the moor, whipping snow into flurries, hampering many attempt to free the stricken engine and coaches. After eight days in a freezing hell the conditions gave way at last, and after tremendously exhausting labour the wheels of the train were freed.

From Princetown the steam railway track leaves the wide open space of the moor via the outer fields of Horseyeat Farm and within a few yards parts company with the old Tramway bed it has more or less followed so far. A patchwork of farmland mellowing into the distant heights of Cornwall is rewarding to the eye as the train heads towards Lowery level-crossing and the keeper's cottage. For 44 years the crossing keeper held this job in picturesque surroundings until warning bells operated by the oncoming train made his job redundant, and his cottage was let.

From the crossing, the lower eastern slope of Yennadon Down is traversed, where trees of oak, beech and hazel skirting the track flit by. Views, almost close enough to touch, reveal spectacular scenery: the spread of Downtor and Combshead backdropped by the high hills of the Plym's deciduous woodland and small granite-walled farms. In the valley below once stood the ancient Manor of Longstone, where the foot of mighty Sheepstor once bathed in the Meavy. But this frameless picture, with the scene's reflections shimmering in the water, was to change with the construction of Burrator Reservoir.

For five years, until the man-made lake was completed and silence again settled back into the valley, the railway benefited from its construction, carrying workmen and materials and of course the curious wishing to see what was going on. But the train ran only as far as Dousland, and the one and half miles to the site had to be walked and materials transported by road.

In 1922 the renowned Great Western Railway wrapped an arm around the little line and pulled it fully into its system. Two years later, twenty-six years after Burrator Reservoir was finished, a halt was built on Yennadon, overlooking the small 'sea' on the edge of the moor, its construction coinciding with the raising of the dam, and bringing in a little more revenue to keep the train on the rails.

The line finished its curving route to Yennadon by once again running along the ghost of the old Tramway, for a while looking into gardens of dwellings, and through the gates of Prowes's Crossing, before entering Dousland Station.

Seasons come and go, with most winters' trials best forgotten, allowing them to fade into history, but every now and then a wild evil strikes in full-blown fury across Dartmoor's barren heights and normal life cedes to the Colossus from above. The years 1891 and 1947 troubled man and beast alike, the latter winter seeming to last forever. The sky blackened and came to rest above the moor as the storm howled its ferocity, drifting snow deep over the bleak landscape, with Princetown and Dousland held captive in its grip. Snowplough engines came to a halt, half buried in a vast sheet of whiteness. Troops were employed to aid the almost impossible task, and the line was cleared then buried again until spring daffodils pushed their greenery through to signal the winter's end. The snow melted away and with it dwindled the fortunes of this delightful little railway.

Aching for better days that were never to come, the line nearly always suffered economically, and as technology advanced other industries so the line's money matters worsened even more. Granite hauled by train from the Walkham quarries was forsaken in preference to concrete products in the building trade. The introduction of the motor car, lorries and bus routes throughout the various districts of the moor took further revenue away from the line. The railway faced the losing battle of survival, with halts being introduced at Ingra Tor and Kings Tor, to interest the hardened hiker and holiday walker, but to no avail. On New Year's Day 1948, nationalization devoured the revered GWR system and renamed it Western Region, leaving history to tell the tales and legends of the romance of the railways.

Steam evaporates over the train as it passes along the embankment overlooking the two dry leats from the moor. The engine runs freely here, hissing, and emitting no smoke on the downhill gradient leaving the saddle on the Meavy–Walkham ridge. Through the cutting it runs and under the iron aqueducts that once carried the water of the leats, and on between the outer dwellings of Yelverton. The village of Meavy is seen against the winter's morning sun, mingling with the trees beneath the expanse of Ringmoor Down, while the train with Engine 4568 pushing the coaches ahead of it, curves sharply into Yelverton Station and the end of the line.

'Praps tiz wispers an roomers, but ther's a yarn gwain roun', they'm closin us down.' For Months despondency reigned in Doom and Gloom, with hearsay travelling up and down the line, telephones red hot with the latest. 'There's no smoke without fire, y'naw,' said one. 'Tiz true, tiz,' said another. The flames of surmising became uncontrollable when in 1955 the rumours sadly became reality. The staff were told officially of the dreaded day and notices were pasted up for all to see.

CLOSURE OF LINE
YELVERTON TO PRINCETOWN
THE BRITISH TRANSPORT COMMISSION
HEREBY GIVE NOTICE THAT ON AND FROM...

Letters of protest came pouring in from various individuals, groups and parties. The volume of passenger traffic grew enormously for the last few months of its life as enthusiasts and sentimentalist came from far and wide to pass on their feelings, to share their thoughts, to look and ride – some bringing their children who had never seen the little railway before, but who could say in later years 'I rode on the Princetown Branchline Train'.

The last train drew out of Princetown Station at 10.06pm on Saturday evening, 3 March 1956, with 200 people packed on board. As the two engines and six coaches disappeared out into the moor, dusk fell into darkness and the line was to be travelled no more by train.

Within twelve months, 73 years of the branchline's history was picked clean, devoured by the vultures of demolition, leaving just the track-bed skeleton weaving its path into visual oblivion and a ghost of fawn and brown to drift in a hazy existence in one's own imagination.

Five years later, the Plymouth to Launceston line fell like a severed limb from a rotting tree, amputated to suit the economic strategy of Dr Beecham. There is nowhere emptier, quieter or lonelier than a country station when the last train disappears from view and its sounds fade into nothing. A final signal-box manoeuvre and a short tuneless whistle from a porter were all that met the dying embers of the day when Yelverton Station closed in 1962.

Colonel Spencer or, just plain Dick to all who knew him well, reclaimed the station land back again for his family and asked that all buildings, including the turntable, should be dismantled and taken away, leaving just the platforms and tunnel. He then allowed his wish to run its course, letting nature declare its presence and brush a touch of magical Eden over a natural developing wildlife reserve. Now the tunnel and the cutting's sheer twin face back-drops a sanctuary for all but the permanent presence of man.

Tunnel at Yelverton Station today.

It has become a translucent wonderland,
In all shades of green,
Exuding the colour, gently touching, gently kissing,
A lovely secluded scene.

Wandering through this haven,
Passed plumes of graceful fern,
Songbirds sing and rays of sunlight,
Warm a peace we yearn.

Water oozes, seeping, shimmering,
Dripping from the slate;
Ivy pendulates, over red brick platforms,
Gone is the station kissing gate.

Great beech trees tower over all that is there,
Looking down on the changes,
Through the seasons of the year.

Variegated Lamium silver and green,
And creeping buttercups carpet the floor,
Where the rumble of wheels and sounds from the station,
Are gone, to be heard no more.

I can fully understand the fondness that is felt locally for the late Colonel and Mrs Spencer. I met them for the first time after making a telephone call wishing to see the site of the station: 'If I am not here, Dick will be,' Mrs Spencer assured me, with her throat sounding as if liquid refreshment would take the rasping away, apologizing for the state of her early morning voice before putting the receiver down. Half an hour later, I pulled up quietly alongside the white-painted house, tyres crunching on the chipping driveway as I came to a stop. In front of my car were bantam hens with chicks scratching, feeding, the more colourful cock bird head held high strutting, uttering, and white doves, wings fluttering.

'Good morning!' from a cultured voice was the welcome, along with a firm but slightly quivering handshake. 'My wife tells me you would like to see the old station site.'

We spoke for a while about who we were and delved a little deeper into what I wanted to do there. I immediately felt at ease in the company of this old soldier. In the mid-morning early summer sunshine, he wore a tie slackened slightly in its knot, a sports jacket, twill trousers and heavy brogues, yet not a drop of perspiration showed on his brow, while my shirt clung firmly to my back.

The conversation drifted from today, as he reminisced, talking of times gone by, of how the station staff preferred to catch their drinking water from the dripping slate, a bowl-shape dug out of the cutting's face and a length of pipe placed just so, to act as an ever-running tap, never stopping even in the driest of summers. A smile turned almost to a chuckle when he told of how the men would help themselves to eggs for breakfast from a poor old hen that had made a nest in a nearby hedgerow. How in the depth of freezing winters when the trains weren't able to run, icicles formed curtain-like at the tunnel entrance, smashing to smithereens when the first train ran again.

He proudly recalled how just after the Second World War, his daughter won Show Jumping Championships three years in succession at the White City in London. Boarding the train at the station, pony and all, they would alight at Paddington and walk the animal through the streets of the capital to its stable for the night; compete the following day and journey back to Devon after the event, arriving at Yelverton completely elated, shattered and worn out. He went on to tell me of how she triumphed a fourth time without breaking the sequence, but that year, he said the event was held at Harringey and they were living in Somerset. The Colonel mused in contentment, happy with his life and with that which surrounds him.

'The house,' he suddenly exclaimed, in a livelier tone of voice, as if waking from a dream, 'it's an old longhouse, built in Drake's time, typical of the day; cattle to the right, living quarters to the left.' He went on to explain how when he came there to live after leaving Higher Elfordtown, much of the house had been altered, the open cart shed attached to the house had had a wall built across its entrance to provide the dwelling with another room, which is now his studio. The windows he said with a certain amount of sadness in his voice, had been altered to let in more light. He had since found a discarded mullion and put it back in place in the kitchen window.

I followed as he led the way in to the compact little dwelling, the low doors and ceilings charmed an air of cosiness, warmly wrapping itself around you. Pictures hung all over the walls and sentimental curios adorned anything with a horizontal surface. Flowers decorated the hearth, hiding the winter's ash from view, and framing their prettiness stood a massive granite mantel.

A doorway gave access to a carpeted spiral staircase. The stairs of the Dartmoor longhouses are normally of granite, but these, the Colonel assured me, were of wood. The hole in the bottom of the door, 'the legacy of a rat, I think.' he said, and thought it added character to the place.

We passed the parlour and entered his studio. This was a very private room where fondness and passion seeped into every item to be seen. The room was littered with old works of art leaning against one another, as if hiding from today. Paintings of landscapes, butterflies and horses draped the walls. Books, paints, brushes, pencils and other materials for his work lay about at random, he no doubt knowing exactly where to find them. Here is where he busied his days, restoring paintings of any age, and not strictly to receive financial remuneration, but for friends and personal gratification. The adroitness of his skill was painted in a satisfied smile, which widened his face as he exhibited to me a piece of finished work.

I suddenly felt as if I was intruding into this lovely person's life; it passed through my mind of how vulnerable he was in this modern age, when doors and windows have to be locked. Merely a voice on the telephone had given me licence to enter his home and the sincerity of this old gentleman, in his mid eighties, had accepted my presence as if he had known me for years.

A car stopped outside and footsteps brought his wife like a force-ten gale into our company with her hair fashioned by the same storm.

'Hello, good morning, you must be the man who telephoned earlier. I'm making coffee, you will have one won't you,' she said, and went about it as if no tomorrows were imminent. She placed the drink on the table with the saucer taking the spillage, and went on, 'Dick has told you how to get to the station, we have not been up there for sometime, have we Dick?' He raised his head and smiled in reply. Her pace relented a little but still standing with one hand on her brow as if some tide was sweeping her uncontrollably along, she began direct-ing me to where I wanted to go, at the same time, begging me to heed a warning about the wooden steps they had built sometime ago, into the embankment, which climbed to the old track bed.

A light breeze blew, mellowing the sun's warmth as I reached the embankment, my sudden arrival here startling a couple of pheasants that speedily took refuge beneath rhodo-dendrons in full bloom. Time lapsed whilst immersed in these surroundings new to me. When I arrive back at my car the old army officer and his wonderfully impetuous lady had gone out for the day. 'Our granddaughter is soon to be married and we are preparing for Yealmpton Show where we are judging. We must make a move. Come again when it's all over and time is a little more sparing,' were her last words to me, two and half almost non-existent hours before, when I had left their company.

Every once in a while, someone enters into the frame of one's life and casts a deep and lasting impression. Colonel Spencer and I became acquainted for only a few brief moments, sadly those very small fragments of time were the only moments I was to spend in his company, for just months after our meeting, in the early days of February, 1994 illness came and took his life away and passed him back to his Maker. Now, thoughts of this gentle, caring man, drift through my mind on occasions and broadens my face with a smile.

The track bed back to Princetown can now not be followed wholly, except on the open moor. Higher Elfordtown can be seen clearly to the left as the curve of the bed leads away from the overgrown sanctuary, but soon the density of blackthorn, hawthorn, brambles, young birch and ash make the way impassable. The footpath to Gratton does not exist any more, the fencing gone for cattle to graze where footsteps once made their way to and from the station. A kissing gate lies dumped, abandoned, to be forgotten half hidden in the undergrowth at the foot of the embankment. Fern, pennywort and succulent wild strawberries, grow from the stonework of the arch in the fields of old Gratton Farm. This is the only bridge to be seen standing complete amidst the lanes and fields of the in-country, the others being dismantled, leaving their abutments still to verge the roadsides. The triple arch which spanned the cutting that once gouged through the fields of Ride-Out-Lake still stands in all its shape and form but, alas, lies buried unceremoniously along with the aqueduct's granite legs. Filling in the cutting reclaimed useful acreage for Farmer Ellis, who later had a bunga-low built where the ghost of a train may well trundle beneath its foundations.

Besides the bungalow of Southella Road, other properties now stand astride the track bed between Gratton Cross and the moor at Yennadon.

Dousland Station.

> *There are Dwellings large and small,*
> *With Gardens at the front and back,*
> *Where Runner Beans and Winter Greens,*
> *Now adorn the old Railway Track.*
>
> *There was, a corrugated iron Coal Store,*
> *A Goods Shed topped with Slate,*
> *And a windowed brick-built Ground Frame,*
> *Which controlled the Crossing Gate.*

With a few structural alterations, the Dousland Station buildings now comprise a consider-able bungalow, where Mr John Anscome lives, wrapped totally in railway nostalgia. Ladies once read, chatted or knitted in the room where John now sleeps. Cosy lounge furniture, television, hi-fi and soft lighting warm the main waiting room, while cooking smells drift from a kitchen that occupies the ticket and parcel office, with serving hatch still available for use. And hot water fills a bath tub where ladies once spent their pennies. The signal box was dismantled for the use of its foundations to create two more bedrooms, the whole then brought together with the construction of an exterior wall topped with glass to form one long conservatory beneath the old station veranda. Framed photographs of the branchline's stations, halts and trains adorn the walls; lamps once used for various railway duties sit on window sills; sleeper chairs and the pointed bulbous tops of signal gantries, brightly painted red, deck the patio here and there where passengers once strolled up and down whilst waiting for their train.

'It is sad,' said John, 'when you think of its past, the line today would have been a wonder-ful tourist attraction.'

Conifers still sway in the breeze above this fascinating enigma of time, where the name Dousland is fixed to the old brick platform face. All around, if one wishes to look, are reminders of the railway's past, mixed with the clinical straight lines of today. The Station Master's house, the path to the coal yard that's gone, and the Manor Hotel that once quenched the thirst of the train-travelling moor walker, now opens its doors as the Burrator Inn.

Less than half-a-mile stroll along the Burrator road, Iron Mine Lane descends from Yennadon Down, passing Prowse's Crossing Cottage on the way. Here Mr Dewdney clearly relishes living in the midst of memories of the old railway. Like the Station Master's house, the cottage no longer gives the appearance of a once functional railway dwelling, altered in fashion to suit the wishes of previous occupiers since the properties became redundant from railway duty. Even the giveaway hump in the road where the level crossing sat, has been taken out to lessen a problem for the modern motor vehicle's suspension.

'As soon as we saw the property on the market , we just had to buy it.' enthused Mr Dewdney, 'Coming here to live was a joy.' Yet, his avid interest in railways is not wholly enjoyed by his wife, although she does caringly share space for his enthusiasm. On walls are framed prints of powerful old steam trains, an old GWR manhole cover and other bits wait in the yard for permanent homes. Nevertheless his pride and joy sits in place in the garden. He proudly explained of how when he and his wife were tidying around when they came here to live, he hit something extremely hard under the soil, digging down they unearthed short pieces of railway line, lying side by side, and discovered they were the capping for an old well, presumably sunk for the cottage water supply by the Princetown Railway Company. Mr Dewdney then went on to reveal how he employed a local mason to rebuild it into the lovely garden feature it is today. On my way out, after saying goodbye, I noticed on the gate, a little above the latch, a plaque with the wording:

GREAT WESTERN RAILWAY
ANYONE FOUND NOT SHUTTING THIS GATE
WILL PAY THE SUM OF FORTY SHILLINGS

'Amusing, don't you think,' he said, as he closed the gate behind me.

An aching sadness is felt in the loss of this railway as Yennadon Down is traversed. Way before the fenceless rusting kissing gates of Burrator Halt are reached, the Meavy valley begins to spread its splendour in full. No matter what the season, it is totally exhilarating, the scenery being nothing less than spectacular, even more

Rusting gates at Burrator Halt.

so when dressed in winter colour and a touch of frost glistens in the early morning sun.

From Prowse's Crossing to where the expanse of the Walkham watershed commences to unfold its charm, the track bed rises one hundred and fifty feet, in a little over one-and-half miles. Here the sad remnants of Lowery Crossing Cottage are no more than foundations in the ground and a piece of brick or mortar to tell a stranger that once an isolated building for some purpose stood here.

The Walkham hills are contoured for a full five-and-a-half miles before entering into Meavy country again, where the home signal to Princetown Station stood. All gone are any immediate visual indications that a railway station and its sidings once lay just beyond a bridge built over the line to convenience the crossing of wandering livestock. Riding pony grazing enclosures now occupy the area where carved figures tell us the station yard once spreading itself here was the highest in England. Gone are the main functional buildings: the waiting rooms, ticket office and signal box, the engine shed, cattle pen and the table where the engine turned from front to back. Only the attractive dwellings built to house the work-force remain, facing the redundant site, seeming un-associated with any bygone railway. Here also stand the dilapidated stables, while red bricks and mortar litter the ground and certain convenient fence posts are utilised for present-day purposes.

Young boys dreamt of steam engines in days gone by, drivers and firemen their heroes. They stood on station platforms or beside some railway fencing to collect engine names and numbers and watch the train trundle or hurtle by, gazing in amazement at their magnificence, in awe of size and power, fascinated by the thunderous belching plumes of smoke and ear-splitting hiss of steam.

After 73 years Princetown lost its railway and with it the pleasure of working in a pleasing environment. For fourteen years Ron Hext enjoyed the company of this beautiful railway, firing the engines up and down the line. As so often happens, it was by chance that I met Mr Hext, delving into the past and searching for characters who were actually a part of it, and he helped to create its image and paint it in colour. Such research can be exhausting and frustrating, leading to nowhere, into alleyways of confusion, into darkness and the deceased, but more often than not into pleasurable conclusions. For months I explored various avenues until an acquaintance told me about his friend who had at one time on occasions fired the train on the Princetown line. He had worked on the railway actually stationed at Laira engine sheds, where Ron a few years earlier had done his training. Horace Northam was the friend and this gentleman introduced me to Ron by kindly obtaining his telephone number and address, telling me, 'He's the man you want to talk to.'

Within a few days I was sat comfortably in Ron's Newton Abbot home letting him take the reins in our conversation, leading me into the past, dipping into time gone by. His wife Isabel was inclined to conceal herself in little chores around the house, politely allowing her husband to have centre stage, only dropping in and out of our little world to prompt or nudge his memory when temporarily it failed him.

Ron's father was a stonemason employed at Swell Tor quarry. The family lived into the now-ruined Mistor Cottages where Ron was born, one of ten children. They moved a couple of times within the Princetown area before settling to accommodate the large family at Blackbrook Farm. When the weather laid the quarrymen off, there was cruelly no pay; this at times made life extremely hard, the cupboard shelves were so very often bare when there were so many mouths to feed.

Princetown Station in its working days.

Ron left school at fourteen and went to work for people called Bolt, who owned the town's general store.

'Mrs Bolt often helped us out when we never had much,' said Ron. His normally satisfying little smile turned down to remember those days. After a period of shop work, Ron went to work on the farm at Tor Royal, but eventually his love for railways led him to Laira engine sheds, for training, cleaning, washing and polishing the great engines. Legends of the Great Western Railway could be seen at work, the Halls, Castles and the fabulous King Class locomotives. After twelve months, through a chance opportunity, he was back working at Princetown. A fellow worker was pencilled in to fill a vacancy on the Princetown line but didn't fancy a job up in the wilderness of the moor, unlike the old stalwart Bill Gough who came to Princetown from Southall in smog-ridden London.

Ron was offered the position and gleefully accepted the good fortune to be home again with family and friends, to become the youngest fireman on the branch. He loved the line and all that went with it. He was at home in the company of men he knew, including his uncle Gilbert, the renowned Bill Gough, the Stevenses and Jack Brockinshire who worked the signal box. It was at times hard work, with certain drivers being hard taskmasters. Early turn meant up and about before the lark sounded the new day's beginning, walking through Princetown in the early hours before 4.00am, to rake out the engine's ash pan and light the fire before driver Stoyle came on duty.

A passion simmered constantly for his work and the area in which he lived. Smiles and chuckles of happiness came from Ron and Isabel as they recalled fond memories of local moorland places they knew. Yet not all memories allowed for smiles; the war years brought grave concern, the air raids over Plymouth could be seen clearly from the higher elevations of the line; searchlights criss-crossed the night skies and fires burned all around, while the shuddering sound of explosions shook the city as bombs rained down leaving the next morning's daylight to bring the sight of smoke rising from smouldering debris.

Mostly the sun shines in life and, as in nearly every story, a romance unfolds in such idyllic settings. Isabel was a local girl, her father was the crossing keeper at Lowery, where the remnants of the cottage are no more than foundations in the ground. He also at times worked Prowse's Crossing where Mr and Mrs Dewdney now live. Isabel recalled conversations about the well in the garden there, but never knew exactly where it could be found. With her local childhood upbringing it was inevitable that she and Ron should meet. Everyday his work took him across her path, allowing time to introduce them to one another and it wasn't long before the pretty fifteen-year-old lit a little something in the young fireman's heart, eventually casting the net of charm to bring him fully into her life. Four years later brought the wedding in the month of February 1948. For nearly nine years, Ron lived in bliss with the girl, the job and the place he loved. Then crash: his world fell off the rails, the impending closure of the line came about causing severe upheaval, destroying the rustic peace in which he lived; he was a country boy through to his very soul.

He knew the Moors and where to walk,
He knew the people and how they talk,
He knew the closure, would bring heartache and pain,
He knew that going away, may mean, never to return again.

Life's twists and turns are set in the fate which is cast and Ron was transferred to Old Oak Common in London, coming home as often as he was able. For twelve long months he endured the capital, before coming back to the Westcountry and Newton Abbot to work and live, where two people unfulfilled, now look back, sadly disappointed at losing their branch-line and their way of life they had thought at the outset should have lasted for ever. For them, memories of the railway are no more than mere shadows in the mind.

CHAPTER 2
North Hessary Tor

To encourage the lungs to exercise, and the heart to beat just that little bit faster, the climb to North Hessary Tor rises something like three hundred feet in about three-quarters of a mile. It lies a little west of north of Meavy Head. From this unassuming pinnacle, eyes open to a fabulous panorama. Every prominent feature on the distant skyline is normally clearly identifiable, but on this particular visit the sun was pulling up the wet from the night before's heavy rain, inducing a frown on the Lady's brow, when the Lizard headland couldn't be seen.

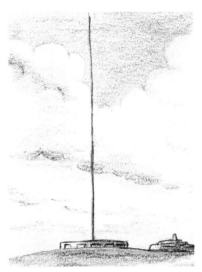

Television aerial.

She had climbed to the same spot from a few hundred yards behind my ascent, a rather pleasant dumpy lady, a local preacher's wife. She was puffing slightly from exertion, with tiny beads of perspiration dotted on her flushed red cheeks. She wore merely a pair of patterned above-the-knee-length leggings and a loose fitting T-shirt, yet the late summer breeze was fresh and had fostered the reason for me to be wearing my fleece jacket. For the little while she spent in my company she chatted away, allowing a slight accent to display that her origins were from a lot farther north than the spot on which we stood. Disappointment shed her contentment for a moment, for a friend had told her that on a clear day the Goonhilly dishes could be seen on the Lizard peninsula. All the while, her canine company, a young beagle, sat quietly beside her feet, uninquisitive, unplayful, submissive, adopted from a rescue centre, its young life had been tethered to the experiments of science. At the moment it is incapable of anything other than eating, sleeping and normal bodily functions: 'It is sad, very sad,' was a low utterance from the lady's voice, as she turned to walk away, leaving without a smile, her little friend walking, perhaps not knowing why, alongside her stride.

North Hessary Tor.

Scanning the near and distant hills and valleys, the church of St Michael de Rupe seems always to warrant the first attention. Built in the middle years of the twelfth century, it stands on the peak of Brent Tor, in silhouette fashion against the hazy north Cornish landscape, scalloped in the dip between the much nearer rock piles of Great Staple Tor and Roose Tor. Visually traversing the landscape from Roose Tor, in a clockwise direction: Great Mis Tor with its huge battlement-like rock formation, rises six hundred feet and more from the Walkham waters it overlooks. Beyond, in the middle distance the hills swollen above the Lyd hold proud their presence, the massif of Great Links Tor, claiming the glory on the highest ground, sitting like some imperial majesty, on a throne. Near the ruin of Bleak House, the old peat works manager's dwelling, the salmon-coloured tors of the twin Dunna Goats and Green Tor occupy areas on the banks of the Rattle Brook, and above to the right of Woodcock Hill, the escarpment contouring over the West Okement stretches and climbs to Fordsland Ledge and, less steeply, on to High Willhays, at two thousand and thirty eight feet, the loftiest peak on this wonderful wilderness.

On this particular day slow-moving clouds were casting shadows on the middle ground of the northern moor, where Cut Hill and Fur Tor sit, desolate, wild, yet beautiful, miles from the sight and sounds of the modern age. From my perch, I can see all the peaks straddling the higher elevations of the West Dart, and crowning the skyline to the north-east is the long ridge of Hameldown and the conjured magical tors named Honeybag, Chinkwell and Bonehill, mountainous above the village of Widecombe, lying deep in its valley. Looking out over Teign country to the sea are the much visited rock piles lining the Ashburton–Bovey Tracey road. Surveying the skyline still farther to the east, Buckland Beacon can be seen standing guard over the Commandment Stones and the picturesque hamlet of Buckland-in-the-

An uninterupted view towards Great Mis Tor.

Moor. Protruding above the Swincombe on the horizon is Ter Hill and Nakers Hill and just showing above the never-ending stretch of the Langcombe ridge is the cairn of Eastern Whitebarrow. Where the east mingles its pointers with the south, the moors on Shell Top stand at fifteen hundred feet before dropping down to the in-country and the city of Plymouth, where across the mouth of the Tamar the sea meets the Cornish coast. Coming full circle, the hills in the west, stretched along under the sky to fuse again with the tors above the Walkham, hold in their fold in the middle distance the church of St Michael de Rupe.

Sitting on North Hessary Tor, I feel seduced, robbed of my inner self, in awe of this, my arcadia; quiet in mind, in thought, very little flowing through my head but an incoming sense of fulfilment. This place, this view, that has passed through the ages, the baton of time, from era to era, from generation to generation, could I am sure, inspire a symphony or, empty the ink from a poet's pen.

Somewhere in the middle of October 1951 a rather disturbing piece of information filtered through various channels to the lovers of Dartmoor, that there was advanced thinking by the British Broadcasting Corporation of building a medium-powered television transmitting station right on the plinth of the Tor. Heads spun and stomachs sickly churned at the mental picture of concrete and steel defiling the rock pile. From miles around the hill would be seen without first having to search the skyline, for the mast would reach 750 Feet into the sky.

Devon County Council had been approached and asked for planning observations. The council's response was written with cautious reverence, requesting for time to lapse for a while until the thoughts of others had been considered.

Very little of the Meavy watershed would be occupied by the boundaries of the station and its mast, but the dominance of its presence would be seen from most areas of the beautiful valley.

Horrified concern leapt immediately to defend the landscape's beauty. Those dedicated people of the Dartmoor Preservation Association took up the challenge practically before the gloves of the fight were laced, using very descriptive wording in their newsletters to portray the gravity of the situation.

On 9 February 1952 the subject was on the agenda, at a Dartmoor National Park Committee meeting. The BBC were represented and put their thinking into words, but to some in attendance, their words seemed to lead suspiciously in favour of nowhere else but the granite rock pile of North Hessary.

The committee listened with interest to all aspects of the discussion, then leant tactfully on the side of caution, with no decision reached, except to wait for further technical advice and the completion of Wenfoe, a high-powered transmitting station being constructed near Cardiff in South Wales, which would, when finished, relay television signals to the Westcountry and the decided location of the transmitter.

Television relay station, North Hessary.

Brent Tor through the stay wires.

But the DPA, finding no comfort in the meeting, shook their heads and concluded that the little tor was in deeper trouble than was first anticipated. They had, however, the good fortune of employing the generous voluntary services of an Admiralty radar specialist with a great deal of television know-how, who gave the worried a little space in their minds to loosen the strains of anxiety, when explaining that no definite site could be chosen for the project until conclusive radiation tests had been carried out.

Just a few months later in June, gobsmacking news shattered the uneasy calm. With several members who shared an empathy with the opposers unavoidably absent, the Dartmoor National Park Committee shocked everyone with a sudden reversal of their February decision. When the show of hands were counted the fors and against were equal, till the Chairman arrested the conclusion with his casting vote of not waiting for the completion of Wenfoe.

Where was the reality in these people having even contemplated making a decision, knowing they had no jurisdiction over major developments in the Park? They were merely watchdogs who were not members of the Council nor of any Planning Authority, their presence was to wrap a caring arm around the consequence of minor matters. Other than that, their strings were pulled this way and that by the County Council, who supposedly cradled the welfare of the moor.

Like most problems in life they disappear only when they are finally resolved. For a few more weeks the issue rumbled in the moans and groans of thoughts and conversations, then on 17 July, disaster tore the heart out of the debate. Heads again shook in total disbelief and chins dropped slowly to the chest, when the County Council itself acquired a solid resounding vote in favour of North Hessary being terminally defiled. Right through the matter in question the atmosphere in the Council Chamber and gallery was fraught with tense anticipation, some eager for a conclusion in the direction of their choice, others pensive, deep in thought, until pandemonium ruled the proceedings from when it could be clearly seen which way the verdict was wanted to go. Hoots, cat-calls and whistles dominated the commotion and somewhere in the midst, notions and ideas were angrily vented, bellowing verbal accusations at the perpetrators of the motion eventually carried. The accusations were not of infidelity or corruption but of being misled, duped into thinking Devon may lose the chance of television within the near future if planning permission was not permitted forthwith.

Within no time at all, support from many other organisations who had been watching events with sympathetic concern from outside the immediate arena of dispute, came to the fore and united with the protesting little army of Dartmoor lovers. The war for the tor was now truly on and necessary defence on various fronts was imperative, issues of historic interest had to be addressed and evaluated.

Up to this stage in the proceedings, no other site at all appeared to have been contemplated by the BBC. August 1952 saw the first concentrated movements to establish the testing apparatus on North Hessary, with still no certainty of the site being the chosen one. Access to it was extremely difficult, even the shortest and most obvious route became a steep, oozing black quagmire once the virgin moorland surface was broken. BBC personnel and their vehicles hauling heavy equipment up to the trial site came to a slithering messy halt, bogged down feet deep in a thick dense soup of self-churned vegetation and peat. When eventually the materials arrived at their destination, a temporary slimline 110-foot aerial mast was erected to radiate signals to vans packed with all sorts of technical television paraphernalia, moving here and there through the lanes of Devon and Cornwall to measure and register the strength of signals received from North Hessary. Within a few weeks the engineers had exhausted the use of the slender mast and introduced a hydrogen-filled, silver-coloured balloon to the sky, floating a thousand feet above the moor, this re-employed and extended the duties of the slender mast, sending more television data through the airwaves to the roving vans until the experiments were complete. Before the real cold months set in to stiffen the moor, all the BBC equipment had been removed leaving just the experimentations, remnants to be sniffed at by inquisitive livestock, the permanent occupiers of the waste.

It was argued that there were alternatives to North Hessary, which would have given better reception for both Devon and Cornwall. Even independent expert opinion confirmed that the Modbury area of South Devon and Hensbarrow near St Austell in Cornwall, would have jointly better benefited the prospective viewer. The BBC was clearly not really prepared to reason, their finances, they had said, could stretch no further than the cost of one transmitter, but for the sake of appeasing their niggling tormentors, tests in the New Year of 1953 were carried out on Shaugh Moor and Horner Down at Halwell near Kingsbridge.

The DPA, the obvious backbone of the opposers, considered Halwell to be ideal and congratulated their efforts in nudging the BBC's thoughts towards the totally acceptable off-the-moor location. Shaugh of course presented a different line of thinking. Although the site was on the periphery of the Southern Moor and indeed not even within the confines of the National Park, the station's conspicuous mast would have still displayed itself well above the skyline, to be seen from many miles around.

The door, perhaps of unintentional delusion, was open and for a few months the uncomfortable tension of suspense abated, the far more agreeable move by the television people flipped the coin to come down in favour of respite, ridding the molested mind of anxiety and allowing the concerned heart to beat more aptly for better health.

Spring was now painting warmth and colour on the once uneasy scene and liberated smiles touched again the cheerful face of optimism. Feeling free from the stress and strain of embittered confrontation, the DPA wrote to Broadcasting House, asking if the North Hessary was now spared from the destructive hand of ruination. As if keeping a distance, a polite yet rather discomposing reply came back from the Director General himself. There was no mention at all of the very subject in dispute, yet it stated quite categorically without further statements as to why, Shaugh Moor had been rejected and tests were now being made on Horner Down.

Doubts were creeping back as to the authenticity of the BBC's contribution to fair play and integrity, especially when a few months later, Horner Down too, was not considered suitable, that the tests there were not as satisfactory as those up on North Hessary.

It was believed from the outset of the controversy that the BBC wanted only the little tor and all along they had been playing the game of cat and mouse.

What else could be done to save the Moor from a hideous eyesore being forced upon it, to defile and degrade, to violate the skyline and embarrass the beauty for miles and miles around? It was realisation living in a nightmare, trapped in a situation unable to move one way or another, with all the aces held firmly in the strong hand of the aggressor. All possible channels of deliberation had been attended throughout the struggle, every notion and opinion had felt the full weight of honest self scrutiny, men and women from all walks of life had championed the cause, among them respected public figures, and MPs from both sides of the House asked questions in Parliament.

For nearly two years, the dispute simmered and boiled, till the Minister of Housing and Local Government intervened and ordered a public inquiry. It was set for 10.00am on 29 September 1953 at the Castle in Exeter.

Among other groups standing alongside the DPA at the inquiry, were the Dartmoor Ramblers, the Commons Preservation Society, The Council for the Preservation of Rural England, and the Youth Hostel Association. The BBC had regularly reminded that there were no corners to be cut, even if strings could be conveniently pulled, the fight would go to the bitter end.

What was all the fuss really all about, when relics of past industries which have scarred and disfigured the landscape's every hill and valley, are found fascinating enough to be preserved, with the happy wanderer forbidden by law to move a stone or shed its covering of vegetation. Such relics' very presence intrigue archaeologists to the point where they band together students in their own field and enthusiastic volunteers to officially, with patience and dripping sweat from sheer hard work, bare the ancient remains and try to ascertain their origins and discover how their functional workings performed. When the building of Burrator Reservoir was completed and filled to overflowing, it drowned the higher middle reaches of the Meavy valley, submerging old farm buildings and moorland pasture. Though very sad, it was necessary. Plymouth's population and industry was in need of more water.

Now everyday the reservoir reflects the sky's ever changing mood and amplifies the multi-colours of the seasons, that in turn display to the world an area of outstanding beauty, attracting thousands of visitors to enjoy its surroundings. Unfortunately this in turn, we know to our cost, encourages the odd delinquent who steals and disrupts, but the bad penny turns up wherever we choose to spend our time at leisure.

During the height of their mighty differences with the BBC, the DPA were at loggerheads with the construction of a lay-by, just a few yards long, beside the road below the prehistoric remains of Grimspound, arguing that it would be used as a car park with the usual discarded litter desecrating the heather-clad surroundings. My experience contradicts these conjectured theories. It is true that over the years since the few yards of tarmac was laid I have seen the odd misdemeanour, but in general the people who use it are level headed, litter conscious and considerate. The lay-by is very convenient for those people who are physically incapable of walking very far, or haven't the instinctive desire to trek miles across the moor, yet wish to see and absorb a piece of our past to be mused over, only yards from where their car is parked.

If the past was to flash through time and appear today, would the opposers of the television station seek to prevent the industries of their ages from ever existing? If this was so, Crossing, Worth and many more authors would have had very little to write about. Indeed my computer would not be writing these words today. Magnificent as it is, Dartmoor would be merely a landscape and nothing more; nothing there to stimulate the inquisitive, nothing there to seek out and investigate, nothing to relate the past with today. To have prevented a part of the past we forego a piece of the present; just as if we have no present, we certainly have no future.

We all feel the need to protest at times, to try and keep a sense of proportion to prevent ourselves from being trampled over, but some want to take their thoughts just that little bit further. Not so long ago one particular lady wrote of her wishes for the future of Dartmoor, in a local magazine. One wonders who she wanted to trek on the moor when among her words were the three of 'free from tourism'. Did she want the wide open space wandered over only by a selected few?

One can sympathise with the argument of conservation on Dartmoor, when we relate back to 15 August 1951, for that is when the wild and uncompromising upland was designated a National Park, so why wrap an appreciative arm around it one minute then throw disrespectful unconcern in its face the next.

The Inquiry stretched into three long days, costing the DPA and their allies to delve deep into their financial pockets. All but the professionals attended at their own expense and inconvenience of being absent from personal affairs. Many individuals affiliated to the protesting groups tucked themselves somewhere into the crowded room to voice an utterance of support, a sigh or a smile, while calculated expertise volleyed skilfully around the arena of proceedings as arguments for and against fired the debate into a tense and highly-charged confrontation. At the end of the Inquiry, all were pleased with how things went and felt that applause and pats on the back were deserved all around.

Six months later, in March 1954, came the Minister's judgement, announcing with the sharp edge of his axe, thrusting deep into the granite of North Hessary Tor, the little pinnacle was doomed to extinction, the visual imbalance of a 700-foot mast standing in its place.

It was felt by some individuals on the losing side that at sometime, somewhere, behind the scenes, local politics had put its devious finger into the long-running dispute's unsavoury pie, fretting that votes may be lost on future polling days if television did not come to the Westcountry soon. This thinking fostered the notion that the Inquiry was a complete and utter sham, being merely an extravagant and expensive veneer to overlay the already concluded decision.

Very few local people knew of any protests over the station and its mast. Talking to local residents during my research today, I found that very few knew of any protests; it seems that a majority of those who had to live under and endure the site of the monster above were not asked for their opinion. Winifred and Gilbert Warne of Princetown remember nothing of any protest. 'It just went up,' said Winifred. Despite her 84 years, Mrs Warne displayed remarkable reasoning, saying that herself and 87-year-old Gilbert were privileged to have lived in an era which had seen all manner of technical and mechanised developments. They merely viewed the television station and mast as just another unfolding of man's ingenuity. They didn't like it: 'It spoilt the surroundings I grew up in, stuck up there,' said Winifred. For a while, she reminisced deeply, as if living the time again, saying how as a young girl she walked a little over a mile to school and back to Blackbrook Farm, 'not there any more', then up on to the moor to turn the peat for drying, that her father had cut in the morning for the fire. She spoke of picking juicy whortleberries up in Whistman's Wood, how she experienced the tractor and other motor vehicles gradually replacing the horse, and oil lamps for lighting going out, doused by the much brighter, far cleaner and odourless electric bulb. One could see her reaping pleasure from seeing the pictures in her mind. I hesitated before intruding into her almost dreamlike realm of self indulgence, half afraid of missing out on even the smallest snippet of information through an untimely interruption.

'Blackbrook Farm,' I said, 'that's where Ron Hext once lived as a boy.'

'Yes, that's right, his family took over the tenancy from mine when we moved out.' Gilbert, one of the very few Dartmoor tin miners left to tell the tale, sat quietly in his favourite armchair, with his hands together on his ample tummy, his eyes gradually closing as his head nodded forward, as if reluctantly fighting a nap. But an utterance in a soft low voice of a much broader local pronunciation than Winifred's, would now and again break into the conversation when a difference of opinion was met.

Mr George Dunn who farms at Brisworthy, remembers the mast being erected. As a young man he lived in the Walkham Valley at Horseyeat, with his mother and stepfather. 'I rememberin gwain' up, back 'een th' early fifties. They ad uh liddle theen one tu start weeth, then uh barrige bloon wen up, great zilver theeng twuz, then after that up went the one that's ther now. Uz wachen day be day, till they finish een. Us didn knaw anythin bout any protess.'

Ron Hext the former railway fireman and his wife, Isabel, lived for a couple of years under the shadow of the mast before moving to Newton Abbot. They also knew very little about the controversy related to the tor above, recalling merely what they had read in the *Western Morning News*. Similar stories were told by a vast majority of the people I spoke to who were old enough to remember and had lived around the area at the time.

Because of the ever-increasing advancement in technology, it was quite rightly thought that the tor should be spared the indignity of destruction. Future technical know-how may well determine the transmitting systems of television and radio obsolete and the mast redundant, leaving cranes and spanners to dismantle and clear it away, allowing the moor once again to wake in the morning without the great scar pushing up into the sky and the panorama to return to its uninterrupted 360-degree halo, without having to view it through a huge lattice framework of silver grey steel.

For what seemed an eternity, the BBC eventually saw logic in the reasoning when rational thinking caught someone's eye and the tor was granted a total reprieve from execution. It was looked upon, as a moral victory, by the protesting fraternity, but their thoughts were not yet ready to rest on contentment.

Although the fight for the tor was won, the conflict still simmered on, with the DPA still snapping and snarling like an aggravated terrier, questioning the right for the Corporation to nonchalantly presume it could enclose twenty-five acres of Walkhampton Common without going through the appropriate statutory channels of procedure.

Walkhampton, like all the other parishes around the periphery of the moor, is a Venville Parish and its farmers, owners and tenants alike, enjoy Venville Rights, passed down through the ages from the dim regions of our past. They have historical licence from the Crown to graze their cattle on the Commons of the moor, the right of turbary to cut peat for the hearth, glean stone for walling and sickle reed for thatch. By enclosing areas of the Common, these rights are restricted. Permission to fence must be sought from the Minister of Agriculture who, when assessing the situation, takes into account the value of the Commons grazing.

The wrangling festered again into solicitor and parliamentary involvement with questions from local MPs being asked in the House, and letters going out to those responsible for the deep

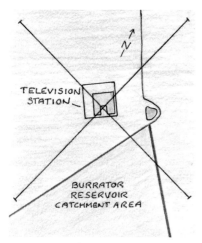

Reservoir catchment area.

frown upon the brow of the DPA. There was concern as to whether the BBC would take the fair road of credibility and seek the Minister's nod of approval or merely purchase the land and fence it without giving consideration to others. The area required took the BBC to three different venues, the Prison that Thomas Tyrwhitt had built on Duchy soil, the Lopes family and the Plymouth City Council. On Walkhampton Common the city bought their land in 1917 from the Lopes as part of the rainwater catchment area that empties into Burrator Reservoir.

The BBC did purchase the acreage they wanted, late in January 1955, with the consent of the Minister of Housing and Local Government, but they were restricted to fencing just two-thirds of an acre to accommodate the station, mast and vehicle space. Also a strict code of conduct was written down and had to be adhered to, stating that the BBC were answerable to the water engineer for any misdemeanour concerning pollution.

Another battle was over, with the DPA smiling, content to lodge no objections to a much smaller area being enclosed, sensing that after the expensive debacle at Exeter in September 1953, another Inquiry would serve no purpose at all.

Television broadcasting initially went out from North Hessary on 17 December 1954, in time to add another dimension to Christmas entertainment.

Words from a short essay, kindly given to me by the BBC, written by a Mr Massey an engineer at the station from the outset of its origins, now retired, illustrate quite graphically what working life was like for those employed there. The station was a mere temporary affair consisting of three caravans linked together by corrugated asbestos corridors lined with hardboard. One caravan housed the office, kitchen and the only toilet, another the controls, two 200W sound transmitters and the reserve 500W television transmitter. The third, which was used for the BBC's first outside broadcast during the Coronation of King George VI, housed the main vision transmitter and power supplies. Vision signals were received off air from Wenfoe and sound from two incoming Post Office feeds, one from London via Bristol, the other via Plymouth. The coverage from the temporary mast splayed about twenty miles in all directions from Plymouth.

Getting to work was sometimes a feat in itself before the tarmac road was laid. Access to the site from the entrance at Rundlestone was one slippery ride on a surface of ever-sinking railway sleepers. Often in winter, when the roads were deep in snow, the Princetown railway replaced the car, till the line closed in 1956, then a long walk across the moor was endured from wherever the local garage's Land Rover could reach.

Three months of arctic conditions delayed the start of building, which eventually began in March 1955. Mr Massey goes on to say, that manpower from the local Moormen was found to be the only method to dig through the solid granite and bottomless peat; their horse and carts were far more effective than mechanical transport on the open moor. So the ultra-modern station was built with age-old techniques.

It was during the process of construction that the subject of preservation had its final words of war with the BBC. It was to do with a small Bronze Age barrow near the tor. During Ministerial negotiations relating to the television project, it was agreed that the barrow should be either spared intact or scientifically excavated before its ruination. Those who cared for the little monument, could foresee damage being done to it by total neglect of thought from ignorance of its existence, or an arrogant couldn't-care-less attitude towards what may be seen as nothing more than a hump on the ground. Intervention by those who feared for its wellbeing encouraged it to be temporarily fenced, to save it, as the DPA newsletter put it at the time 'from the bulldozers and the feet of sensation seekers, who swarm open-mouthed over an area they never thought of climbing to before.'

Very early in this dispute, a Mr Ralegh Radford was asked by the DPA to identify, visually examine and report upon the barrow. Putting it on paper, he wrote:

The fenced barrow at North Hessary.

North Hessary Tor half a mile N.W. of Princetown on the rounded summit of the hill, at about 1600ft, and about 100ft N.N.W. of the O.S. mark on the summit of the Tor, is a small Barrow, the mound about 20ft across and 18in above the natural surface, is surrounded with a circular ditch about 7ft wide and now barely 1ft deep. Overall measurement of the monument, about 30ft. The mound is mainly composed of soil with a number of medium-sized split stones on the edge, particularly on the North side. The bottom of the ditch is soft. The surface is disturbed, but the mound does not appear to be rifled. The monument is probably of the Early Bronze Age, possibly with a cist and peristalith, the latter robbed for the adjacent newtake wall.

Much later on during the upheaval of the station's construction, the BBC unwittingly provoked controversy by complimenting itself in a local newspaper over the care and regard they had shown to the barrow. This gave rise to contradiction by the DPA who claimed that the surrounding ditch and peristalith had been destroyed. Here confusion begs further explanation, for the DPA appeared satisfied with the initial fencing of the barrow, yet later complained about the sorry state of its condition. If the protective fencing did not meet the requirements of the monument's safety when it was first erected, why didn't the DPA say so? Perhaps only conjecture can reason as to why,

Whitehall of course got to hear about the ditch and peristalith, but the words used by the DPA, as if the circle from the outset of discovery was complete, were a little hypocritical, bending reality to suit their own ends, especially after damning the BBC of all sorts of wrong-doings. Ministerial letters of rebuke arrived at the BBC causing the erection of a second fence, enclosing the two ruined features. No wonder the Devonshire Association representative who climbed to the site to view the situation for himself was completely bemused by it all.

Mr Ted Lock, employed as a technical assistant, was away on a course when the building work was being done; the mast was up and terminated, according to Ted, at 720 feet but full power did not radiate from it till nearly twelve months later. Ted, like Mr Massey, remembers the times when the staff were living on a diet of crisps and chocolate whilst marooned for three days with no electricity, BT cables down and aerials blown away. 'Home Office engineers came in by helicopter to find out what was going on, then disappeared again, leaving no provisions of bread or milk or good cheer, particularly galling when the water was frozen solid and snow had to be shovelled into the diesel cooling system as it boiled away. Helicopters flew by to drop fodder on the moor for the livestock, only for the staff to see the machine fly off again without so much as a wave. Another winter, during severe icing, a huge chunk of ice the size of a dustbin, came away from the mast and nearly penetrated the switch room roof.' Ironically for Ted, rapidly advancing technology pressured him into a happy and contented retirement at early age of fifty-five.

Over the years, changes in TV such as colour and stereo have materialised and in 1986, the mast was reduced in height by fifty feet. Now television only radiates down the hill to Princetown; the station is owned by an American company and sends FM Radio and other users' facilities.

Still today, during a thaw, spear like slivers of ice come crashing down off the mast, but the station roof is now reinforced to take the battering and staff are compelled to wear protective headwear while outside the building. On a clear night, from dusk to dawn, the lights on the mast can be seen flashing from miles away, sending out their warnings to the sky.

North Hessary wasn't the first to have a great elongated needle-like object erected on its actual doorstep, to cause concern for the Dartmoor lover. Looking down and along the Meavy valley, the acreage of Peak Hill can be seen jutting out from behind the great feature of Sharpitor. In comparison, its prominence doesn't always stand out to catch the eye when viewing one's surroundings whilst sitting on the rocks of North Hessary. Yet at one time it was definitely different, for during the Second World War an RAF radio station and its mast of 240 feet was built right on its very summit. The structure was of a lattice design and fashioned out of wood, and there it stood alone on the hill surrounded by corrugated Nissen huts, till the Air Ministry decided to replace the wooden mast with one of steel, along with a much taller height of 350 feet. As well as the new mast, permanent buildings were being proposed to accompany it.

Stay wires and the TV relay station.

Without the station and stay wires.

It was begged that the Air Ministry find a site elsewhere, North Hessary had already been defiled, now another fight was on the hands of those who cared for their moor. The usual protests went to the highest authorities in the land and questions again were asked in Parliament. The Ministry did mention another site and shook the protesters to the core. Great Links, the fabulous prominence on the northern moor, was supposedly their chosen alternative, they said, to Peak Hill. But was this a game being played out by the Ministry; were they pulling the strings of craftiness to steer the argument in their chosen direction.

Words at the protesters' meetings made it clear to the Ministry that neither Great Links Tor nor Peak Hill would do, above all, that Great Links would not do, and that no more large masts could be tolerated on Dartmoor unless it could be proved beyond all doubt that there was absolutely no other alternative.

Like the horrendous nightmare situation with North Hessary, great noises were made by pen and voice throughout the dispute. Fretting, sweating brows were constantly wiped and hearts missed a beat or two before the confrontation came to a unsatisfactory close, with the protesters saying that Great Links Tor has been saved by the weight of public protest.

Having backed off from supposedly wanting Great Links Tor, the Air Ministry dug their heels in concerning Peak Hill and would not be dislodged from their stance. By October 1957 although agreed to be only twenty feet higher than the wooden lattice object, the steel

View from Peak Hill towards Leather Tor.

mast was up and its associated buildings in place, just over two years after the fight was lost up at North Hessary.

The mast's life on Peak Hill, was not expected to last beyond 1966 but it did not come down till the spring of May 1971.

Luck was on my side when leaving North Hessary on that late hazy summer's day. I was strolling away when a young man called out to me, saying that I had left my camera behind. He and his girlfriend, holding hands, had climbed the hill from the Rundlestone direction and sat with their backs to me, on the other side of the Tor, looking down towards the lower Walkham Valley. I had heard their youthful chatter and laughter, interweaving nonsensically with the breeze. Apart from these mingled utterances, I paid very little attention to their presence. With a coy and humble thankyou I retrieved my camera and went on my way with a refreshed belief that the vast majority of youth are as good and honest today as they have ever been. Heading back down towards Meavy Head I am always compelled at intervals to hesitate in my stride, reluctant to leave a view, as individual spreads of scenery dip out of sight.

CHAPTER 3
Old Tin Workings

Part way down the hill, after passing beneath the railway bridge, a spring pushes out from the ground and quickly runs down the slope to join the infant Meavy. Before uniting, both streams find their way through the spoil heaps of old tinners' workings, until meandering almost aimlessly through a confusion of silt and vegetation. Within a few yards, before flowing under Devil's Elbow bridge, it becomes a true and proper stream. After leaving the little structure, that is no more than a culvert, the Meavy for the first few hundred yards is, in places, no more than twelve inches wide. Here the man-deepened valley is narrow and through it the water meanders, busily twisting and turning, bubbling and gurgling where tumbling tiny cataracts fall splashing and sparkling in the sunlight. The pace subsides and quietens where the streambed widens and in the more tranquil water, broad-leaf pondweed waves to the flow of the much slower current, and in places the little leaves of duckweed mat the water's surface. Springs here and there issue crystal clear rivulets to weep quietly into the stream from bulging mounds of moss that display in splendour various vibrant shades of glowing greens.

Only a few yards farther on are the tumbling waters of Black Tor Falls. Here below this lovely feature are the ruins of two stamping mills, one on each side of what is now, with its gradual increasing volume, becoming a river.

Like all the Dartmoor tin mills, these two are in a ruinous state, the right hand mill displays a scene of fallen masonry with just a few feet of walling to identify it. On the steep slope beside the waterfall is a large stone; a keen eye will discover a small rust-stained groove worked into it, where the mills waterwheel shaft rotated. Another bearing stone can be found at the bottom of what remains of the mill's walling. The waterwheel was employed to crank a set of sturdy poles up and down. These poles, called stamps, crushed the tin ore that was placed on a conveniently-shaped piece of granite called a mortar stone. The continual pounding of the stamps in the same place over a period of time created saucer-shaped depressions in the stone that eventually became too deep to be effective; once this happened they were discarded. Among the fallen debris, within the inner portions of the mill, are two such stones, one of which is only a half and has only one depression sunk into it, the other, a whole one, displays three depressions of irregular proportions, with the middle one overlapping a much larger one in size. Two other

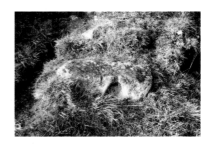

Mortar stone in the river.

Mortar stone on the right bank.

What could be an unfinished Crazing Mill stone.

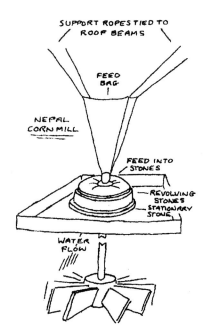

Nepalese Corn Mill.

mortar stones are there to see, one in the water, the other a few yards away from the mill, set in the banking that is negotiated when clambering down to the site. There is also in the water a stone which someone had ideas of splitting, but didn't complete the task.

Farther downstream, jutting out from a spoil heap, is a large stone that I found years ago. Its shape intrigued me as I made my way down over the side of the mound. I could see it had a fairly smooth surface and most of the rim of its circumference also looked as if it had been dressed, but it wasn't until I managed to push my hand between it and its exposed section's covering of vegetation that real excitement pulsed through me at the thought of discovering a crazing mill stone, or at least a mill stone of some description. Hidden for who knows how many years there was a hole, smooth to the touch of my hand. What the rest of the upper surface of the object is like only the stone's removal from its captive position can reveal. The stone I believe, because of its rough and unworked under surface, was discarded when perhaps broken during its making. The radius of it, from the centre of what would have been its pivot hole, to the distinctively recognised area of its circumference, measures thirty inches, which would obviously have given an overall diameter of five feet. Across the hole and through it, to the unhewn underside, measures four-and-a-half inches.

If at sometime it is proved conclusively to be an unfinished mill stone, it would have been rather large, larger than any other found and recorded on the moor. But who is to say what dimension a particular article is supposed to be? Beside the Deancombe Brook, the Outcombe mill stone, measured many years ago by the renowned R.H. Worth, which now cannot be found, was a clear one foot one inch smaller in its diameter than the Gobbet Mine stones which can be seen lying on the grassy right hand bank of the River Swincombe near Hexworthy.

Whilst trekking among the Nepal Himalayas, especially along the Kaligandaki and Marsyangdi Valleys, I had the opportunity to visit several corn mills, a few whilst in operation. The stones there differ a great deal in diameter from one mill to another. It is not known exactly how the stone revolved in the crazing mills on Dartmoor, one can only imagine them operating in the same manner as the those in the corn mills of Nepal, that is, of the mill house itself sitting over the leat or stream of water, with the vertical wooden shaft driving the upper stone, protruding through the floor of the mill house where the water is directed on to wooden blades that are fitted to the tail-end of the shaft, each blade measuring about eighteen inches by twelve, with an unplaned inch-thickness, its length set at right angles to its driving force, and each blade set at a certain degree of tilt so as to catch the full force of the water.

Back at the falls on the left hand side of the river is the other stamping mill. This building consists of two rooms but it does appear that the smaller room was annexed to the main structure at a later date. Time hasn't ravaged this building quite so much as it as its partner already mentioned. Here a great deal more survives: the doorway, the only one to be still in situ on Dartmoor is in excellent condition. The large granite lintel is still perfectly placed on top of its door jambs, but whether the Roman numerals cut into it which translate to the number thirteen, supposedly the works number which was registered at the stannary town, are genuine or not, is open to debate. On the underside of the great slab can be seen the small circular cavity in which the door's top pivoting 'hinge' lodged, passing through the doorway from the outside. The position of the left-hand door jamb indicates

The tin mill on the left bank.

clearly that the door opened outwards, allowing more room to be utilised inside. Two mortar stones can be found within the walls of the mill. The stone lying on grass near the centre of the larger room cannot be missed, unlike the stone hiding its depressions in the annex. This object, which is partly submerged, is not mentioned by any known Dartmoor writer past or present, and can be located at the foot of the eastern wall. Also there, beside the mortar densely-clothed in moss, is an axle-bearing stone.

On a quiet summer day this tranquil little dell overflows with charm. All around the tumbled masonry the grass is nibbled neat and tidy by the foraging livestock, goat willow splays dappled shadows on to the cascading waterfall, glinting silvery white on its travel to the pool below. Looking down the valley towards the lower slopes of Raddick Hill, stunted rowan grows among the tinners' spoil heaps, while above their heads the mountain-like peaks of Leather Tor and Sharpitor sit grandly on the skyline.

Mortar stone on the left bank. The spectacles on the stone give some idea of its size.

Taking one's thoughts into the past contorts the mind to see wavering images; it reaches almost into the realms of visionary make-believe when one endeavours to conceive the medieval picture that was played out everyday under the shadow of Black Tor. Dimly portrayed in faint pastel a rustic scene of men toiling in the earth of the moor, beads of sweat oozing to trickle down across skin stained by the ever-changing patterns of moorland weather, hands like shovels, hard, cracked and heavily gnarled, and hair fashioned by the grime of the day. Water rushes along leats fed from farther up stream, providing the power for the waterwheels rotating beside ruggedly built little mills tucked conveniently below the cascading waterfall. The mills, busily refining the work of excavation, drown the song of the lark; the perpetual thud of the stamps shod with iron, clanking up and down, gradually pulverising the crude ore, shovelled on to the mortar stones, into dust. For hundreds of years the valley was alive with the sound of industry.

It is not conclusively known when this beautiful rugged upland was first delved into for tin. My theory is that it was mined during the period of the Bronze Age. The very term bronze, suggest this to be a reasonable and logical assumption, for by mixing tin and copper, it formulated the first alloy produced by man. Whether these people imported the materials first, from their original homelands on the Iberian peninsula where it is known to be found, or merely brought the knowledge and expertise with them to later exercise the mining of it, is a matter for speculation.

Another hint towards dating the age of tin excavation was read in our history books at school. They told us that way before the comparatively modern mariners of Columbus and Drake came to seafaring prominence, the Phoenicians, those people of early enterprising commerce from the eastern shores of the Mediterranean, were, a few hundred years before Christ, sailing the seas to Britain to trade for tin.

But it was not until the early years of the thirteenth century that anything was produced in writing concerning the commercial importance of tin. In only the third year of his reign, King John had the Manorial Lords seething, baring their teeth in anger, for with just a few strokes of a quill in the first ever Charter of the Stannaries, he set free their Serfs, free from tied labour, liberated to be their own masters, to work for themselves digging and streaming for tin. His Highness had wilfully conjured the needy, the graft and sweat of the nonentity, to unwittingly earn revenue for the Crown and the greedy rapacious John.

One can only endeavour to cast the imagination back into the dark torrid days of early medieval serfdom, to wonder in awe at the courage it surely took to take up the challenge of the unknown, thrown to the unenlightened by the King. To give up the security of a rude dwelling which sheltered family and kin, and to pitch a claim for tin, perhaps on the wild open moor, and work at something completely alien to whatever one had done before. Or, maybe the adventure wasn't that daunting, merely one of leaving the tethers of a tyrant Lordship after having served an enforced apprenticeship of digging and streaming for him. Now the King had perhaps inadvertently laid the foundations of hope and prosperity.

The area a tinner chose to work was referred to as a sett. It was first mapped out on the ground with miniature cairn-shaped heaps of turf or stone, placed here and there, till the area of the sett was framed. Then came a trudge, of maybe of several hours, to the appropriate Stannary town with four witnesses who were necessary to register the claim.

It is not known exactly how the tin was smelted in the early years of the industry, it is generally surmised, that the ore was built into a fire similar to the system employed to make char-coal, the resulting liquid tin then found its way into a small pit in the ground below. The ingot, of course, would have been very crude in its content with all sorts of foreign matter getting into it from the fire above. A far greater heat would have been needed to rid the ingot of other unwanted mineral and chemical elements within its structure, so a jaunt to the Stannary furnace was necessary for a firing in far more clinical surroundings. Here, after setting, the ingot would have been stamped with the seal of the Crown before its sale could take place.

The whole of Devon was once laid out in description as Stannary ground, allowing people the chance to dig for tin anywhere in the county. The Charters down through the ages differed very little in their wording but the little in which they did differ caused problems.

King John gave licence for the tinners to work only the moors and wastes, and the lands of Bishops, Abbots and Counts, not to delve into the private acreage of others. In 1305 two years before he died, Edward I, decreed differently, allowing tinners to dig for tin and turf for smelting, anywhere in the county.

As the industry came into documented history, it was found that the Jewish communities had by far the greatest share of influence over the streaming and digging of tin. There are shadowy thoughts to reason, that Jews were brought here by the all-conquering Romans, as slaves, during their near 360 years of occupation of Britain. By the year AD400 the Romans were gone, but the slaves stayed on to use their wit and industry, to gradually climb out of the mire of slavery, the pit of despair, to become leaders in commerce. By the thirteenth century, they were prosperous and wealthy, even loaning finance to the Crown. However, behind certain closed doors jealousy boiled, and enraged feelings ran high against them, encouraging the Crown to look elsewhere for financial help. The fate of the Jew was sealed and the downward spiral of their British existence began. Cruel persecution followed, with killings and massacres, until their expulsion from our shores was complete, in the early winter months of 1290, leaving deserted the tin setts.

It can be seen on record that at one time the Devon and Cornish tinners were under the jurisdiction of one Stannary Parliament, which was held every seven or eight years on the Cornish side of the River Tamar, on Hingston Hill, near Callington. No one can be sure why, but somewhere amidst the reign of Edward I, the two counties went their own way, when their administrations paired off into separate entities, with the Devon towns of Tavistock, Chagford and Ashburton named as Stannary market places, and with their Parliament sitting on Crockern Tor near Two Bridges.

Edward III or, his mother, perhaps even his mother's lover, Roger Mortimer, in 1328, relieved Tavistock of its Stannary status and installed Plympton to take on the duties. A couple of years later, young Edward married, still in his teens, and took the reigns of the Realm when he personally arrested Mortimer and had him hanged for the murder of his father. He then imprisoned his mother for the rest of her life. It was at about this time that the tax revenue from the tin was delivered into the hands of the King's first son, Edward of Woodstock (later to become the Black Prince), when he was made the first Duke of Cornwall.

Sometime during the fifteenth century, Tavistock was reinstated as a Stannary town and the bounds split into four. The outer limits of these divisions ran from the middle of the moor to the sea. Each one of them developed problems which fostered agitation between the property owner and the tinner, with complaints being heard at Westminster – disputes arising from men not knowing the rules within their own jurisdiction, and tinners digging for tin on land out of bounds to them.

On the moors and wastes they were permitted to mine by Charter, and in a roundabout way they were allowed to undermine houses and highways providing the disturbance was corrected when the delving was done, but they were absolutely forbidden to disturb church-yards, corn mills, gardens and orchards. At times total ignorance was pleaded, with apologies accepted, but often tempers flared in the heat of exasperation, when contemptuous bloody-mindedness ruled the argumentative confrontations. Occasionally fist flew when the more sinister attempts of extortion were suffered: from villainous threats to tear homes and farmbuildings to the ground, or to rip up fields full of maturing crops. Rather than wait for the seemingly eternal Parliamentary procedure of legislation to come to fruition, the injured parties would sometimes take the risky road of retaliation, blocking or turning leats to run back into the river, damaging waterwheels and smelting houses, stealing tools and ingots, causing tinners to hide their tin in caches.

Water itself was a constant cause of aggravation between the rivals. Rivers and streams were a precious source of energy, turning the waterwheels of corn mills that lined the river banks from the moor to the sea; they fed leats that contoured the countryside, feeding drinking and culinary water to outlying farms, warrens and ordinary dwellings. Yet a tinner had the right by Charter to tap the leat dry, and could also at will, run the rivers low without having the slightest worry of the consequence for other users farther downstream.

Who were these tinners, people often labelled as foreigners, that caused all this aggravation to their neighbours? It was the man up to his armpits in water and grime; the delver, the sweating grafter. Others profiting from the enterprise, the owner, the merchant, carpenter and smith were all invisible to the blind eye of retaliation. All those earning from the spoils of tin regarded themselves a tinner when it suited, those peripheral to the trade jumping on and off the bandwagon when the jurisdiction of Stannary law protected their interest. Tinners convened and presided over their own court of law and system of justice, and tremendous beneficial advantages were enjoyed under the cloak of the Stannaries. They were exempt from ordinary taxation and, except from their own tribunals, they were immune from jury service. Once registered as a tinner they were liberated from the constraints of manorial and common law. No magistrate or coroner had jurisdiction over the tinner, except in the case of murder or the loss of a limb, and even then half the jury members at the trial were entitled to be tinners.

In their heyday, the Stannary courts wielded tremendous power, much more than some may have anticipated. Sir Richard Strode, MP for Plympton, in 1512 succumbed to their verdict when he was found guilty in his absence for nurturing trouble at Westminster in accusing the tinners of silting up the estuaries and harbours below the moor with their debris of mud and sand. It wasn't long before the contemptuous Sir Richard was summoned to appear before the Court on Crockern Tor. He failed to do so and his foolhardy approach towards the situation brought further displeasure from the tinners. Bread and water for him to relish was on the menu at Lydford when he was dragged from his family seat at Newnham and incarcerated in irons for a few weeks, down in the dark bowels of the Stannary prison, along with all kinds of miserable wretches, till money changed hands for his freedom.

The term in Lydford prison must have nudged the Strodes along another line of thought: if you cannot beat them then join them, for by 1625 the silting problem did not seem to concern the family any more. According to their documented records, a Sir Richard Strode of Newnham, had interest in over two dozen tin operations registered in the Plympton and Tavistock Stannaries. One joint venture on the land of Walter Elford, gent of Shittestor (now Sheepstor) refers to pitch at Higher Helebeame at Bickleigh. Here they eagerly took from under the very nose of unfortunate Robert Dingle, who pitched the Tynworke at the court the year before 'but had not fower tynners att the warning to be witnesses, wherefore his pitch was void by the statute'.

The Stannary Parliament was presided over by the Lord Warden of the Stannaries, who represented the Crown; in his absence the Vice Warden sat at the helm. Devon's own famous Sir Walter Raliegh was appointed Lord Warden, along with being granted other rewards of high office by Queen Elizabeth I. His chivalry of draping his handsomely embroidered cape over a puddle of water, allowing Her Majesty to pass by without soiling her dainty footwear helped him, along with other feats of daring, to win her deep affection. Whether the gallant gent ever sat his backside on the cold stone of Crockern Tor is open to question. Ironically it was during Elizabeth's reign that the industry was on the steep downward slide.

One can imagine the assembly on and around the tor. A full entourage of the Lord Warden, the Clerks and Stewards and two dozen tinners from each Stannary, and no doubt others relevant to the proceedings, all with their horses tethered on the lower slopes of the hill to a gorse bush or stake, and of course the odd convenient boulder lying around. On a fine summer day the scene can be easily depicted, but in inclement weather, when the welcome from the granite is wet and horizons hide behind the misery of dense mist and saturating pervading drizzle, it issues to the mind a picture of forlorn aimlessness and the tor abandoned even before the session even began. No wonder a room at the White Horse Inn at

Moretonhampstead was sought out and adopted to become the Parliament's regular venue, after first being officially opened on the tor.

It was not until 1837 that the Stannary Parliament sat down and seriously considered the question of who was a tinner. The debate eventually concluded, that all who gained from the production of tin were tinners from the spalliard, right across the industry to the shareholder. At last, after well over six hundred years, the span of six royal houses, from the Plantagenets with King John, to the Hanovers and Queen Victoria, through twenty-nine reigns and goodness knows how many battles and wars, through the tragic years of the Black Death; the plague that devoured almost half the nation, when the industry stood still. Sixty years after their prolonged subject of identity was resolved and the industry on Dartmoor was in the painful death-throes of extinction, an Act passed at Westminster lost the tinners their much enjoyed independence, with Stannary jurisdiction transferred to the County Courts.

Throughout the years of tin mining on Dartmoor, there appears to have been five different methods used to excavate the ore. Streaming took advantage of ready-formed alluvial and eluvial sedimentary deposits, the former was found in the valley bottoms, the latter in depressions on the escarpments. For thousands of years this material, in the shape of large stones, rubble, sand and tin particles, washed off the higher hillsides by rain and swollen streams, settling where the lie of the land stemmed its flow. In places the conveniently available material lay several feet deep. Picks and shovels were employed to break down the compact conglomeration. The tinners utilised the larger material by placing it to one side, gradually building a confining bank to prevent the working stream from getting too wide. As the load was worked away from this bank, so another would be formed. The flow of water arrived at the site by diverting it in the form of a leat from farther up stream, or from a reservoir specially constructed above the place of work, to catch rainwater. The flow was carefully monitored in its gallonage and speed, so as to flush away the much lighter materials back into the rivers, leaving the reward of sweat and toil to be rewashed on a dressing floor called a buddle, before the heat of the furnace turned it into liquid metal.

According to R.H. Worth, who delved into the files of the Plymouth Municipal Records, Sir Richard Strode in 1654, along with four others, leased a tin works, known as Black Tor Tin Works, to Mathew Yandall and Roger Williams the Younger of Walkhampton. This could only have been the mills below the falls and perhaps some of their adjacent ore excavations. The whole area is an uneven mass of landscape, disfigured humps and bumps of trial pits and multiple lodeback workings, deep gerts (rift-like openings on the hillsides extending from top to bottom), all now partially camouflaged in a shaggy coat of rugged moorland vegetation.

A stone that appears to have been placed in position here is, I believe, a tinner's sett marker of a comparatively modern age. The stone may well have been put there at the instigation of Strode and his partners, wanting to secure the identity of their working area. It stands very close to being upright with a height of 42 inches and almost square in section. It overlooks the top end of the gert or openworks, on the south-west slope of Hart Tor. The gert is by far the most expansive tear in the ground above the falls; it widens considerably as it runs down towards the Meavy and divides into a number of sections where the tin lodes were obviously followed. Huge boulders manhandled to one side of a once profitable lode sit here and there, left abandoned after the lighter material was washed away to end up on the spoil heaps or turned to molten liquid in the furnace. Now rabbits with their burrows at hand, scurry around them to safety when human presence is near. At the gert's confluence with the Meavy hides a neat little cache where, when the tinners' day was done, the tools of their trade were hidden from site. In the days of active working, the whole area would have been bare of vegetation and a stone placed in the small entrance to the cache would have cleverly rendered it just a little extension of its neighbouring spoil heap.

After the easier streaming material had over the years been eventually worked out, the gert method of excavation came into being. It still employed water to aid extraction, but in a slightly different way, for here the excavators followed earth-bound tin bearing veins, or lodes as they were called. After the vegetation was taken off the area to be worked, the water was brought to above the site to wash away other unwanted materials such as soil, peat and growan (decomposed granite); these materials no doubt finished up in a river to be carried conveniently away, saving the time-consuming task of manhandling it to a waste heap. Once exposed, the lode was then broken up and taken piece-by-piece to the mills for refining and its eventual smelting.

As one can imagine, the tinners were reckless in their pursuit of the all important ore, giving very little consideration towards other man-made structures in their way. Their ignorance, or arrogance, or the sheer necessity to feed a hungry family, gave no consideration whatsoever for the care of monuments still standing that were built in times gone by. It seems that the unsatisfactory harvest from one tin lode was the saviour of the Hart Tor prehistoric double stone row that trails away from its much-ruined cairn. The gert had cut right through and eaten away at sections of the avenue before excavation was suspended. Far more of the monument would have been in peril if the value of the lode had encouraged those mining the gert to go deeper. The workings also decimated the lower end of the rows, leaving now only the Meavy's close proximity to allow us the slightest hint as to where the alignments may have terminated.

A single row of stones which runs a little more to the true south-west than the double, has suffered far more from the depredations of modern man, with only a dozen or so stones of the avenue remaining in its line, the majority of which seem to stand defiant in front of their associated cairn waiting for the hand of the robbers to return.

The so called lodeback pits, of which there are many in the Meavy valleys, dictate the wanderings of curiosity in my mind. Here I am not setting out to demean or deride the thoughts of the professional archaeologist these lodeback pits are miniature quarries of no great depth in the ground, some of them are lined up side by side with their extremities almost touching one another. Other pits found are single, with evidence, although now visually scant, of collapsed adits that supposedly led into their shaft-like interiors. In these cases, water was obviously employed, with the adit utilised not only for entry into the working area but also for drainage and retrieving the wanted ore. The depth of the lodeback pit excavations go no deeper than the average gert, so why the little quarries in a line almost touching one another, when the lode could well have been extracted merely by working the ground like a gert as a elongated open works?

Just a short ramble downstream from the mill ruins, over the awkward ankle-jarring stones of spoil heaps, the Hart Tor Brook empties out of a valley that hides from the rest of the moor. All around its perimeter, ridge like hills cocoon its midst into a secluded empty wilderness. Today, but for song of the lark and pipit and the occasional call of the raven, the valley is quiet; tracks of olden days appearing as shadowy remnants, crossing the fords on the brook to ascend over the horizon to wherever they led, and leats, long ago forgotten, traverse the hillside to the gert that runs down to the Meavy from the slopes below Hart Tor. There is, under the long early-winter shadows of Cramber Tor, the trace of a prehistoric enclosure of considerable size, with a small cairn set within its confines. There is no evidence of any kind that man had ever occupied this secluded valley; there are no visible signs of any hut circles, no remnants of any structure that man may have lived in except on the left bank of the brook, near its confluence with the Meavy. Tall seeded grasses undulate, like waves on a lake of liquid gold, masking the sodden wetness underfoot where the tin people have wrenched every bone out of the valley's long elongated spine. Livestock forage quietly among huge mounds of tinners' waste, adorned now in a flamboyant coat of ling and bell heather. Thousands of large boulders lie around, scrubbed clean over the years by frost and rain. Two especially are of extraordinary size; seen from afar, sitting among their much smaller inferiors, the monsters appear alien to their surroundings, one resembling a giant marble has been utilised for the rear wall of a lean-to tinner's hut, the masonry of which is now very ruinous, lying in an untidy line among the bracken. From the Meavy to the middle reaches of the brook, can be seen classic examples of row after row of parallel spoil heaps.

As it leaves its valley, the Hart Tor Brook drops steeply through a small gorge, then immediately loses its independent flow as it merges with the bulk of the Meavy in the confining concrete walls of a sluice, from where it is promptly delivered a few yards downstream via a pipeline to the Devonport Leat. The meagre flow of the Meavy's water that eludes the sluice, trickles on down beneath the leat's aqueduct. Keeping to the river's left bank, progress on foot until the Stanlake Brook on the right is met, is a mischievous labyrinth to thwart the walker. First, getting over or under the aqueduct has to be managed before areas of sodden, squelching black holds the thought of which way to proceed; sopping wet carpets of sphagnum moss, here and there oozing spring water, encourages a diversion. There are tinners' waste heaps to climb, rivulets to jump, stunted head-scratching, clothes-snatching hawthorns to avoid or stoop under, prickly gorse bushes to squeeze between, and toe-catching rocks to trip over hidden below a canopy of bracken. And all the while, the little river alongside to the right, tumbles, slashes and gurgles under the shade of goat willow and rowan.

The tin operations on the little Stanlake are somewhat intriguing: the depression running down the hillside displays three separate types of operation. The lower section was worked by streaming, one can see the alluvial parallel rows of spoil running more or less downhill, whereas the eluvial rows are found to run diagonally to the vertical, so as to restrict the velocity at which the water was required to flow, thus preventing any loss of the much-valued material being harvested. Both utilised the flow of water that the little Stanlake stream produces. The third operation, occupying the upper section of the same depression, was of the gert or openworks system. The stream of water for this came from a reservoir above, on the other side of the Yelverton to Princetown road. One can assume the reservoir to have been in place before the gert was worked, for a faint line of a leat can be traced running from the reservoir's direction down the gert's right hand side to the top end of the streamworks. This feature gives licence to one's thinking that streaming at one time preceded the gert right up to the highest elevations of the depression.

From the foot of Stanlake, under the evergreen and deciduous canopy of Raddick plantation, a stony and sometimes muddy track, undulates and meanders its way to Norsworthy Bridge, beside the orchestrating sounds of the Meavy. Half a mile along this rugged little thoroughfare, on the left, is the one-time whereabouts of Riddipit stamping mill. In R.H. Worth's time of tramping on Dartmoor there were four complete mortar stones to be seen here, now remain just the sad fragments of three, coated in layers of moss. These are located lying in the grass just in over the wall, on the higher ground near to where the ruins of a dwelling once stood. During the mill's productive periods, a Joan Dunterfilde held the lease for seventy years, till 1565, when it was 'counterpart leased to John Gyll, Robert Gyll his son, and William Bryce, son of Robert Bryce, from Nicholas Slanning, gent. of London'. The description of the place, displayed on the document, was of 'a knocking mill and half acre of ground at Reddapitt'. Among the bramble, gorse and bracken-choked ruins of the dwelling will be found, if a search is made, a neatly fash-ioned stone with three holes bored into its top; the middle one of the trio is partially filled with a stub of iron that may at one time have formed part of a ring.

Other interesting features to see whilst in the area are two potato caves; one a little way back on the track, on the right. A climb over a stile is now needed, to find the cave that is tucked just around the corner out of sight. This frost-free hollow was at sometime furnished with a door, the other cave may be easily spotted by passing up the lane towards Leather Tor Farm. Before passing up the lane, a bridge is crossed, this is one those gems of man's creation. Leather Tor Bridge spans the Meavy using great sturdy blocks of granite, cut to measure by the tare-and-feather method to fashion a clapper with the unusual feature of parapets along both sides of its path. The callous hand of the timber industry slightly mars the scene, with the vertical trunks of conifer standing characterless in an area where the oak or sycamore, or any deciduous example, would turn the picture to oil on canvas.

From the clapper bridge, the track within a few minutes runs beneath a beautiful canopy of magnificent beech, which for some reason or another, were spared by the lumberjack.

Before the scant remains of old Norsworthy Farm is met, a climb down to beside the river will discover the almost total ruination of a tinners' mill; just a fraction of its masonry now remains tucked against the bank below the track to Norsworthy. Here, including a fragment, are ten worked stones of various shapes and sizes left abandoned, lying around for the future to contemplate their once-busy uses. Counting the stone in the river adjacent to the site, there are four mortars with two depressions worked into them; there is one with three, another has four, and one displaying six, that, after its use as a mortar was spent, became employed to carry the axle of a water wheel. Also among these features from our past is a stone with a square section cut into it and two with elongated slots cut into them; these, were no doubt, fashioned to hold the mill's timbers in place.

Across the river, just a little way up under the canopy of oak, is another tin mill ruin. In close proximity, standing on its narrow side, is a large mortar now dressed in lichen. Its employment at the mill seems to have been short lived, for the depressions sunk into it are extremely shallow. Another mortar can be found on the same side of the river, where it can be spotted farther downstream close to the water's edge half hidden among the tall water-loving plants, but here the likelihood of a wet foot can be had if care is not taken. This stone, I think, may well have been deposited here from the left bank mill during a huge flood. It can be rightly thought that one of these two mills may well have conducted smelting operations, for only a few yards farther on, wedged among a conglomeration of various sized stones, is a unfinished mould stone, into which would have been poured the liquid tin produced by the furnace.

Back upstream, and best reached from the Leather Tor Farm track, is a magnificent cache, partially hidden from view in a steep slope that drops down towards the river. In full summer when the grass and bracken are at their best, this most interesting of features is difficult to locate. Once found, a peer inside is a most valuable experience for those who are interested in the subject of the tinners and their work.

Mortar stones at Norsworthy on the left bank.

Mortar stone on the left bank.

Mortar stone up on the higher ground, right bank.

Mortar stone on the river's edge, downstream, right bank.

Cache entrance, up in the woods, right bank.

Interior of the cache.

Keaglesborough Mine adit entrance.

Overshot launder at the same mine.

The mine's wheel pit.

On the hillside above Riddipit, are the remains of Keaglesborough tin mine. Up here in the midst of the conifer plantation, we are far from the idyllic scene of a little rectangular building beside a stream with mortar stones lying around. There seems to be no evidence of any shelter, no fallen masonry that once may have stood to give cover for the function of mining; the pounding of the stamps could well have been out in the open, to echo unbridled down through the valley.

For just over a mile from the Hart Tor Brook, the water for the mine's use rippled along the now overgrown leat that traverses the steeper and rockier slopes of Raddick Hill. Two waterwheels turned their days away up on this hillside, each employing the same stream from the same leat. Still to be seen, practically unscathed by time and the elements, is the embankment that carried the overshot launder from the leat to the first waterwheel. One look at the two wheel pits that housed them, tells the observer that this wheel was the larger of the two. It could well have been that the larger wheel came into existence when the works were perhaps upgraded, leaving the smaller one to become redundant. Also to be found with a good old search around are filled-in shafts and the mine's adit, if a careful eye can spot its half-hidden entrance down in the depth of Riddipit Beam. The entrance these days has a grid just a couple of feet inside barring the adventurous from entering any farther; also the ground above to the right has slipped down to almost block the way in, leaving a matter of a few inches for the inquisitive to peer inside.

In 1623, a century and more years before these structures were placed here on the hillside to do their work, Sir Richard Strode and Walter Elford of Shittestor, pitched a sett for labourers to stream for tin at 'Keaglesborrowe, it liethe in the Tavistock Stannary, lying between Glasawill and Reedapitt Beam streaming into Peikes Park'. Strode had one half and Elford the other. A reward for the rambler who makes a way beneath the conifers is the various fungi that appear here in the autumn months; among them the beautiful but poisonous fly agaric. Out on the open moor to the north-east is the lonely Crazy Well Pool (the Clasawill of 1623), an mine pit of ancient date. The substantial spring that keeps the acre of water to the brim, not only aided the tinner to excavate this great hole for his mineral reward, it also created the gert that runs downhill away from it. Through the years of its flooded existence, stories of strange tales and nightmares have been evoked by the pool, evolving into moorland folklore.

The exact depth of the pool isn't known, but the tale handed down though the ages tells us that it is bottomless, for at one time many years ago, the bellringing ropes of Walkhampton Church were brought to the site and tied together end to end. Gradually the 510-foot length was slowly lowered, foot by foot, into the pool till the hands clasping it touched the water. The exercise confirmed to those gathered around that the great hole full of water had no bottom. The story could well be related to another belief, that the water level of the pool lowers and rises with the tidal waters of the sea down at Plymouth. Superstition plays a leading role in local legends. One should never look into the pool on Midsummer's Eve, for the air all around will become still, and the rippling water slowly calm, then the smiling face of the next person in the parish to die will gradually appear from the darkness of the water's depth. Farmers and their families who lived in earshot of the pool must have gone to bed at night with wool stuffed deep into their ears, for sinister is the word used to describe the calling in the night of a voice, ghoulishly shouting, foretelling to the moor the name of the face in the water.

Crazy Well Cross.

Early one autumn morning in 1998 this flooded old pit, took a life for itself. A young and dedicated Royal Marine Commando exercising on the moor with his unit was, like his comrades, ordered to swim across the pool, fully-clothed with full pack on his back. The water-saturated weight was far heavier than the struggling soldier could bear, resulting in the chillingly cold water taking him under.

Just a stone's throw or so from the pool, silhouetted against the eastern skyline is the aptly named Crazy Well Cross, one of three standing on the northern escarpment of the Newlycombe Valley, doing duty as guide post along this section of the ancient monastic way. This cross, like the Newlycombe emblem of Christianity standing just over half a mile away to the east, was re-erected in 1915 with carefully chosen lengths of granite crowned with the original heads and arms. The work was thoughtfully carried out under the watchful eye of the Rev. Hugh Breton, and now still stands, acceptable again to the eyes of the valley; unlike the third cross still farther along the hillside, mounted on the edge of a huge boulder. Here, I reluctantly disagree with some commentators, for who am I to judge another man's values on what they conceive as beauty? It is not the most handsome cross, it is too neat and characterless, not fitting to stand in such beautifully rugged surroundings. It is a replacement cross erected in 1968 by a Lt. Commander, in memory of his mother; a truly endearing gesture, but I often suspiciously wonder if someone of lesser standing would have been granted the same privilege.

Newlycombe Cross.

Like a majority of crosses on the moor, these three were thrown down and taken away, or their shafts used as lintels and gateposts after their heads were unceremoniously decapitated, all because the unfortunate Catherine of Aragon could not produce a son and heir for Henry.

The opulent wealth of the nation at the time of Henry VIIIs reign wasn't all down to him selling off the substantially valuable property of the Catholic Church. Tin mining was also spiralling upwards to its headiest profit margins. This is reflected in the shape of the valley today. From head to toe, the Newlycombe was torn to the bare bones of the earth, creating a landscape for the curious now to ponder, to indulge in exploration, and to contemplate the shadowy remnants of the various operating methods employed in the exploitation of Dartmoor tin.

The third of the three, Hutchinson's cross.

Tinner's house beside the Devonport Leat.

Cache, Higher Newlycombe, right of the brook.

Great mountains of waste cover nearly every square yard of space between the streaming scarps. There are two dozen masonry structures that I know of, including stamping mills, tinners' houses, wheel pits, launder embankments, clapper bridges and settling pits. There are buddles, leats, reservoirs and caches too, all to be found along one little stream.

About one hundred yards on up the valley from the interloper cross wedged in the socket stone boulder, through a narrow landscape of pits and gullies, we find the considerable remains of a one-roomed house, tucked snugly into the foot of the hillside. A small group of rowan flourish in the shelter of the lee, standing with their roots partially entwined in the ruined masonry. Nothing is known of this tinner's house, and only speculation suggests that it was first built by them and years later refurbished by the builders of the nearby tunnel carrying the Devonport Leat from the Swincombe Valley through the hill into the Newlycombe. A glance at the surviving fireplace establishes the reason for this thinking, for on the uprights and lintel the semi-circular grooves of the feather-and-tare method of stone splitting (that materialised somewhere between the latter end of the eighteenth century and the beginnings of the nineteenth), can be clearly seen. These marks are also visible on the pillars of the doorway and both items of masonry seem alien to the rest of the stonework which is of uncut material.

Below the head of the valley where the two main headwaters meet, are the remains of a stamping mill, of the mid eighteenth century period. The wheel pit and tail race, still manage to elude the creeping, converging vegetation that will surely wrap it in greenery and hide it from the inquisitive antiquarian.

Beyond the confluence, where the streams run into one, it flows hurriedly through the narrow Newlycombe gorge. Here a little climb up from the water's edge, is a ruined cache, the entrance stonework is still very much in place and parts of the inner walling survives to help hold the massive roof boulder weighing many tons in position. Across the brook on the left bank, hidden from the little warmth the winter sun may give to the day, is a whole range of interesting tinners' artefacts to see: there is a wheel pit with a great deal of its masonry intact, beside it downstream is the area where the stamps did their pounding. Running steeply down the bank, still to be seen, are the grooves where the wooden launders sat to deliver water from the leat above to the buddles below. Adjoining them are the sad remains of a tinner's house which appears to be from a different age, perhaps a contemporary of the cache. A majority of its walling still holds strong but is clothed heavily in dankness where moss and lichen cling to every stone. Whortleberry, heather and fern grow from every nook and cranny large enough to hold and sustain their roots with any nourishment they can find. A few yards farther on but still within the same complex are the walls of a rectangular grass-shrouded settling pit, 44 feet long by fifteen wide. Here the brook is hidden behind a large spoil heap, and when it reappears it takes a left turn and flows immediately in front of the pit's overflow. This outlet I think may have been the trap system, where pieces of wood are placed one on top of the other into wooden slots, trapping back the sediment until it reaches near to the top of the pit walls. Here the material in suspension is stopped, and once the pit is allowed to drain it leaves the ore to dry, ready for the furnace. The unwanted spoil was probably shovelled into the brook.

Just a yard or two across the brook is a retaining wall, built of large squarish stones, holding back a huge spoil heap from the water's edge. The height of the spoil heap here is due to the need to contain it within the narrow confines of the gorge.

Where the valley floor begins to widen a leat, now wildly overgrown, leads away from the right bank of the brook. It traverses the lower slopes of the hillside for just over a third of a mile along old stream workings, under rugged little clappers and on through the forgotten pastures of ruinous Crazy Well Farm, before reaching a small plateau and launder embankment of the defunct Plym Consoles Mine. The waterwheel it fed here is no more to be seen, dismantled perhaps and taken away as part of a new venture at a more prosperous operation, or possibly it merely rotted into the soil at the bottom of the scarp.

Down on the valley floor, squeezed in among the spoil, are the waterwheel's associated mechanisms and inter-related buildings, still displaying their existence in one dilapidated state or another. There are buddles and filled-in shafts, and there is a ruin, probably a tinner's house of an earlier age, that has adopted a section of Crazy Well Farm's perimeter hedge as part of its outer walling. Not far away, water trickles from an adit and seeps into a gully before reaching a neat clapper twenty or so yards away. It must be assumed that this structure, which is eight feet wide, was erected to take the width of a horse and cart. Within the vicinity of the bridge is a tinner's house that still retains a great deal of its shape, and a very much smaller building, a tool shed perhaps, is built into one end of a spoil heap.

Spoil heap beside the Newlycombe Lake.

To reach the next conglomeration of artefacts a walk in the mind is first required, for a straight line will take the feet into a hazardous, nerve-racking quagmire of wetness. It is a well-thought-out little trek that is warranted, over spoil heaps, down steep embankments into gullies and out again, with leaps over rivulets amply widened by weed, reed, and spongy sphagnum moss, whilst all along following boundary field walls, thrown down here and there by the tinner's toil, until a ruinous little structure is found built deep into the scarp. Appearances suggests its age to be the same as its immediate streamed surroundings. Much of the masonry has collapsed but enough remains in situ to determine the building's dimensions. With the north wall being higher than that of its opposite number, it gives the idea that this stamping mill had been capped with a sloping roof. The remains of a wheel pit and

Kistvaens. The three in a group.

tail race front the weather from the west, whilst the entrance looks to have come in through a gap from the south. All share just a few square yards, with the dressing floor buddles only a stride or two away to the north.

Across the brook from this complex, a gentle climb up the slope of Hingston Hill reveals the grassed-over trails of three tinners' leats, traversing their way from farther upstream to tin workings on the escarpment. The higher leat which fed off the middle one, dropped into a small tinners' reservoir above a large gert, that runs down the hill towards the brook, whilst the lower leat met the gert halfway down.

The old grafters of the industry built the middle waterway along the contours of the hillside and inadvertently broke the silence of a prehistoric cemetery, a tiny three-kistvaen affair of what could be thought of as a family burial ground; the size of each grave's dimension, allows some idea of the interred's family status, before the fading of their day was done. The little graveyard situated uphill to the south of a huge boulder, was obviously obstructing the course of the leat from where it could be conveniently brought from the brook on its journey of about one-and-three-quarter miles to its destination on the southern slopes of Down Tor. The kistvaens are in a sad state of preservation; whether their appearance is down to the tinners no one will ever know. We can see that the leat was respectfully taken through them with little or no damage done to the actual stone coffins. When one considers that nearly all the kistvaens on Dartmoor are in a similar state, one is entitled to doubt the theory that tinners took special care not to disturb these ancient sites. The disfigurement of the farmland in this valley is a glaring example of them doing whatever was necessary in pursuit of their goal.

Farther down the valley, where it narrows below the fields of long-ago abandoned Kingsett Farm, are what can only be the tumbled ruins of three related tinners' buildings. Nature has camouflaged their structure and it is difficult to ascertain what their functional purposes were. The much larger ruin of the two, tucked into the right bank, has a couple of features that suggests it could well have been a stamping mill. On top of the bank wall, fourteen feet from the outer side wall of the more recognisable features of a room, are the remains of a stone-lined pit. What is left there to measure, is eight-feet long by three feet wide. Whether these dimensions were ever part of a larger structure, and included a water-powered wheel turning in them, only the calculated delving of the archaeologist could really ascertain.

Another wall-lined pit of about the same width, runs away from the outer walling of the ruin, a tailrace perhaps, that took the used water away to the brook. A little farther on, noticeable only to the investigating eye, is a tinner's house, dramatically disguised by time and the ever-pounding high moorland weather. Just a hint of its four sides are there to be discerned, leaving to history the lives of those who occupied it after hours of strenuous toil.

Where a stroll (ancient farm track) arrives from Kingsett Farm and fords the brook, the third ruin of the trio lies now like a ghost on the left bank, among a dense growth of gorse.

This structure's presence has enjoyed far more attention in the past from the rambler, than all the tin artefacts in the valley put together. The reason may have been the mention of a trough by Crossing in his much admired *Guide to Dartmoor*. In the last few years it seems to have been ignored, for the little granite vessel lies disintegrating half-buried in grass. When Mr Crossing roamed the moors, he spied the object lying outside the doorway of the ruin and suggests that it was a mould stone. As much as I feel uncomfortable disagreeing with that venerable Dartmoor writer, I must voice the opinion that, although the inner dimensions would have been sufficiently sizable, the mason chiselled its walls far too vertically for an ingot to be easily extracted, and the bulk of the stone would not have withstood for very long the intense heat the molten tin would have given out. Hence I believe this to be a trough.

Condition of trough in 1982.

Above the ruin, and hidden behind a field hedge, is a leat that did not at any time feed a supply of water to the building. The artificial waterway is of a far later date and took its water from the brook a few hundred yards upstream where the contour allowed its water to run into the leat. It then ran across the moorland hillside and fields until reaching the great tinners' gert running down to the brook from up under the eye of Middleworth Tor, where a number of twenty-to-thirty-foot trees now grow. Among them, sheltering in this deep man-made gorge, are sturdy oaks, sycamores and beech. It is fascinating to follow this leat, for it ducks and weaves in a seemingly positive and purposeful manner. It curves and S-bends around boulders, runs under field walls and drops down into a large gert, which it obviously post-dates, and runs out again, traversing the opposite side of the working. It hides for a while under a clapper that takes a cart track from Middleworth to the open moor, before again following old stone walls, eventually reaching the great gert that once employed it.

Condition of same trough in 1994.

Strolling along the leat one New Year's Day, my wife Sandy and I came across a cow that had just given birth to a little black calf. The calf was still wet and steaming from its birth; it was slightly arched and wobbly, trying to suckle from its mother who was grazing on the sparse moorland grass. Its presence in the cold and wet deeply concerned my wife, to the extent that the farmer had to be informed of the little creature's plight. It was late afternoon when we arrived home and the light was fading when I phoned the farmer.

'It is late for calving,' I said to the farmer, on the telephone.

'No,' was the reply, 'it's early. The damn bull got out and served about ten, before we knew he was out, it's now thrown our programme out of line. We were aiming for spring calves to sell in the autumn. I'll keep an eye out for them, she'll get down somewhere out of the weather.'

On 16th of the same month I found a little black calf in the gert under Middleworth Tor, dead, bogged down in a small mire, right up to its still shrivelling umbilical cord. Yes, the mother took it to shelter from the winter wind but unwittingly, took it into danger and prolonged suffering until it eventually died. On the open moor, these great gerts present little or no problem to mature livestock or their young, but where the gert is sheltered by the trees, from the drying summer sun, they become wet and saturated, especially where drainage is poor. In these conditions they offer to the weak and unwary only danger and peril.

Tumbling water, Newlycombe Brook.

On the far side of the brook, near to where the gert meets the water, is a ruin. Just scattered heaps of tumbled masonry can be seen when the bracken is high, yet with a little positive foraging, sections of walling become apparent. Except where it is seen running away towards Norsworthy Bridge and its confluence with the Meavy, the ruin is almost wholly screened from the brook by the old tinners' mass of unwanted stones and boulders. Here one is acutely aware of the grafting of the miner's life. Every stone, no matter what shape or size, displays evidence of spent energy, the grunt and groan of sheer endeavour in order to find the tin-rich ore. Like in the rest of the valley, no mortar stone can be found; the only presence of anything that may distinguish this ruin as being the remains of a stamping mill, is a leat, which meanders slightly away from the brook. From under steep banking, about a quarter of a mile upstream, it displays its course quite clearly, until it reaches small green fields as it approaches the ruin. From here merely a shadow runs along the grass, till it fades altogether. It is more than likely that a launder delivered water from here, over earlier workings, to the waterwheel.

Making my way along this side of the brook one November afternoon, I experienced a distinct quietness, only the ever-present trickle of water and the crisp crunch of trodden frost-stiffened grass beneath my footsteps could be heard. Not even a light breeze blew to disturb the silent seclusion. The sky was cloudless, clear and cold, when all of a sudden out of the stillness two dozen or so linnets danced in the air all around me. I watched in total fascination as they flitted here and there, on to trees and bushes disturbing droplets of melted frost, each catching a reflection of the low winter sun to fall like silver rain from fragile twiglets. As suddenly as they came they disappeared, and I remember shaking my head in pleasurable disbelief at the tiny feathered ballerinas' performance. So much so, I wasn't aware of a bullock standing only a foot or so away, a Hereford cross camouflaged among frost-tinted bracken and other seasonally painted vegetation. The animal raised a foot and put it down again while exhaling heavily to bring me back into the day.

Where the mill's tailrace water meets the brook again, sounds of recreational play resound through the trees announcing that the brook will soon arrive at the Burrator reservoir perimeter road, where in-country folk park their vehicles and mingle with the beauty of pure nature. Here is an escape for a while from mundane domestic drudgery. Children scamper noisily, shouting and laughing among the old oaks and boulders, prodding sticks and fingers in the cold running water. The aged mostly come to sit and watch, strolling a few yards to feed the birds that drop from the trees like a heavenly shower of colour. These older folk reminisce of days gone by, of when stronger limbs took them way out into the open moor, back when the lock and key for security never warranted a second thought.

On a good day the ice cream seller does well with people queuing, standing, sitting, strolling, chatting, and licking their choice of refreshment. The sheep have gone, moved to the solitude of higher ground, while cattle in the shade indifferently unconcerned, chew their cud and swish a tail to flick an aggravating fly away. Ponies with coats of various colours, hang around here and there, waiting for the expected irresponsible hand offering food. Dogs bark, run and chase, free to place their excrement wherever they please. Others leashed, wait patiently for their masters to heave on a rucksack and diligently secure their vehicle for the day, for here too comes the spoiler, the vile unscrupulous thief to enjoy the distasteful fruits of so-called petty crime.

Only a few of these people are aware that way before the car was born and tarmac roads were laid, the sights and sounds of tin mining filled the days here. From the left side of the brook runs clear evidence of a leat, terminating where a waterwheel once turned; now only the curious would begin to wonder what the scant remains of the wheel-pit masonry was all about.

Heading towards Deancombe Farm.

Just a little to the south-east from where the ice cream seller settles for the day, a lane rises for a few yards, before taking one on to an undulating path of interest and intrigue, through scenery of breathtaking loveliness and sheer rugged beauty, where the hand of man has carved his endeavours into history and left jagged lacerations, waiting for the caress of time to wrap a caring arm around the wounds and seal them with the ever-forgiving kiss of nature. At the apex of every rise and the turn of every corner one enters into another scene of engaging wonderment and curiosity. To paint the picture with these words is of no exaggeration to the lover of Nature's ingenious beauty.

On top of the first rise in the lane, a look over one's shoulder reveals the tor of Crossing's *Devonshire Alps*. Leather Tor from here towers above all that's around, glistening in the early morning sunlight whilst the valley waits patiently below for its warmth.

At the head of the Deancombe valley, two streams are born from the moorland soil, though eventually combining into one. They each arise from areas of great historical interest, yet intriguingly their origins are thousands of years apart. The Combeshead Brook rises between Hingston Hill and the great mound of Eylesbarrow, weeping as though the moor is crying. Springs ooze to the surface from in and outside the tinners' workings, and for several yards no meaning can be made of its course, just a spread of spongy, squelching mire till the weight

Hingston Hill stone circle and row.

A tinners' waterway.

of gradual accumulation begins to wear its way into the granite floor. Only yards from the infant brook, prehistory has gifted Hingston Hill with a stone row and cairn circle, an amazing spectacle of Bronze Age man's endeavour and ingenuity, a true creation of art, fashioned from the crude stone of the moor.

As it leaves Hingston Hill the maturing brook turns south and drops down through the contours. Cataract after cataract splash into crystal clear pools making bubbles that burst before falling over the following cascade. Here, high above the left bank under the tinners' scarp, sheep nibble the luxury of rich green grass growing in small nooks and crannies, but these verdant areas soon give way to a considerable acreage of spoil. Just around the corner, away from the sound of the brook, the scant remains of a tinner's shelter is protected from the bitter north-easterly winter weather beneath the old working scarp of earlier excavators.

All around is the evidence of tin working: pits and gullies, heaps and alluvial walling, all dressed in some simple form of vegetation, and there are adits, a wheel pit and flat rod pillars running down the hill from Eylesbarrow Mine.

Following the man-made cliff south-east brings the rambler to the soggy beginnings of the Deancombe Brook as it enters into daylight from the higher of the two Eylesbarrow adits. It spreads, turning the slope below it into a bog, before oozing drippingly over a wide area of moss-clad scarp. The lower adit flows from farther south and from much deeper under the hillside. After the two flows converge they make their way through the tinners' debris before running beneath the Eylesbarrow path coming up from the valley below. From here the brook drops busily into the narrow confines of a gorge, where another little streamlet augments the flow. Here for a while, nothing but the precipitous lower gradients of the hill immediately surrounding the gorge can be seen.

Although the terrain of the two brooks differ in character, it is wise to have good ankle support when following either. The uphill side of the Combeshead Brook, just a few yards after it turns to the west, is hidden behind huge spoil heaps and is best avoided because of its awkwardness under foot, but the easy way forward is rewarding to the inquisitive eye, for somewhere in among the upheaval, amidst the silent inactivity of yesteryear's turmoil, a huge flat-bottomed boulder forms the roof of a hideaway, perhaps a suitable shelter for a tinner to eat his midday meal on a rainy day. Visitors to the spot often have the notion that the entrance should be smaller and thus employ the stone lying around to narrow it.

Farther on, still a few yards from the brook, gouged out of the left bank, is an amazing cavern, big enough inside to house a small family car. The entrance itself is designed only for the slight and most nimble to negotiate. It has to be hands and knees and a crawl of a couple of yards before it is possible to stand. Immediately in front of the opening is a small grass bank restricting still further the initial point of entry, thus leaving very little for the eye to discern whilst finding one's way to it along a maze of sheep paths and a conglomeration of heaps, pits, bracken and gorse bushes. Who occupied their time excavating this minor miracle, and for what, no one knows. The entrance and rather awkward location suggests that its use was not for storing root crops, and every thing about it is too extravagant for it to have been a cache. Mr Crossing suggested it may have housed a still for illicit alcohol, distilled by the tinners for their own consumption. The notion, although possibly a little fanciful and romantic, is highly probable.

From the entrance of the cavern, on a still day, the brook can be heard tumbling down the hill towards a ford. In the warm months it arrives unseen from under the low, drooping leaves of willows that line the banks for several yards on both sides of the water. The little crossing carries the path to Eylesbarrow, the same path that spans the Deancombe Brook higher up on the hillside. The ford is paved with flat-topped slabs of peat-stained granite, many of which have either disappeared or been covered with silt and sand.

From the ford, another well-trodden path leads away from the main thoroughfare and travels almost in a straight line up the hill to the north, terminating on a small grass-covered plateau. Here, without doubt, is a true potato or root crop cave. Like the cavern on the other side of the brook, the entrance is walled but here the location is easily approached and one only has to stoop to enter the hollow. It is situated on the land of old Combeshead Farm, the yard and buildings of which lie in near-tumbled ruin below.

Just a couple of yards downstream from the ford, hidden behind a dense growth of gorse, an uncharacteristically shaped boulder forms a one-span clapper. From here the water flows under, over and around huge moss-clad boulders; great silver-streaked cataracts drop into

Cavern. Hiding away above the Combeshead Brook.

A stamping mill lies betwixt the two brooks.

One of four mortar stones outside the same mill.

pools, agitating their depths and sending bubbles sparkling to the surface in spectacular confusion. Willow trees hold strong, with roots entwined securely around stones and boulders, while the water perfectly mirrors their drooping likeness. Tufts of lichen are draped delicately from branches, others of various intriguing shapes coat the bark with their greyish blue-greens. All year round this valley is lovely, with the dress of winter colour being undoubtedly very beautiful, but the songs of spring come nearest to perfection, when it enchantingly serenades all the new-born into life.

Tucked into the foot of the steep embankment, right in the midst of this idyllic place, are the remains of an interesting little stamping mill. A considerable amount of its walling. still stands, veiled in all sorts of greenery. The position of the wheel pit and tailrace, both of which are clearly discernable, give the indication that the stamps were exterior to the building. This dates the mill's working life, I am sure, somewhere between the late medieval period and the mid eighteenth century. What throws the observer into confusion here is the number of mortar stones to be seen lying around, which were, to popular belief, employed only when the stamps operated under cover. Maybe here we are looking at a mill that saw the age of transition.

The wheel pit is a curious feature in that it was built diagonally away from the general line of the mill. With a little exploring the leat to the waterwheel from the Combeshead Brook can also be traced. And not far away, out of sight to the east, is an adit, seeping water to the Deancombe Brook. The floor of its channelled outlet has, over the years, gradually risen and is now choked with grass, reed and sphagnum moss, and the entrance itself in summer is partially concealed by a cloak of hanging bramble. There is no stone-lined entrance to this adit, which make it exceedingly dangerous to even contemplate entering it.

Not too far downstream the two brooks lose their individual identities when they fuse into one to become the Narrator Brook. Making my way along the left bank one early summer's day, I came across an amusing yet sorrowful sight. A ewe was tentatively nibbling the tender new growth of a gorse bush, while its lamb was prodding very gingerly at the lower foliage while occasionally letting out a plaintive little cry, as I drew closer the pair turned their heads to look at me, The ewe made what seemed like a disgruntled bleating utterance before moving off leaving her offspring looking at me with its nose and mouth spotted all over with blood.

Ruins of Outcombe stamping mill.

Sopping wetness is encountered if the right-hand side of the brook is followed, unless, of course, wellington boots are worn, even then, if the eye is not mindful, the occasional bootful of water is likely. It is best to accompany the brook on its left, where one can relax and look around whilst strolling along. Through this delightful little glen, about a quarter of a mile from the confluence, an oak wood is met. This suddenly alters the atmosphere, very much like a curtain rising on a change of scene in a theatre. The only thing to mar the occasion is the lack of accommodating access in the stile for Toffee, my dog.

Like most deciduous woodland, this place is magical, a miracle of nature. All year round, dead leaves rustle underfoot, and pockets of them form leaf-mould several inches deep between the boulders, fostering the ever-present earthy smell of humus. Moss, lichen, fern and fungi adorn every tree. In the later days of spring, bluebells carpet the floor. Nest boxes for blue tits and great tits are secured to several trees, and at times the oak canopy simply buzzes with the sound of their chittering as they search for caterpillars. The tiny wren, who lives here too, can also be heard.

Mortar stone built into interior wall.

The moss-matted ruin of Outcombe Farm can be mused over, almost immediately to the left after descending from the stile. Those just setting out to discover the tin artefacts of the moor for themselves, could be forgiven for thinking that the ruin may be the Outcombe blowing house (smelting house) marked on the Ordnance Survey map. When I first came across this site this was certainly the initial thought hesitantly running through my head. Until I read Worth's *Dartmoor.* I did not have a clue what a blowing house looked like, let alone the tumbled remains of one. It took a little time to search around until I found it, lying only a few strides to the left of the path that meanders alongside the flow of the brook. Tribute must be paid to the old Dartmoor writers for pointing many of us in the right direction.

The function of the mill was in fact for stamping and not for smelting, and a busy place it must have been for there are many mortar stones to be found. There are fourteen in and around the immediate vicinity of the ruin, including one built into the wheel pit walling, which prompts the thought that either the walling had at sometime in its history collapsed and was rebuilt, or that the building was erected on or near the site of an older mill. There are another two mortar stones lying almost undetectable on the edge of the spoil heap a few yards from the ruin's entrance. Another nine are to be seen, where the brook meets the cart track, which runs up to the tumbled stonework of Outcombe Farm. One stands on end at the water's edge, acting rather like a roadside milestone, seven others form a line acting as walling on the bend of the track. In the wall on the other side of the track is another that can be spotted if a little patience is had.

Mortar stone inside the mill.

Mortar stone outside the mill.

Mortar stones on the bend of the Outcombe track.

Ragged Robin.

As already written about, in the rambling days of Mr Worth, there was a crazing mill stone to be seen lying on the floor of the mill. Like a few other artefacts that at one time could be seen in the Meavy valley, it is now no doubt decorating some private garden, or employed as a focal point in the grounds of a public house. With so much ground disturbance in the area, the course of the leat to the mill is not easily located, but the lie of the land near the immediate approach to the wheel pit embankment suggests it came from the Narrator Brook.

The Outcombe track leads out of the wood via another stile, and this one quite sensibly has dog access. Out in the open a long, single stone forms a one-span clapper bridge. Crossing this in early summer and looking into a spring-saturated field on the right can be rewarding, for here the pink blooms of the rare ragged robin grows in plentiful profusion.

The little Outcombe Brook sheds its small flow into the Narrator Brook from a marsh created between the high ground of Yellowmead Down and Leeden Hill. From head to toe it is only a little over half a mile in length. For the first couple of hundred yards it proceeds among a mass of tinners' scars, where tiny streamlets trickle silently, in places almost motionless, until uniting as one near the brow of Leeden Hill, from where it cascades very steeply down through a deep boulder-strewn gorge under a canopy of conifer. To follow the stream up to its source, the area at the confluence with the Narrator Brook is best avoided, for here the ground is a mass of spongy wetness. It literally wobbles, squelches, bubbles and shakes; even the moisture-loving willows are buried up to their branches in the mire. Although the area has a certain atmosphere, it is reasonable to take the easier option and trace the more agreeable steps back towards the wood, turning right in front of the stile to ascend steeply uphill between wooden fencing until the open moor is reached. The view unfolding on the way up is magnificent, cocooned all around with the near horizons of Sheepstor, Peak Hill, the twin rock piles of Sharpitor and Leather Tor, the great mass of Down Tor and Combeshead, and the huge bare back of Eylesbarrow. Climbing the hill one mid-April morning, the song of blackbirds could be heard coming from half a dozen or more places in the valley below; it seemed that little else stirred bar this wonderful sound, and not even a breeze could interrupt the melody.

Near the crest of the rise is an old mine shaft with a hawthorn tree growing contentedly from the lip of the fenced-off hole. About ninety strides down hill, more-or-less parallel with the brook, under the remains of a stone wall, is the adit related to the shaft. The initial excavation was for tin, but china clay was found within the seams. One can see, spread out like a small plateau, the waste contents of the venture, the small quantity suggesting that the life of the mine was short.

Downstream from the merged Outcombe and Narrator waters there are few accessible tin-related features and only the left side of the valley, under the shade of Roughtor Plantation, affords any opportunities find them. What there is, is irritatingly screened with a tangled curtain of bracken and bramble, and a dense growth of young conifer. There is, on the left of the path, a vestige of a post-1750 stamping mill, with just a few yards of its leat to be traced. A little farther on, a foot or two to the right of the path, is a bramble-smothered adit, and another can be found in the same condition on the left, near where the plantation eventually gives way to open space. For those with time there are adit-related shafts to see, but only if a clothes-snagging, skin-scratching search is laboriously undertaken.

The Narrator Brook ends its journey where it meets the much stronger flow of the Meavy, the swollen mother river in turn issuing into the beautiful man-made Burrator Reservoir.

Hidden beneath this expanse of water, somewhere on the left side of the drowned riverbed, is the stamping and blowing mill to which belonged the mould stones that could be seen in Worth's day, near the lawn on the west side of the reservoir. Neither stones can be seen today, no doubt carted away by opportunists who have taken other artefacts from in and around this beautiful area. Only one, double-sided, mortar can be seen now to give a hint that somewhere nearby the tinner had been busy, perhaps its shape not having lucrative value attached to it. There is another mould stone which escaped even the eye of Mr Worth for it lies beneath the water of the reservoir, and can only be seen during times of severe drought. It was most probably a companion of those near the lawn on the west side of the reservoir.

The mill below the water no doubt belonged to the Elfords of Longstone, the ruins of which house can be seen on the piece of land protruding into the water, from the eastern shore of the reservoir. The family, who were Lords of the Manor in their day, had tin interests stretching back to Elizabeth I's time, and probably way before, In the 43rd year of her reign, Alexander and John Elford shared a streamwork with Sir Richard Strode. The bounds lay in the Plym valley, to the East of Trowlesworthy, 'on a rock three arrow shots up from the river, by the West side of Yeaster Brook' (Spanish Lake). At Bickleigh, the same three men had miners toiling for the mineral during the reign of Charles I.

A little way downstream from the reservoir's lofty granite wall, the Sheepstor Brook flows into the Meavy from high up in rock-strewn Burrator wood. The rewards of a spring visit to this place are unbelievably delightful, but care as to be taken for there is no easy walking and good ankle support is needed if a sprain is not to be the remuneration. Even where the blue-bells grow, the hillside is steep and the flowers' foliage is slippery. On a bright afternoon, when the rays of the sun pour in, one's eyes open to the light gleaming through tender young sycamore leaves and huge moss-clad boulders being splashed by white cascading waterfalls, tumbling, falling, plunging in wonderful disarray.

Up on the open moor, the Sheepstor Brook quietly matures from a small but hazardous mire, under the ever-watchful eye of Gutter Tor perched high on the eastern extremity of Ringmoor Down. The head of this little brook is not too dissimilar to others in the Meavy valleys in that it is surrounded by old tinners' heaps, pits and gullies.

The end of the road for the motor vehicle is at Burcombe Gate, only a few hundred yards from the stream's seeping beginnings. It is often congested here with parked cars and mini-buses, and the odd military vehicle. All manner of people use the area as a base for the outset and return from an enjoyable stroll or a more invigorating expedition into the moor. The military find it handy for manoeuvres, with the troops using the old tinners' workings for cover while firing; spent shells by the dozen can often be found among the heather.

Rock Basin on Gutter Tor.

There are all sorts of things in and around the mire to see that may stimulate the grey matter, all within stone-throwing distance from one another. A climb to the tor will give venture-tempting views of a great length of the moorland Plym. Whilst up there on the roof of the tor itself there is a fascinating feature, intriguing to those who see it. It is a depression of some depth, resembling a basin, with its outlet now worn sufficiently enough to empty the hollow of rainwater before it has chance to fill. For thousands of years the harsh elements biting at the moor have eaten steadily away at a weakness in the rock's structure, gradually creating what we see today.

Over the fencing, and a few yards away on a rise to the west, the ruins of a kistvaen can be found, with just three stones of the little monument remaining, protruding clear of the ground. Downhill, more or less to the north, is another in a much happier state of preservation, with all four stones set in what remains of the surrounding cairn; only the capstone is missing, robbed no doubt for use elsewhere. Like the grave on the hill, this one again is considerably narrow.

Old Leat to Yellowmead blowing mill.

Between the Ditsworthy track and the Sheepstor Brook, protruding from the moorland surface like some grassed-over moonscape craters, are the filled in mine shafts belonging to tin workings of the early nineteenth century. These holes in the ground were drained by an adit that was once situated near to where the brook meets the tarmac road.

Before the brook loses its short moorland identity and enters the fields of Yellowmead Farm, a tinners' ravaged rivulet joins its water from near the head of the Outcombe Brook. The two, united, flow under a cart track down into the valley, hiding in the midst of a landscape carved out by tinners; only hawthorn, willow, rowan and gorse softens the rugged upheaval. Here and there traces of the leat that fed the Yellowmead smelting house can be walked along, if a search is made to find it; however, permission from the landowner must be obtained before venturing here.

To see the site where the tin ingot was produced, it's best to ask locally for directions and permission. Once located, bits and pieces related to the tinner's craft can be found, the remnants lying within a few feet of each other. A section of a small mould stone and a large salmon-coloured axle-bearing stone, with animal fat (grease) burnt black and ground into the slot, rest on what could be the very scant ruins of the mill that once employed them. There is also a stone, again of salmon colouring, with a shallow slot neatly cut into it, perhaps employed to hold a structural timber in place. Resting on the bank nearby is a piece of a double-sided mortar stone. Inadequately thin for the pounding it would have taken, the stone is split across the two visible depressions. The piece of mould stone is obviously a fraction of a larger section. Before the split occurred the mould would have produced a very small ingot and, like the mortar stone, it would have been inadequate to last the pace of constant employment, too frail to take the heat of smelted tin for any great length of time. The outer dimensions of the fragment are no more than twelve inches wide and from top to bottom eight and three-quarter inches, the internal measurements span seven inches across the top and five across the bottom, with a depth of only three.

Fragment of mould stone.

Up in the stroll to the north-east can be found, with a little searching, a large stone, almost square in section, with clear indications of a trough being hewn out of it; the chisel marks can be clearly seen. The abandoned shallow surface dimensions cut from it are roughly twenty inches by sixteen. If the finished item was to have been a mould stone, it would have provided the mill with the largest mould known of on the moor.

Mr Worth tells us in his book that there was a float stone to be seen built into the hedge near the mill. This object, like the crazing mill stone he described near the farmyard itself, cannot now be found. These specimens could well have been sold when the previous proprietor of the farm, a Mr Manning, had a farm sale before he vacated the place. It is known that a few stone artefacts were sold, together with machinery and other farming implements.

Broken in two, a double-sided mortar stone.

It was an early summer evening, whilst I was searching for the partly-cut mould stone, just a little before dusk draped itself across the moor, when my attention was taken away from the subject in mind by the sight of four fox cubs playing outside their den, running here and there, jumping and hopping, tail-pulling, and with mouth-to-mouth playful fighting. The earth was large, with holes and earth mounds covering quite an extensive area. A week later, on another visit, there were five cubs just sitting and lying in the shade under the stroll's perimeter banking with the tree canopy overhead. The earth complex being of a substantial size, fostered the thought that the farmer must have been fully aware of its existence, seeing the lambing season was in its early stages. When cubs are born, even when they are sucklings, the adult fox still continues to pursue its prey to fill the larder for a rainy day. I have often watched foxes paw out a hole, place in it a future meal, then nose the soil back over, until satisfied it is covered well and hidden from other hungry mouths.

Two young cubs at Yellowcombe Farm.

Collyton clapper bridge.

Six depressions on one mortar stone..

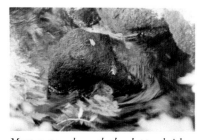

Mortar stone beneath the clapper bridge.

Four depressions on each side.

Mr Palmer, the farmer at Yellowmead, viewed the fox with refreshing tolerance, saying there was a place for everything in life, and made light of the few Muscovy ducks he once had that were too slow for Reynard who eventually nabbed the lot. He went on to say, in a more serious tone, that one year far too many lambs were being taken, and the situation called for some positive head-scratching. In the end the profound thinking initiated a call for a marksman to cull. By the time the man with the gun had left the premises, sixteen foxes lay dead, but not before an unacceptable number of lambs had fallen victim to them.

To follow the course of the brook through farmland, permission from the farmers concerned would obviously need to be obtained as this is all private land. From where it leaves the ground of Yellowmead, the brook meanders quietly through the lower fields of Nattor Farm, or Natter as the locals so nonchalantly call it. In places the ground is wet, boot-filling spongy wet, where it nears Collyton Farm fields worked by the Legassick family.

The brook flows beneath a variety of wetland-tolerant trees and shrubs, through almost inpenetrable clothes-tearing undergrowth. Within a few yards, the brook arrives back out into daylight at a ford before dropping weir-like under the trees again. Now the way is slightly easier, but the awkward ground needs to be paid attention to if a sprain to the lower limbs is to be avoided, and one still has to be aware of what may snag at head level. After a few yards a rugged little clapper is met. Here at one time, perhaps during the late years of the Middle Ages, tin ore was crushed and smelted. The mill is now laid to ruin, under a nasty blanket of bramble.

The only thing remaining unimpaired is the mouth of the tailrace which discharged just below the bridge. Beside it in the water is a double-sided mortar stone resting on the clapper's impost. Immediately above is a mortar, the only specimen I know of on Dartmoor with so many depressions worn into it. There are six on the upper surface and six on the lower. The stone was I should think, finally overworked, leaving two of the depressions at one end split across their centres. Behind this stone there are another two, hidden from sight. Wellington boots are the order of the day if these artefacts are to be detected, and only in good light can anything be seen, but a slender hand can feel that both stones have the saucer shapes worked into them. They seem to be doing duty as pieces of the rough masonry material extending the length of the impost there to carry two bridge-widening slabs of granite.

The bridge is of a much earlier date than this development, for the left-hand slab displays the scars of the feather-and-tare along with a piece of the rusting tare still wedged firmly into it. The other slab seems more in keeping with the age of the bridge; this stone has an aperture worked into it, hinting that it was at one time employed elsewhere, maybe as a lintel over a doorway at the mill, with the door pin swivelling in the hole. There is another mortar on the bridge itself and one just a little downstream on the left bank. Up from the bridge, on the right of the brook, are two more of larger proportions, with four depressions each on their upper and lower surfaces.

Over the fence to the left of the brook, are the cow fields as Mr Legassick senior called them during a thoroughly enjoyable conversation one evening. After one has respectfully straddled the fencing, a stroll along to the right will soon find the tarmac road and the Collyton Farm buildings. Immediately across the road from the field gate is a cart shed that attracts a lot of attention from the moorland artefact-seeking enthusiast.

The top and one side of the shed is constructed of corrugated iron, whilst the opposite side and rear, are built of stone. Used merely as building material and placed in the bottom of the wall, is the item that makes the shed so interesting, a fine example of a mould stone with its cavity facing the daylight, its sharply-hewn edges rounded by the red-hot liquid tin. The stone was more than likely made redundant when the crack it carries appeared diagonally across its face. At one end a small groove, just a couple of inches in length, slopes into the cavity from its top edge. In this, it is thought, a stick of doweling shape was placed, and as the mould filled and the molten liquid cooled the outer portions of the stick burned off, making it easy when the mould was full, to twist and remove it, leaving a hole into which something far more substantial could be inserted to lever the cold ingot out. Also in the stone is a tiny cavity, cut to secure a sample ingot. The stone is now the only complete example to be seen in the whole of the Meavy and Plym valleys, the rest, like the other missing artefacts, may never be seen again.

Mould stone in Collyton Farm cart shed.

The cow fields at one time were littered with the tinners' spoil, until the industrious Legassicks astutely utilised some of the seemingly useless material for the base of their farm-yard floor. Trailer loads were taken away for infill before the concrete was laid. The hard work repaid the family double, with a level and easy-to-clean yard, and the field acreage returned after hundreds of years to a far more useful asset. More of the debris, literally hundreds of tons was scraped up, picked up and pushed uphill to the southern edge of the inner cow field, to infill a large gert, deep enough said Mr Legassick to hide a double-decker bus. Now a huge winter feeding cow shed stands where a little of the tin history lies buried. 'I don't know exactly how deep he was,' said Mr Legassick junior, 'but even heavy rain running off the roof of the shed, disappears before it runs very far.'

The working water that aided the tinners who obliterated the fields, came to the site from near the beginnings of the Sheepstor Brook, via a leat that can still be seen running along the northern slopes of Ringmoor Down, supplemented by another source from the west. The ore from the workings was no doubt crushed and smelted at the mill near the old clapper.

This beautiful valley is at its deepest just down the road from Collyton Farm entrance, under the shade of tall sycamore and beech. Stepping stones and a ford side-by-side cross the brook to a gate that opens to take the eye up to the magnificent rocks of Sheepstor, nearly four hundred feet above.

One of the Kit Mine Blacksmiths' shops.

One of the buddles at Kit Mine.

From this lovely spot, a few twists and turns along the road will find Kit Tin Mine, all the necessary apparatus to work the ore ready for the furnace could be seen in operation if one passed by the entrance gate in the first quarter of the twentieth century, all no more than a dozen yards from the road. Permission from the landowner is needed to enter.

Compared to the mill near the clapper, this mine is modern, three to four centuries could well separate their working years, a huge chasm in time. Yet production methods were not too dissimilar. Just a hint of the clothes drying house base can be detected on the left, as one passes by to investigate the more substantial remains to be seen. The house, now with the corrugated iron roof, was the forge where the smith would have used his ingenuity to create a piece of mechanism for some particular function in the mine. The house now is utilised as a shelter for livestock when respite from inclement weather is needed. On top of a rise, near the rear of the old building, are three circular buddles, a system of dressing the tin that differed from the old stamping mill method, replacing the drag where the crushed ore in liquid suspension ran into a shallow rectangular trough-like pit, set on a slight incline. The tin being the heavier dropped first, the other materials falling as the water lost its pace near the outlet of the drag. The buddle did more or less the same, except that the material in suspension was delivered on to a stone with a convex upper surface sitting in the centre of a round trough-like basin, where the floor inclined slightly to the basin's circumference. When the material in the trough reached the level of spilling over, the flow was stopped and the contents allowed to drain till dry enough to be handled with a shovel. First, the waste, sandy material which was lighter and which settled at the periphery of the trough was taken out and discarded, then the 'middlings' as they were called, were transferred to another buddle that was designed to catch the tin particles that may have escaped the first dressing. The tin being the heavier, was in general the first to lose its suspension and accumulated closest to the point of delivery; this was now ready for the furnace.

Sadly mosses now coat the buddles that are cracked and disfigured by the roots of hawthorn, hazel and ash that shade the abandoned and neglected site. Some of the waste that was thrown out to one side of the buddles, and now nurturing various forms of plant life, can still be seen when the mole in its own excavating brings it to the surface in small grey-brown heaps. The Legassicks, when Mr Manning worked Yellowmead, took away wheelbarrow-loads of the material, mixing it with cement for rendering the farmyard shippon walls, giving them a smooth washable surface.

The stamping mechanisms, which were of the Cornish type, pounded up and down just a yard or two uphill to the south of the buddles, but no trace of their existence can now be found. The wheel pit which could be cleaned out and used again today, reveals more or less the dimensions of the wheel that powered them, but here again nothing of the wheel. By all accounts it was allowed to rot and collapse, with time taking it down to nothing, leaving way for the sycamore to flourish in its place.

The launder bank behind the pit, though gradually being eroded by the feet of livestock, is still there, but the wooden launders that sat on it have long gone. Mr Legassick remembers seeing pieces of the timber which, he said, were an inch and more thick. He also told me that the water was delivered to it via a clome pipeline, that still runs beneath the Collyton fields. At times even today it collapses under the weight of the tractor, leaving a hole to be filled in. In turn the pipeline itself was fed by a launder from the Sheepstor Brook. The intake is crude in construction, but nevertheless effective still today. It is hidden and forgotten under the dense growth of vegetation where the brook ran through before reaching the old clapper. With permission from the landowner, it can be located, just inside the boundary hedge of Collyton Farm.

Although the whereabouts of the mine's adit entrance is clearly discernable, it is nevertheless blocked, and displays none of the character of its working era. It lies on the far side of the field to the west of the mill buildings. The roots of a mature oak now feel their way in and around the interior, where during its days of activity, volunteers were asked to enter and ascertain the damage, and whether it could be restored to working order after the roof collapsed midway along its 300 yard length. Mr Legassick remembers his grandfather telling him of the event.

To follow the adit's travel out in the open, we have to walk uphill to the south, in the direction of Ringmoor Down. Up in the right-hand corner of the same field is the old explosives house, now roofless. Between the stones of the neglected masonry grows the dainty maidenhair spleenwort by the hundreds. Over the hedge from this house and a little farther on up the hill, a depression in the hillside is found, apparently caused by the collapse of the adit. The crater is quite a substantial size, about twenty feet deep and several yards in circumference at the rim. A coppice of hazel and blackthorn are among other small trees now hiding the crater from the open skies. A little farther on to the south, the adit traverses the Collyton property, where the shafts, and trial pit and their thrown-out waste heaps were once seen. Today only different shades of green in the grass give a clue to the past. The Legassick's over the years have to a great extent levelled the area, patiently refilling each time a depression seems to be deepening.

The Sheepstor Brook runs along beside the road like a dog beside its master, quietly compliant to the tether of disciplined confinement. The rush from the moor is stemmed for a while as the gradient levels out, leaving just the sound of the ripple over a bed of small granite stones. The flow runs below the pretty village of Sheepstor making its way behind the cottages, hiding even from the church where only the loftier stonework of the tower can watch it go by under the road-side wall. After flowing beneath the little bridge in Portman Lane the brook loses itself for about a third of a mile to the fields of private land, until reappearing again in the steep cascade to the Meavy.

Wheel pit at Kit mine.

Kit Mine leat intake from the Sheepstor Brook.

Sheepstor Church.

Circumstances have changed since I first photographed the items of interest at the next point to occupy our curiosity. Permission then had to be obtained from Mr Williams who works Yeo Farm, the buildings of which lie away to the left of the Meavy, just over a third of a mile downstream from its confluence with the Sheepstor Brook. Fronting the farm at the entrance then was a nigh-on derelict dwelling, quite a large residence, far more spacious than the house up on the higher ground where the Williams family reside. The old derelict house, built by the Woollcombe family in 1610, was sold by the Maristow Estate in the mid 1990s to the Thompson family, who have done astonishing work in restoring and revitalising the house and its immediate surroundings, bringing to the area a scintillating breath of fresh air.

The family first spotted the property for sale in the *Western Morning News*. Mrs Thompson viewed it while her husband was away with the armed forces in Norway and fell in love with the idea of living there. On his return home, she took him along to have a look at its potential. The rest of the story can be seen in the sheer determination that has produced what we see today. Livestock had used the house for shelter; they were fed there, they slept there and their dung likened to a foot-deep sponge, layered the floor from wall to wall. Most of the timbers upstairs and down had to be replaced, including the roof joists, only a few of these survived to stay in place. The interior walls had to be taken back to the stonework and replastered, and new slates were purchased for the roof. The annex at the rear of the house had a gaping hole in its eastern wall, apparently the legacy of a runaway tractor that careered down a nearby gradient. Before restoration took place, I took the annex, which was only a single storey, to be an outhouse, but in fact it did originally have an upper floor where the servants' quarters were. Here again the feature has returned more-or-less to its former self, with an upper floor back in place.

In Mr Worth's days of exploration there were three mortar stones to be seen at the farm. One built into the foot of the northern wall of what he thought was the outhouse, the other two lay in the yard, with an iron ring inserted into each of them. When I first visited the site there were only two to be found, one partially imbedded in the yard flooring with the ring having been either cut or knocked off, leaving just a small stub of iron, barely noticeable, rusting away between the depressions, and of course, the stone built into the foot of the masonry.

Now, with Mr Thompson rediscovering the third, or a third, and finding another to make it four, all can be seen in place around the property. All four display only two depressions each, but the one tucked up close to the wall near the back door of the house has two on its reverse. Neither of the other two now built into walling had depressions on their reverse side 'If they had,' said Mrs Thompson, 'we would have left them free standing in some other location.'

The distance between the depressions in the mortar stone built into the driveway drystone walling being wider than those in the other three, suggests that at sometime alterations had been made to the stamps at the mill. There is another stone of interest in the wall, being

Mortar stone built into outhouse wall, Yeo Farm.

The same stone. Now built into house wall.

Mortar stone at the foot of the building.

The same stone. Found to be double sided.

Mortar stone built into the yard wall.

Mortar stone being built into the drive wall.

pillar shaped with a slot chiselled out of it. It fires the imagination into thinking that it could well have been a part of the stamping system.

The Woollcombes may well have enjoyed the odd drop of cider, for the most exciting find for the Thompson family was a magnificent apple-press stone in wonderful condition. It was discovered when the area was levelled to the horizontal base that the drystone wall now stands on.

Only the mortar stones tell the story that at one time the tinner was active somewhere nearby. One has to delve into records to find that the Woollcombes themselves had associations with the industry. A John Woollcombe shared the streaming at Higher Hele Beam (another term for a gert or gully) at Bickleigh. This was the pitch that was taken from Robert Dingle, involving Richard Strode. A Hugh Stutworthy warned Walter Elford of their plans. Those present to witness, no doubt servants, were a George May, William, Northam, William Watte, Stephen Knight and Mark Stutworthy (a pitcher himself). John Woollcombe also had interest at Willabeam near the higher reaches of the Newleycombe Lake, with William and Richard Woolcombe, Strode, John Dunning, Richard Peike, Thomas Windiate and Edmund Dunritche.

The letters on the porch of the Thompson's house are the initials of John Woollcombe, the letter T below was the first letter of his wife's name, Tamsania.

One of the stones that held the mill's stamping frame.

High up on the moor sharing space with the forgotten fields of Aylesborough Farm, are spread the dilapidated remains of what is known today as Eylesbarrow Mine. Its (mostly) dressed tumbled stonework gives the hint that a majority of what we can see is of comparatively recent origin. The mine did in fact operate during a large part of the first half of the nineteenth century, until eventually sending its grafting workforce down the long road to the valleys for the last time in 1852. By then time had built a small industrial community on the hillside in the depth of the moor. There was, apparently, accommodation for all, including houses for the manager and captain, and barrack-type quarters for the labourers, there was a blacksmith's shop, a place for the carpenter, a turf house, timber house and a powder house. Stamps pounded and water wheels turned, including two employed to push and pull the flat rods that were part of the mechanism that kept the water levels down in the workings underground.

A visit to the site, is best got from parking the car at Burcombe Gate and walking up the track that passes the much-refurbished Scout hut. The ground under foot is rainwater washed and uneven, so care is needed, with eyes to the floor most of the way. Looking into the hill for nearly a mile makes the track seem endless, with all the majesty of the views hidden behind one. To make the long haul more engaging, a little ferreting around on a slight detour to the left of the track, near the brow of Leeden Hill, will reveal a ruined kistvaen set in the grass-covered remains of its cairn. Over the brow, the ground levels out on the saddle that arches over the landscape between the Meavy and the Plym, before rising again to an area where the eye catches the fallen masonry of tumbled buildings.

Ups and downs, successes and failures, are a fact of life for all industries, what with peaks and troughs of production and sales, market fluctuation, the sensitive area of cash flow and the need for more investment. By turning the pages of the mine's short history one finds that on a few occasions during its working life Eylesbarrow certainly seemed to have met each of these individual hurdles, leaving both workmen and managers alike reaping the wages of profit or feeling the brow-sweating fear of wondering if a job was there when they woke in the morning. Each time when it looked as if the hillside was to fall silent, a saviour came along with fresh enthusiasm and took hold of the controlling reins with a hand in the capital purse. On each occasion the enterprise adopted new names, like Aylesborough, Dartmoor Consolidated, and the last and short lived, Wheal Ruth.

It is best when reaching the saddle, to stroll to the left, down towards the Deancombe, aiming for the tinners' scarp. When below this cliff-like feature, a concentrated search along to the right will reveal an adit. A steady flow of shallow ice-cold clear water runs from within its darkness. Care is needed if entering, for although everything seems set and well established, one never knows; there is already a collapse about seventy feet in. When I measured it from the entrance to the foot of the fallen heap, the tape showed sixty-six feet, a guess of about four feet would take it to where the rock gave way. It would be totally irresponsible and foolhardy to even try and ascertain the exact measurement, for one stone disturbed from its long ago installed resting place, could bring the lot crashing down.

This little orifice in the bottom of the hillside is known, quite naturally I suppose, as Deep Adit. Using rough uncut stone, only masters of their craft could have lined it top and sides so neatly. How far it is lined along its length now is anyone's guess. On average it measures four and half feet high by two and half wide. Heather and slender polypody ferns grow from the entrance stonework. Inside it curves gently to the right until reaching the heap that joins the ceiling to the floor. Beyond the fall the adit turned south-east until connecting with deep shaft it then turned to the east along Eylesbarrow's south load. The area immediately above may well have been excavated after the adit became redundant, for the ground is in places no more than a foot or two deep. The open excavation of the area would also explain why the adit entrance is so far away from the scarp. It appears to me, that the damage was done to the adit, when a large stone of boulder proportions, now resting at the foot of the scarp, tumbled down on to the roof from above. The distance from the entrance to the boulder reflects more or less the same distance from the entrance to the collapse. Here, close to the adit's entrance, was situated a powder house and a dressing house.

Deep Adit entrance.

The same adit's interior.

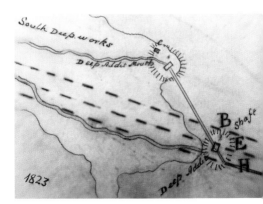

A plan of the lode.

There is no easy way to the shafts on the hill above that the adit once drained. Climbing the almost vertical scarp immediately above the adit is a totally unrewarding exercise, fostering a lot of huff and puff, to be met by several yards of ankle-jarring tussocks. A preferable way is to follow a livestock trail to the right, keeping tight to the scarp on the left, where one has a gentle ascending stroll, negotiating the odd stone and boulder till eventually making it to the top of the climb. Looking down the valley from here brings a satisfying contentment and, before one realises it, one's breathing to normal. From here pits and shafts have to be weaved around by following the tracks that sheep have made their own in their follow-the-leader wanderings when looking for better grazing or shelter.

A few strides on through awkward tussocky terrain brings one to a large mound of heather-clad spoil, where there is another little streamlet. Following this to its source will

Two Brothers Adit.

Looking back to the entrance.

Cavern-like niche on the right.

The author up to his knees.

require more than wellington boots to keep the cold water out, for here again the flow is coming from underground. This is the Two Brothers Adit where fern and heather pendulate from the stonework and the water issuing from inside is, in places, more than knee deep. Access to this black, black hole is unquestionably uninviting. The walling from side to side is just two foot six inches and from the floor beneath the water to the ceiling is a crouching three foot eight inches. The stonework advances only twelve feet, then by design it ceases, the adit opening out, unlined, cavern-like to seven foot wide by six foot high. There is a small niche on the right about twenty-five feet in, and at about forty feet it angles to the right and lessens in proportions, the height more-or-less staying the same but the width narrowing considerably. For those with whatever it takes to enter this intriguing time warp, a pair of waders is a must, for when my friend Bob Williams and I first ventured inside, only spare socks and trousers rolled up were the accessories of the day. The water is cold, bone-chilling cold. After satisfying our interest and emerging out into eye-straining daylight and warm late summer sunshine, it took an age to bring our lower limbs back to normal, even after drying and donning fresh thick walking socks and boots, bones continued to ache for about three-quarters of an hour.

Iron guide rings for flat rods.

Just a dozen or so yards to the right of the adit one looks down into the largest pit on the hill. This at one time was Jenkins' Shaft, but it collapsed and was later utilised to site a water wheel. Looking down now one sees the remains of the wheel pit; only fractions of the masonry survives and where the rest has gone only the past can tell. Speculation would suggest that through the comparatively short space of 150 years since its redundancy, the huge un-mortared stonework has sadly fallen in on itself. The year 1845 saw the birth of the wheel that turned in the pit, with a huge fifty-feet diameter it was the largest on the moor, sited at the head of what I perceive to be the most beautiful valley on Dartmoor. I cannot even begin to contemplate what today's preservationist would have thought of it defiling the moor. One can imagine the task of transporting the materials across the moor by horse and wagon and assembling it in situ, for there could have been no other way. Stone for the wheel pit was at hand in plenty, but it still had to be cut and dressed to fit, some of considerable size, for the walling had to be robust to withstand the weight of the giant wheel that was to rotate in the pit. A stroll among the ample clitter lying around reveals the occasional failed attempt at cutting the stone for the project, abandoned with the grooves of the feather and tare displayed on the course of the chosen line, only for the other side to split along a contrary direction. The wheel turned to push and pull a flat rod system, employed in connection with pumping out water from the workings below ground. These rods reciprocated to and fro from the wheel via two iron rings fixed loosely for manoeuvrability into the upper face of a sunken boulder near the rim of the pit. From here the rods rolled on a series of axles that rotated in semi-circular slots on the top inner edge of twin stone pillars. These pillars formed a line

Flat rod stones overlooking the Deancombe.

Burnt grease from a flat rod stone.

One of Eylesbarrows old shafts.

Double row of flat stones. Runs parallel to the mine track.

until reaching the shaft to be drained. The stones, each un-hewn and of no particular fashion, and several with time-baked grease streaked down their inner face, run up the hill now in a totally haphazard way, like a troop of disorderly drunken soldiers, some leaning this way and that, others having fallen. Most, although a little unruly to the line, have stood the test of time and still stand for livestock to rub themselves against. The tallest stone is three foot, all but an inch, whilst others barely show above the ground. The axle sitting in the slots of each set were at most twelve inches long, while the sets on average were spaced about twenty feet apart.

While following the line one needs to be wary of what is underfoot for dense moorland vegetation hides toe-tripping stones and potholes. The profuse growth of heather on this west-facing hill also needs to be respected. On top of the rise, nature has altered its choice of vegetation giving the walker the humps and bumps of the tussock, this in turn hides the row's change of direction, but a little searching reveals the way until its destination is reached 1144 yards further along the way.

Up here only the skyline over the Plym bears witness to the landscape's origins. Everywhere one looks, the surface of the moor has been transformed into a chaotic confusion of filled in shafts, load back pits, open works, reservoirs, waste heaps, leats and fallen masonry. The whole is scythed through by the continuation of the mine track running on towards ancient Nun's Cross.

In the midst of the mine's remains, when the cloud is down, it is like no other place on the moor. Another dimension drifts it into eeriness. With so little to see and only soft muted sounds to hear, the whole place takes on an almost ghostly feel, especially when drizzle drips and a light breeze whispers around the half-tumbled stonework. Out there somewhere a sheep will bleat and the sound of footsteps gradually come to the ear as though someone else is out here alone.

From the end of the row take the compass point reading east, this in no time at all finds the track. Turn right and the spread of time-ruined mine buildings come into view after about a quarter of a mile. Just after passing a fork in the track that circles a shaft and its spoil heap, a pair of small axle-bearing flat rod stones can be found on the right, almost beside one's stride, hidden amongst the heather. These are a part of a dilapidated row of which more substantial members can be seen more clearly farther on. There are breaks in the row and I am sure that the missing stones served to assist the completion of the flat bed system mentioned above. No doubt several other stones lie buried close to the track.

Beyond the next section of surviving stones another break in the row is met. Here on the right is a filled-in shaft, still deep enough to warrant caution when approached. It isn't until the open moor is met again that a little more searching reveals the row once more, lying in a shallow trench. The stones here are again small, some of these display the axle as having rotated in a hole six or so inches down from the usual slot on the top. The idea could well have been experimental, a notion perhaps of confining the rods to prevent them from straying. Whatever the reasons were, the method certainly wasn't so easy to grease and maintain. Beside it here is a far more conspicuous row made up of stones of larger proportions. The pair now run side by side, with the stones coated in heather and moss, until we reach the ruins of their related wheel pit.

The water that powered the wheel and aided all the others during the mine's occupation of the hill came from the Langcombe Brook. The intake of the leat was situated just below the impressive cairn and kistvaen of Grimes Grave. The stonework of the intake, apart from one, is still in place. Until the leat gets into the hill properly and begins to traverse around to Deadman's Bottom, it is merely an impression in the sheep nibbled grass. Nevertheless the line of it is clearly discernable. It is not till one can actually walk in the little waterway that it becomes no effort at all to follow. Wellington boots are required if wet feet are not wanted for, although it is only a shadow of its former self, it continues to catch water from the higher ground above it. It can also be awkward in places where stones and pits are hidden beneath long grass, heather and gorse.

Leat intake from the Langcombe Brook.

The leat crosses Deadman's Bottom where it conveniently caught the headwater of that stream. From here it follows its guiding contour around the hill towards Calveslake, within sight of Calveslake Tor it loses its identity completely as it takes a course to the north-east. Cattle that often graze and laze here I suspect are the culprits of the area's erosion. The leat ran between the little tor and the quite impressive kistvaen above it. It is noticeable again just a couple of yards before it snakes its way across the higher reaches of Calveslake itself, where again it caught a spring or two. The redundant waterway then runs along under little Gnats Head until meeting the Plym.

The river here below Plym Ford, is more or less still in its infancy. There is no sign of the leat anywhere near the riverbed and no evidence of a weir that may have encouraged a flow from it into the leat. It could well have been that the river was crossed by aqueduct, with a launder controlling a certain volume into the leat, from farther upstream. The leat comes into view again once out of the river's reach and weaves in and around the old tin workings of Wheal Katherine. With the leat taking the higher ground above a bridge, a little more erosion spoils the going for a while until, again, the course reappears to follow the hillside around to Evil Combe. Here confusion reigns for several yards with waste-high reeds filling the leat and a squelching spongy bog, coloured brilliantly with sphagnum moss swallowing all traces of its existence. Here once again the designers of the leat cleverly caught another volume of water. Once on the other side of this saturated obstacle, the leat is easy to relocate; a comfortable stroll around the hill under Higher Hart Tor will have brought by now tiring strides 3.5 miles into the old stream working of Drizzlecombe and the reservoir that fed the water wheels of Eylesbarrow Mine.

Leat near Wheal Kathrine.

Eylesbarrow reservoir.

The reservoir, which has a long and slightly curving rectangular shape, measures 220 yards from one end where it receives the Langcombe Brook leat, to its discharge that feeds the water wheels. The width varies, but it is on average about ten yards, the depth from bottom to overflowing when measuring the downhill, south-western walling, that is partly stone lined, is approximately four and half feet.

A little to the north-east of the reservoir, as its outlet approaches the mine track, a rivulet issues from the much silted, now blind entrance of Shallow Adit. This stream of water eventually arrives into the Drizzlecombe Brook but not before it spreads itself bog-like over a little of the moorland terrain. The scant remains of six mills remain for the interested to muse over if the leat that fed them from the reservoir is followed. The ruins of the first three leave very little to appreciate in respect of masonry evidence, except for the second, where an end wall still stands in full with its window looking out over the most wonderful view. Other than this feature all three have tumbled into almost oblivion, leaving mere imprints hidden beneath a coat of vegetation. The sites in one way or another camouflage the usual wheel pits, dressing floors and buddles. Yet there is associated with the first mill, right beside the mine track, the more noticeable ruins of a Reck House. It was one of four such buildings that were sited between here and the last mill in the line of six. The word 'reck' was a term used for a buddle; which was a secondary system for gleaning the tin particles that had escaped the first washing. The method employed planks of wood lying horizontally and angled to a certain degree, with one most probably overlapping the other, similar to that in slate roofing. The

Engine wheel pit.

Ruins of the third mill along the line of six.

Number four mill's wheel pit.

The ruins of Eylesbarrow smelting house.

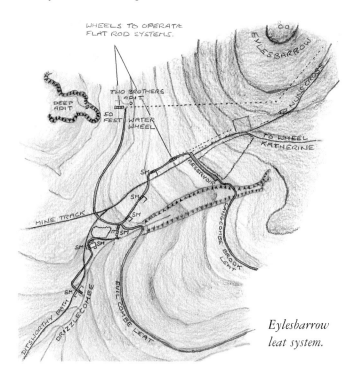

Eylesbarrow leat system.

Flue of the smelting house furnace.

material to be rewashed was introduced to the top end of the inclined structure in liquid suspension and, as it ran down the planking, it separated in the same way as it would have if introduced to the circular buddles down at Kit Mine.

The remains of the lower three mills are more substantial and everything about them is far more evident. The fashioned stonework and the buddles are larger and in a much better state of survival. The fourth mill is fascinating, for here there is quite a comprehensive variation of leats, buddles and settling floors. The launder banking to the wheel pit still survives more or less intact, as does a good section of the wheel pit itself, although one wall of it has fallen into disrepair. A little farther on down the valley, the fifth mill in the line, which was a smelting house, attracts far more attention from the walker than the rest put together. Perhaps Worth's *Dartmoor* provides the reasons for this. The popular and much respected writer in his coverage of the blowing houses on the moor details every aspect of the fallen structure, but makes no reference at all to the other mills along the line. Likewise there is little mention of the complex as a whole in any of the more widely read popular books there are to be had. Mr Worth said that this building was the last place on Dartmoor to smelt tin ore, although he dismissed it as not being a blowing house as such because it employed a reverbatory furnace. However, according to a plan of Eylesbarrow (spelt Ellisborough) dated 1814, there was a stamping mill and a blowing mill here. Nevertheless, gone were the days when the odd tin particles escaped from the blast furnace into the roof and had to be recovered by occasionally burning the thatch. This mill when upgraded had a seventy foot horizontal flue on top of the banking behind it to catch the wayward particles. This structure today is in a bad state of repair and something needs to be done to stabilize its condition so that a relic from our not-too-distant past may be saved for the future.

The sixth and last mill along the line, can be found tucked into the brook's banking just around the corner from the smelting house, where the hills on both sides of the stream climb more steeply away. The launder to the water wheel spanned the Ditswothy-to-Eylesbarrow track from its embankment that still protrudes from the hillside. The leat fed into it from the smelting house tailrace, and maybe a little more water came from the brook. Although the whereabouts of an intake is not obvious it could well be smothered with sphagnum moss and reed. The leat from the reservoir that aided all six mills in their time also sent water to the huge fifty-foot wheel. The branch off to it can be seen before it reaches the ruins of the fourth mill. Here is a fascinating junction of dry waterways where sluice gates must have been employed to send water to wherever it was needed. Here also another feed arrived at the complex from the lower elevations of Evil Combe. To supplement the need for extra power this leat would have also caught the springwater rising from higher up on the Drizzlecombe. Just a few yards below the leat, another intake comes in off the brook to feed the smelting house. This, after running under a little clapper, in turn caught the drainage from the fourth mill. The Evil Combe waterway commences from the Plym and makes its way through the lower area of the wicked little mire. At first sight it disappears at the edge of the mire but, if one is prepared to wobble on the saturated moss and investigate a few yards farther, the run can be found again.

During the period of Eylesbarrow's development, expansion and final demise, Queen Victoria was born, Humphrey Davy the Penzance Chemist invented the miners' Safety Lamp, continuous famine in Ireland led to thousands of its citizens emigrating to the land of promise on the other side of the Atlantic, the Tolpuddle Martyrs were banished to Australia, slavery was abolished, Victoria became Queen, and Charles Darwin sailed from Plymouth in the *Beagle* to voyage round the world, in search of the origin of species. Almost oblivious to these momentous events, the miners up here on the hill might have looked up to see Darwin's ship sail out of Plymouth Sound. Along with these happenings, the postage stamp came into being, Constable created his famous works, Dickens wrote his novels, Victoria had had six children and conceived another in the year of the mine's closure. Eighteen years later a census tells us of a George Worth residing here, still working the fields of Aylesborough Farm.

From Evil Combe, the headwaters of the Plym are about a mile and a quarter up the valley. Unlike Meavy Head this place is, on a still day, dormantly quiet: no dwellings, no railway track bed, no roads, no tourists by the thousands passing through in coaches and cars, and the only sign of human activity was created by the tinner who ventured where not even prehistoric man made his usual indelible impressions.

Cradled between Crane Hill and Great Gnats Head very little of the outside world can be seen until the river turns its flow to the south-west. Here, above the right bank, tin workings become far more apparent, with great heaps and pits and elongated gerts (or 'openworks' as the archaeologists prefer to call them). Hidden among this maze of disturbance, squeezed between the mine track and the ancient Abbots Way, just above Plym Ford, is a well preserved wheel pit. Quite a large wheel rotated in this cavity, one wall that is in almost perfect condition measures seven feet from top to bottom. After the breeze stopped waving my tape about, twenty-three feet was found to be its length and a wheel of forty-two inches, if not more, could easily have been housed here. Down in the bottom's lowest corner, a neat tailrace conduit protrudes in a curve for twenty-one feet out into a gert that runs down towards the river. The leat that carried the water to the wheel, is not so clearly discernable; nature has left only the occasional scar of it to see as one endeavours to trace it back to its source. With this pit situated where it is, hidden among the heather-clad workings, it isn't clear what its function could have been. One can only surmise that it was employed to work in conjunction with the nearby shafts.

If the track near the wheel pit is followed to the south-west, a glance to the right after a hundred yards or so will reveal what appears to be a rectangular three-sided storage bay, built

Wheel pit at Wheal Katherine.

most probably to hold the raw material extracted from the multitude of nearby delvings. Two small grass-covered heaps can be seen resting against the bay's seven-foot-high interior walling, the beginnings perhaps of fresh heaps for processing   The rest of the bay's dimensions measure sixty feet by forty four feet.

A little farther on the track reaches Crane Lake, a small stream that weeps to the Plym from the wet ground on the south-east flank of Eylesbarrow. It is here, where the stored heaps would have come to be crushed, dressed and washed. Here, all in close proximity, is the conglomeration of masonry ruins of Wheal Katherine tin works, a venture belonging to the early to mid decades of the nineteenth century. Also here is the Langcombe/Eylesbarrow leat, weaving its way through a miscellaneous assemblage of pre-Wheal Katherine masonry structures belonging to the older Crane Lake Mine. As one meanders here and there in the

Bay for storing raw material.

Ruins of Wheal Katherine stamping mill.

Dressing house at Wheal Katherine.

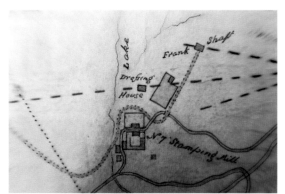

Plan of Wheal Katherine.

seclusion of this little combe searching to satisfy a curiosity, the ruins of Wheal Katherine's stamping mill stands the tallest. This venture, although tucked out of site in the depths of the moor, had a working relationship with Eylesbarrow. The stamping mill here in 1817 was numbered No.7. The tailrace issuing from the mill, now choked with reed, runs beneath the mine track before discharging into the Crane Lake stream. Sitting up on a knoll, like some miniature castle keep, are the substantial remains of the dressing house.

Up on the immediate higher ground, more or less to the north-east of the fallen stamping area, are the tumbled ruins of a small dwelling. Enough still remains to see that it comprised two rooms and a tiny front garden with a walled path running to the dwelling's doorway. This little abode, out here in the middle of nowhere, no doubt housed someone responsible for the older stream workings of the Crane Lake mine. They could well have kept a small amount of livestock, a cow for milk, a pig for bacon and a few chickens for eggs, for a walled field surrounds three sides of the ruined abode; a good deal of the walling of the fourth side has fallen into the deep elongated gert that completes the border.

A small reservoir and its associated leat system for excavating the gert can be located on the higher ground above it. This vegetation-coated openwork could well have resulted from the toil of the Wheel Katherine men, devouring the old field walling with their spoil.

Blachford bound stone.

As the Crane Lake stream miner left his abode for his work, the view from the doorway would have been exclusively of open moorland. The hill running up towards Great Gnats Head dominates the scene across the river Plym. The Abbots Way curves up around its western flank towards the out-of-sight Broad Rock, a huge natural boulder, with the words etched on it indicating the boundary limit of the ancient Blatchford Manor. With its back to the winter sun, Calves Lake Tor can be seen standing like some juvenile rock pile beneath the great expanse of Langcombe Hill that spans across the southern skyline. To the west the drop of Hart Tor Hill to the Plym allows just a little of its lower tor to peep over the horizon. Meandering away out of Crane Lake and over the hill, more or less in the same direction, is the cart track to Eylesbarrow and the in-country. When the rain is persistent and heavy, the track for nearly two-thirds of its length is like a stream, gathering volume and speed as the route becomes flooded from the saturated ground above it.

Just a short way downstream, from where Wheal Katherine's ruins sit, the area appears like the vegetation-shrouded aftermath of an intensive World War II bombing raid. Literally everywhere the ground around the confluence with the Plym has been obliterated by years of delving in one form or another, no doubt the toil of the Crane Lake tin works.

Tucked below the scarp beside the right bank of Crane Lake is a tinner's hut, just a short stone's-throw away another can be found beside the Plym, both are in a very ruinous state of preservation. Their days no doubt belonged to the age when the alluvial beds here were streamed.

One of the mortar stones on the right bank of the Plym.

Double-sided mortar stone on the left bank.

As all moor walkers learn at some time or another a straight line is not always the easiest or quickest route between two points. It is very much like this with getting to the next place of tinning interest, for the bog-ridden area of lower Evil Combe has to be approached with care. It is best to climb away from the river and on to the higher ground, where a weave around the boulders on the hillside between the combes is necessary before dropping down on to softer ground, near to where the little boggy combe begins to widen. From here a safe sheep's track can be followed through the reeds until, with lengthening stride, one crosses the stream and firmer ground is met.

A short stroll to the south, over the lower Plym to Eylesbarrow Leat, brings one on to meet the Plym's banks once more. From here, where the slopes of Hart Tor Hill touch the river, a leat not marked on the Ordnance Survey map fed water to a stamping mill, about three hundred and twenty awkward and irregular steps from the intake. A good look around below where the leat appears to lose its identity locates the whereabouts of the site. Very little of the old workplace exist today, broken down by the harsh moorland elements thrown at it during its time of disuse. The area has almost completely gone back to moor, leaving an utterly confused state of preservation for the interested to scratch a puzzled head over. In a slight hollow on the banking two stones lie among a pile with the usual depressions worked into them, revealing that the tinner once crushed his crude ore here.

On the left a little farther downriver the site of another old mill can be found, just as ruinous, hiding among multiple spoil heaps and a mound of its own fallen masonry. A mortar stone with large twin depressions, appearing like sunken eyes staring across the river, stands on one edge, at the waterside foot of the ruin. With a little knuckle-bruising squeeze one can feel smooth depressions on the reverse side of the stone. The leat to the mill isn't traceable, no doubt over-shadowed, widened and deepened when Mr Phillips in the 1830s used the same contour to take water to his clay works at Lee Moor.

A hundred yards or so farther downstream the Langcombe Brook arrives into the Plym from the south-east. It is very much like most other streams on the moor, nothing too out of the ordinary to see where the subject in hand is concerned. Each of its tributaries, including Dead Man's Bottom, have been reshaped down the years by the tinner. Here is the usual disarray of humps and pits, but near its confluence with the Plym are classic examples of alluvial streaming, row after row of elongated mounds spreading themselves at an angle to the brook along the right bank.

From the confluence, the Plym drops in steps until the valley widens, where Mill Corner comes into view. Just a little way down this noisy stretch of tumbling water the ruins of a tinner's hut can be found, tucked into the steep left bank. How this shelter kept feet dry when the river was in flood only those who used it could tell, for here the high-water level leaves floating debris among the fallen stonework.

In places, almost into Mill Corner, the left side of the river can only be followed twenty foot and more up on the higher ground. Down below the water divides its flow around an island then tumbles on until the final cataract where the sound of the river is hushed as it meanders between the boulders in its bed. Above, an ash tree bows itself precariously over the river, and every year a crow nests in the branches of the wind-ravaged tree. One season, now sometime ago, I followed the bird's activity in refurbishing its nest. Among the materials to make it comfy was horse hair and nylon bailer cord. When the eggs came, their colours varied in different shades of green. Then one by one the young broke their shells to arrive as nestlings to squabble and struggle for survival. My only regret is that I wasn't there for when they flew the nest.

Young crows in the nest.

Although I take a great deal of interest in nature, I have never been one for climbing trees, to nose into a bird's breeding time, but sitting on the north-west slope of Giants Hill observing the birds putting their home together, nurtured thoughts of being a partner to the proceedings and a wish to see Nature's process through to fruition.

A few yards up hill from the tree one will find an old leat that took water off the first cataracts farther back up the river. It can be clearly followed from the water's edge, to its delivery at Mill Corner. Here below the scarp are the more visible remains of a stamping mill. As one looks down on the site, the wheel pit is instantly recognisable, with the much narrower tail-race running away from it. Built into the masonry at the top of the pit walling is a mortar stone with two depressions worked into it, placed there to be re-employed as an axle-bearing stone after its initial use was spent. This semi-circular groove can be seen quite clearly. Not so noticeable though is the fact that the stone was at one time lying at right angles to its present position, for on one end of the same surface is the abandoned uneven wear of another groove. There are other mortar stones lying around the place, broken during their working life. They are often moved from one place to another, in fact it seems that every time I make a visit to the site someone has used tremendous energy to alter their previous positions on top of the old mill's collapsed ruins.

Stamping mill at Mill Corner.

Back on top of the scarp a short walk around the contour to the south reveals the delightful Shavercombe Brook. When in the area during the warmer months a little time-consuming detour to this lovely spot is a must. For wildlife it is a shelter, a heather-, moss- and fern-clad haven in the middle of the moor. The tinner has laid bare its higher elevations, but from about halfway down the brook, where a waterfall drops into a crystal clear pool from about fifteen feet, another story can be told. I remember making my way upstream one morning when a wonderful sight left an indescribable feeling inside me, thrills of absolute untouched and pristine pleasure. Just where the high banks close in on the water's edge, I saw a heron standing motionless, patiently waiting for a meal, until it eventually spotted me and flew off leaving its intended prey to live, to see another day. I passed a lizard basking in the warmth of the sun, a grey wagtail flitted from one stone to another, and up in the secluded theatre of

Broken mortar stone at Mill Corner.

the falls, a mallard startled me when it flew without warning from its nest. Rewardingly the nest revealing to me four warm eggs. A wren, also unseen for a time, outvoiced the cascading water, and all the while Mr and Mrs Crow seemingly oblivious to all, getting on with life in a rowan tree that overshadows the falls. The idyllic time spent here, reaping its pleasing ambience, was a little begrudgingly cut short to allow the duck an earlier return to its eggs.

The Shavercombe joins the Plym among a vast sea of streamworking, acre after acre of moorland here has been churned by the pick and shovel. From here the Plym flows for over two miles between the ancient Dartmoor rabbit warrens. Where the valley bottom narrows again for a while below Ditsworthy Warren House which can be seen on the hillside to the north-west, the river is checked by a weir built to raise the water level and send a proportion of its flow through the adjoining sluice gate and along the leat to the china clay works. The waterway runs around the moor through the old abandoned warrens of Hentor, Willingswall and Trowlesworthy, crossing the brooks of Hentor and Spanish Lake (at one time known as the Eastor Brook), and under the rabbit bridges before arriving into Big Pond to await distribution to the high-powered water jets down in the clay pits.

The digging of this leat in 1825 caused quite a stir; in fact it blew up into a full-scale dispute involving trespass, civil law and the ancient Stannary Laws. The leat was originally nothing to do with the clay industry, it was excavated to carry water all the way to Bottle Hill Mine, situated on the far southern tip of Crownhill Down.

The dispute erupted fully with a man-to-man confrontation on the 12 July 1825 when William Nicholl, the tenant of Trowlesworthy Warren, approached a Nicholas Fezzey, the supposed Captain of the mine, and ten other men who had already begun work on the leat. When asked what they were doing, Fezzey explained that they were cutting a channel to Bottle Hill Mine. When requested to stop he quoted his right to dig under Stannary Law. The warrener then handed to Fezzey a notice from his landlord, Mr George Woollcombe, to discontinue the work. Fezzey took the notice and slipped it into his pocket book, and whilst doing so, said that he had been threatened many a time before with such pieces of paper, then with his men carried on with his work.

Six days later, on the 18 July, a letter was sent to Fezzey on behalf of George Woollcombe. On opening it he read,

Sir
We apply to you on the part of George Woollcombe Esqr, in relation to you having made a Trespass on Trowlesworthy Warren, in digging a trench to carry water from thence to Bottle Hill Mine, as an acknowledgment of you having no right to do so, we have instructions to commence an action against you.

The letter went on to tell him that his pretence of digging the trench under the protection of Stannary Law did not frighten the Woollcombes, for Trowlesworthy was not and never was part of the Duchy of Cornwall lands where the tinners could work at their profession to the inconvenience and discomfort of others. The letter concluded by stressing that if he neglected to take notice of the letter, a writ would be immediately served as a commencement of an action for damages. The wording in the letter was read and a reply sent almost without delay told the Woollcombes that the channel would by no means, be discontinued.

On the 21 July, Fezzey received further correspondence explaining how George Woollcombe would not quietly submit to the deprivation of his property and, however unpleasant it will be for him to be the Plaintiff, an action would be forthcoming.

In the meantime closer observations reveals to the Woollcombe family that Nicholas Fezzey, who claims the privilege of a tinner, is not known as such. Fezzey is a merely a labourer along with other labourers who are committing a trespass; 'he shows no interest in any mine, he is neither the proprietor of the soil where any mine is now working, nor is he an adventurer in any mine, but states himself to be a Captain that is a Foreman of labourers in a mine, distant from this estate, two or three miles, being in another parish'.

When the Woollcombes received this information, it gave them an unexpected headache, for now looking at 'Fezzey as a man with no substance, could be to the complete detriment of the plaintiff, for if damages and costs were awarded, Fezzey could abscond and leave them as badly off as ever'. They decided that 'Under these circumstances, we feel reluctant to go to trial when we fight at such disadvantages.'

George Woollcombe didn't have to worry for too long about being the plaintiff, for his barrister **Mr Coleridge** suggested the tenant, William Nicholl, should face the discomfort of the court proceedings. However the writ up to now still hadn't been issued as Mr Coleridge had not made up his mind against whom the action should be brought, Fezzey alone or all the men who joined him in committing the trespass.

When it got to court Fezzey stood alone to face the action directed at him. By now the damage to the warren was considerable. The court heard that 'they made trenches of 1,500 yards, of the breadth of 10 yards and depth of one yard. Using spades and mattocks and other instruments they threw up the earth and soil of the closure and destroyed 50 rabbit burrows their being of great value to the wit of 50 pounds and there and then drove out and expelled the rabbits.

In throwing up the earth and soil stopped and damaged up a certain other trench gutter or channel in the said closure by along which a certain stream of pot water then and there flowed and of right ought to have flowed and still of right ought to have flowed towards and into the dwelling house for the convenience and enjoyment of the warrener, to benefit in a large and ample manner running to his house.'

Fezzey's leat.

From the day William Nicholls first approached Fezzey on the warren, the Woollcombe family knew the sweat of a confrontation would show on their brow. They professed to have knowledge of the Stannary Laws and, by Fezzey's determination to carry on digging, knew their case would have to be prepared well before going to court.

Mr Coleridge seemed not amused when the court went along with Fezzey's plea for proof of ownership, saying: 'The endorsement would not have been so specially referred to if the deeds had been there before him'. A letter to the Woollcombes concerning the case displays quite clearly that Fezzey was by no means a man to be pushed to one side with ease; he clearly knew the rights of the tinner, and knew how powerful their privileges were when it came to carrying out a task concerning his profession. The letter dated January 31st 1826 read:

And the Sd Nicholas Fezzey in his own proper person comes & says that the Court ought not to have or take further cognisance of the Plea Afsd. Because he says that the Sd Closes in the Sd Declon mentioned & in which &o long before the Sd times when &o & also before & at the time of making the Charter hereinafter mentioned were & from thence hitherto have been & still are within & parcel of the Ancient Stannaries of the County of Devon & at the time of making the Sd Charter were part of the Demesnes of Edward the 1st formally King of England to wit at the Parish Afsd in the County Afsd. And the Sd Deft further saith that long before the Sd time when &o to wit on the 10th day of April in the 33rd year of the Reign of the Sd late King Edward the 1st. by a certain Charter under the great seal of England bearing date at Westminster the same day & year last Afsd & which Sd Charter the Sd Deft now brings here into Court the date whereof is the same day & yearlast Afsd the Sd late King Edward the 1st did grant for himself & his Heirs amongst other things that all Tinners working in the Afsd Stannaries which were the demesnes of the Sd late King Edward the 1st so long as they worked in the Sd Stannaries should be free & quit of Pleas of Natives & of all Pleas & Plaints in any manner whats touching the County of the Sd late King & his Heirs so that they shodnd answer before any justice or ministers of the Sd late King or his Heirs of any Plea or Plaint arising within the Afsd Stannaries except before the Warden of his Stannaries Afsd for the time being Pleas of Land Life & limb excepted nor shouls they deport from their works by the summons of any of the Ministers of the Sd late King or his Heirs except by the Summons of his Sd Warden Afsd or his Deputy should hold Pleas arising between the Tinners Afsd and also between them and other Foreigners of all Trespases Plaints & Contracts made in places in which the worked within the Stannaries Afsd likewise arising & that the Sd Warden should have full power to justice the Tinners Afsd & other Foreigners in such Pleas & do justice to the parties as was right & as theretofore those Stannaries had been accustomed as by the Sd reference being thereunto had will amongst other things more fully & at large appear and the Sd Deft further saith that he the Sd Deft before & at the Sd time when & was & from thence hitherto hath been & still is a Tinner working in the Afsd Stannaries so being part of the ancient demesnes of the Sd late King Edward the 1st that is to say in a certain Mine called Bottle Hill Mine situated & being in a certain Village called Plympton St Mary within & parcel of the Sd Stannaries & in which Sd Mine a certain Tin works for & during all the time last Afsd & still is in working & that the supposed Trespass & causes of action in the Sd declon mentioned. If any such were committed or arose were & each & every of them was committed & did arise within the Stannaries Afsd. & within the Jurisdiction of the Warden of the Sd Stannaries or his Deputy there & that the Sd. Several supposed caused of action & each & every of them do concern the Stannaries Afsd. & the rights and privileges therein of such working Tinners as Afsd to wit at the Parish Afsd in the County Afsd and the Sd Deft further saith that the most & able Francis Charles Seymore Conway Marquis of Hertford before & at the Sd times when & was & from thence hitherto hath been & still is Warden of the Stannaries Afsd & that John Cocks Gent was for & during all the time last Afsd. & still is Vice Warden & Deputy of the Sd Warden in the Sd Stannaries to wit at the Parish Afsd in the County Afsd. And by means of the several premes Afsd the Sd Warden or Vice Warden & Deputy had for & during all the time last Afsd. & still have cognisance of the Plea Afsd. And this the Sd Nicholas Fezzey is ready to verify wherefore he prays Judgment if this Court will or ought to have of take further Cognizance of the Plea Afsd.

The deeds did prove without doubt that Trowlesworthy was never in the Royal Demesnes and therefore not subject to the Stannary Courts of Devon. Although partly in Latin and partly in legal French they clarified the ownership from the Traylsworthys to the Woollcombes. The land was originally granted by Charter by Baldwin De Redvers, the first Earl of Devon, to Samson de Traylsworthy, way before Edward I was born. It was to be passed down through time from heir to heir, before going out of the family and eventually, via other named proprietors, into the hands of William Woollcombe.

Throughout the dispute, it appears that the leat took its source from the Eastor Brook, but in fact that is where the trespass first took place, when the digging of the leat arrived there, for the Brook was the boundary of Trowlesworthy.

Mr Henry Woollcombe, George's brother, in an unfinished letter, said 'that he was making some enquiries about the subject formally in dispute between his brother George and a Captain Vezy of a Mine Company, but his investigations cannot find any papers relating to the action, either among his brother's at Hemerdon or his own in his office'. His recollection of events is not at all clear, although he remembers the writ being served and the declaration filed. He went on to say 'but I believe there was no appearance entered and the impression on my mind is that the action was not followed up, from the circumstance of Captain Vezy not being a responsible person, this certainly is the impression on my mind.' He further states: 'they must pay for any damage it occurred and did pay William Nicholls the late Warrener, for such damages and do at this moment pay Henry Lavers the present Warrener

Parallel tinners' heaps, looking north.

The same parallel heaps, looking south.

Four or Five Pounds per Annum, this the Mine say is paid for keeping the banks of the channels in repair to prevent further damage to the warren.' The date on the letter heading is 31 May 1881, fifty-five years after the dispute first went to court. In 1877, four years before the part letter was written, the mine that fomented all the trouble closed, after which the full flow of its leat went to the local china clay pits.

From the leat the panorama one sees today when looking down the valley towards Cadover Bridge during a sunny weekend resembles a scene at the seaside, A multi-coloured sea of cars extends down the left of the Plym and beyond the Plympton–Yelverton road. Dotted among them are deckchairs and windbreaks and the odd smoking barbecue. Camper vans, the occasional tent and of course the inevitable ice cream van are here. Below the warren's entrance road, youngsters dive into Deep Pool, where the water is dammed to give the area of river a little more depth. Mums and Dads along with their children spend hours retrieving stones of all sizes from farther downstream to create this paddling and swimming pool, only for a flood to wash it away again, very often by the same sudden downpour that encourages them to pack up and leave for home.

Just a few yards farther downstream, the Black-a-Brook flows into the Plym. As one walks along beside this little stream, for the first few yards it appears rather unassuming with nothing out of the ordinary to take the eye. However its valley gradually widens and rivulets from springs flow into it from all angles; in most places the ground below one's feet is sodden where moss and reed clog and spread a spongy wetness to encourage the walker to take another route. The tinners were here; their toil has devastated the whole length of the stream, literally torn the heart out of it, leaving scarps in places fifteen to twenty feet high. And the valley floor is churned upside down with mounds of all shapes and sizes spread everywhere. Out of all this upheaval there is much for the inquisitive to take interest in, including the classic parallel rows of spoil heaps to be found near the top end of the valley which are the best by far on the southern moor. The figure standing at the north end of the tinners' spoil heaps in the lower picture (opposite), gives some idea of the rows' dimensions. It appears that flooding or later streaming has washed the ends of some of the rows away.

After one has somehow crossed the Plym, from where the Brook meets its much heavier flow, a meander will take the wanderer over the considerable calamitous acreage of Brisworthy Burrows, another area where the tinner has turned the land upside down. A vast majority of the people walking at leisure here on a sunny day haven't a clue how the humps and pits were created, or even think about them being the work of man. They are convenient to play hide and seek in, or provide a little privacy for courting couples and a place to spend an urgent penny. The area of land takes its name from the small hamlet that lies up across the fields to the right as one follows the river down. The small cluster of dwellings is mentioned in the Domesday Book as Brittensworthy. By 18 July 1559, in the second year of Elizabeth I's reign, the name had changed to Brightisworthy. That was the day a blowing house and tin sett was leased to Harry of Mewy, John and William and the sons of Harry, from Elizabeth Fortiscue of Spriddelston which, in the time of the Conqueror, lay in the parish of Brixton. This document Harry signed:

To all trewe Christian people to whom this present written indented shall come Elizabeth Fortiscue of Spriddelston in the County of Devon widow and Nicholas Fortiscue gentleman the son of Louis Fortiscue deceased send greating in our Lord God everlasting known ye be the forsaid Elizabeth and Nicholas by one assent and consent do have granted sett and leased and by this present written indented do grant Sett and leased unto Harry of Mewy John and William and sons of the forsaid Harry al that our Tent and Mill called a Blowing Mill with his appurtenance Sett lying and being at Brightisworthy in the parish of Mewy in the County afforsaid with all and all manner of courses and conveyance of water there onto belonging and appertaining the which Blowing Mill with his appurtenance Elizander Webb before held to have and to hold all the said Tent or otherwise called a Blowing Mill with his appurtenance to the said Harry am John am William am and their assigns for two of their lives and to the longest liver of them yielding and paying therefore yearly unto the forsaid Elizabeth and her assigns during her natural life three shillings and four pence of lawfull money of England and after the decease of the said Elizabeth unto the said Nicholas and his heirs three shillings and four pence of lawful money of England to be paid at the usual times of the year that is to say at the Feast of Saint Michael their Angel the birth of our Lord God the annunciation of our Blessed Lady the Virgin and the naturity of Saint John the Baptist by equal portions and if it happen the said yearly rent of three shillings and four pence to be behind unpaid in bit or in all by the space of half a year after any feast of the feast aforesaid in which it ought to be paid and lawfully applied and sufficient distress in and upon the same tent otherwise called a Blowing Mill with his appurtenance may be formed that then it shall be lawful to the said Elizabeth and Nicholas and the heirs and assigns of the said Nicholas to the said Tent otherwise called a Blowing Mill with his appurtenance to rent and the same to have as in their first and former estate any thing within this grant to the contrary notwithstanding and who truly the said Elizabeth and Nicholas and the heirs of the said Nicholas all the said Tent otherwise Called a Blowing Mill with his appurtenance to the said Harry am John am William am sons of the forsaid Harry am for two of their lives in manner and form above written as well against the High Lord or Lorde of the fee thereof for the high rent sute to court heriot release and all other customs and service going out of the same against all the people shall warrant against defend by these present and farther know ye that we the said Elizabeth and Nicholas by these present to have constituted ordained and in our place to have put our well beloved in Christ John Bowden and John Brownsson our true and lawfull attorneys jointly and singly to grant in our name and stede into the said Tent otherwise called a Blowing Mill with his appurtenance and thereof to take possession and after such possession so taken and had to allured in our name and stead full and peaceably possession and session of all the premises to the said *Harry am John am and William am* sons of the forsaid *Harry am* according to the strength form and effect of this our present written indented and all and any thing that the said attorney or one of them shall do in the premises the said *Elizabeth and Nicholas* shall at all times ratify and allow by this our present written indented in witness were of as well we the for said *Elizabeth and Nicholas* as the said *Harry John and William* to these presentindenture interchangeably have put to our seals given the *18th day of July* in the second year of the reign of our Sovereign Lady *Elizabeth* by the grace of God of *England France and Ireland* Queen Defender of the Faith.

Brisworthy blowing mill lease.

The mill, now a complete ruin, is situated below the Brisworthy fields beside an old garage at the time of writing owned by the Tossell family. As well as a blowing mill the place obviously housed a stamping system, for lying on the grass nearby is a large square-shaped mortar stone, worked far more successfully on one side than the other. Another mortar stone displaying clearly only one depression can be found set into a kerbside walling.

Mortar stone near the garage.

Mr Worth wrote in his much respected *Dartmoor*, that at one time there were mortar stones within the confines of the ruin but they had since disappeared, leaving just one outside with two depressions worked into it. Worth was lucky to be able to view the ruin; today there is very little to see other than mere shadows of its whereabouts. Just a meandering twenty yards or so of the mill's leat system is now traceable, hidden among stunted hawthorn and gorse. The rest of its run has been swallowed over the years by ground levelling made during land improvement in the Lower Brisworthy fields. Worth also mentions a stone at the mill which he says was lost years ago. He at first considered this to be, as he put it, the mill's furnace base, but later rejected the notion in favour of it being a pigsty feeding chute. The stone, hewn out of pink granite, has since resurfaced and can be viewed up at the hamlet with the consent of the owner. The last time I saw it it was almost abandoned, lying on top of a heap of field-clearance debris, half hidden among a confusion of perennial weed. The conformity of the stone suggests to me that the shallowness of its chute was more likely to be employed to run off the smooth flow of liquid tin rather than an uneven lumpy flow of pig swill. A few yards from where the float stone lies, a muddy lane runs down between fields. Part way down on the left, built into the bottom of the hedge, is a boulder with a debatable fifteen depressions of various dimensions worked into it. I say debatable because it is so difficult at times to see them clearly. Worth thought the stone to be an unusual mortar, when in fact it belongs to prehistory. To see the object at its best I make a visit during the winter months when the brambles that partly shade it are bare of foliage. This allows the low sun on a clear day to strike across the depressions nearer to an horizontal angle, leaving a majority of them with one side in the shade, thus enhancing its appearance especially for a photograph.

Mortar stone set in kerb track.

Float stone at Brisworthy Farm.

While researching the warrens and their history I had the pleasure of meeting Mr and Mrs Cyril the tenants of Trowlesworthy. As Mr Cyril finished showing me around the place, we stopped to chat when we arrived in the courtyard looking down at a small trough half full of water. I couldn't believe my eyes, and with no hesitation at all went straight over to it for a closer look. It was partly hidden by logs for the fire, but there was no doubting what it was. Mr Cyril was quite surprised at my reaction to the object and asked why I found it so interesting, saying nonchalantly that he placed it there conveniently for the dogs to have a drink out of. It was a tinner's mould stone, with the outer dimensions of seventeen and a quarter inches by fifteen and nine and half inches high. The inner measurement at the top are twelve and half inches long by nine and half, its depth is four inches with the bottom measuring ten

Map showing whereabouts of the mill on the River Plym.

Cup stone, of prehistoric date.

Mould stone at Trowlesworthy.

and half by six and a quarter, chiselled out of the rim is the familiar groove. This trough, I should be able to categorically conclude, came from the Mill beside the Plym at Brisworthy Burrows. When asked how it had arrived at its present site Mr Cyril told me a rather interesting story. 'It was a good job I was here,' he said 'otherwise it would have been gone. When the outbuildings here were being altered, the contractors doing the work found it built into one of the walls, they were about to put in the back of their vehicle when I saw what they were doing, that's how it came to be where it is.' Lucky for Dartmoor, for without Mr Cyril's intervention it would not be here today.

Back down at the burrows, not so very long ago a dispute over the parcel of land where Harry of Mewy and his partners busied themselves, took ten years to resolve. It was all about the sorry state of a prefabricated bungalow owned by a Mr Tossell - Ted, to all those who knew him well. Ted wanted to pull the old building down and put up a permanent structure, but the West Devon Council refused planning permission and requested the eyesore be demolished. From here the conflict simmered on with solicitors being brought into the feud, until eventually the Minister for the Environment became involved. He sided with the Council where a new bungalow was concerned but recommended that the council buy the land from Mr Tossell, seeing it wasn't of much value to him if he could not live there. This, the council agreed to and offered Ted £500.

Ted of course laughed and promptly rejected the offer. Eventually the dispute came to an end, with the council paying £5000 for a concrete base and a tumbled down shack, they too, could do nothing with. Ted had bought the property just after the Second World War, from a Mr Elford. On the deeds and clearly marked was the blowing mill.

Ted was as hard as nails and as strong as an ox. We met up one day during my research as he was making alterations to his garage. Then in his mid seventies, he was manhandling a ten foot long steel girder while standing on top of an empty forty-five gallon oil drum,. After a few heaving grunts and several choice words the steel beam was put in place to his satisfaction. He kindly gave me the time of day, offering along with the conversation a cup of tea from his flask and a biscuit from an old tin box. Sadly Ted has left us, leaving his son the land the council didn't want where once Harry of Mewy, John and William and the sons of Harry once carried out their mining activities.

CHAPTER 4

Water

Ted's little old bungalow was devoid of all modern conveniences; there was no mains electricity, no gas and no mains water supply. Ted's son, Mike, remembers from when he lived there as a boy, that there was a tank in the roof space that filled a bath, flushed the toilet and generally supplied water for all the other household necessities, including the making of a cup of tea. Mike recalls from deep in his bank of distant memories, that the water was pumped to the tank from a small stream that ran down from somewhere up at Brisworthy.

Leat.

Most of us now, take turning on the tap in the comfort of our homes for granted, until perhaps when the water bill is pushed through our letterbox and drops on the doormat.

Dartmoor is saturated like a sponge; for countless thousands of years, numerous springs, streams, and rivers have teemed their waters to the sea but, like Ted's little stream, all have been tapped for one need or another, to supply tin mill, corn mill, farms for domestic and agricultural purposes and to many an isolated dwelling dotted around the moor and its periphery.

Until the late years of the sixteenth century, the Meavy or Mewy as it was then known, ran more or less unchecked to join the Plym beneath the rough crags of the Dewerstone. But down beside the sea, in the fast growing town of Plymouth, insufficient water was giving the Corporation an ever-increasing headache, for as well as a supply for domestic and commercial use, the town was also obliged to provide water to an expanding naval fleet anchored in the Cattewater.

Burrator Reservoir.

Many an idea of how to get more water to supplement the wells and streams of the town was contemplated; the Corporation even employed the water divining knowledge of a Mr Forsland, a tinner from the Bovey Tracey area, to investigate a possible flow from the Meavy. His findings must have pleased them, for just a couple of years later, the Corporation paid Mr Lampen of St Budeaux to survey the course, although again nothing instantly materialised. From the first notions thirty odd years were to pass before the pick and shovels, crow bars and running sweat joined in the excavation. Meanwhile commitments to other projects, and the continual hostilities with Spain, soaked up Plymouth's manpower, leaving the plans to gather dust in a drawer at St Budeaux.

The eventual contract to excavate the seventeen-mile artificial waterway (leat), went to Sir Francis Drake. He was born one of eleven children on a farm just a little to the South-West of Tavistock, at Crowndale. He certainly wasn't from the privileged classes, yet after going to sea at an early age, he quickly rose to become the Vice-Admiral of the Fleet and the occasional favourite of Elizabeth his Queen, He was her licenced pirate; she touched his shoulder with a knighthood in 1580 for being the first Englishman to circumnavigate the world (or was it for returning with an hold full of Spanish gold and silver?). For whatever reason, she rewarded him so handsomely that he was able to purchase Buckland Abbey from Sir Richard Grenville.

The years Sir Francis resided at Buckland, saw him become Mayor of Plymouth and landlord of several properties in the town, yet he was always at the ready for a call from his Queen, especially if it came to aggravating the Spanish, such as at the defeat of the Armada. But, he didn't always shine bright in the woman's eyes, for her notorious fickle-mindedness painted a long-lasting scowl on her face when only twelve months later he led an unsuccessful raid on Lisbon. With the word defeat never entering his vocabulary, Drake had the notion of destroying the remains of the Armada whilst it was anchored in various Spanish ports, and then with Don Antonio of Portugal to overthrow the powerful Phillip II of Spain. When asked for her support, Elizabeth, encouraged by his earlier escapades, backed him enthusiastically to the tune of £60,000. He set out in his usual cavalier manner with one hundred and fifty ships and eighteen thousand men, but the expedition was a total disaster and he returned in complete disgrace, bringing home less than half the men he set out with.

With his head held not quite so high after the Lisbon debacle, Drake took a longer break than was usual from the sea. It was during this time that he began taking a lot more interest in the Devonport leat. History has always credited Sir Francis with bringing water to Plymouth from the Meavy. He did no doubt, as an international, figure inspire and encourage and, as a Member of Parliament (for Bossiney near Tintagel) give the Bill a proverbial 'kick up the backside' and see its passage through Westminster with a little more urgency. However, the responsibility for the idea and groundwork for the leat was definitely that of the Corporation.

On the leat's completion, a fanciful story relates a tale of trumpeters playing a fanfare whilst Drake, with the flamboyant flair of a showman, rides on horseback in front of the oncoming water, with his cloak draping the ground as if enticing the flow along.

Make-believe may be commingled here with reality, for the crafty old sea dog would have wanted the system up and running, for he as an individual was certainly going to benefit from it. Not only was he happy with the fee for the initial contract, and claiming rightful compensation for the leat running through his land, but he also benefited handsomely from building lucrative money making mills along sections of its seventeen mile length.

For a man whose father was a lay preacher and who was brought up to fear the wrath of the Almighty, Drake never seemed to display any scruples where a cunningly devised quick profit was concerned.

Also compensated was Sir Walter Elford, Lord of the Manor at Longstone. He was given the hundred deal boards left over from the construction of the leat-carrying launder, £4.14 shillings and the Freedom of Plymouth. Yet compensation, if any, came slowly to others. The millers on the Meavy below the Head Weir had to grudgingly whistle for any recompense when their profits drastically dwindled owing to the ever-open mouth of the leat devouring the water that had once turned the wheels of their mills. They, along with the Priory Mills at Plympton, took the matter all the way to Westminster in the shape of a Bill to close the leat mills down. But their efforts never stood a chance, for sitting on the Bill's committee as Chairman, was Drake.

Where the tinner was concerned, any stream of water was there for the taking, and generally with the taking came controversy. A flow around the contours of Roborough Down, where very little natural water even trickled, must have seemed like a present heaven sent to anyone with the cheek to tap it. Mr Crymes, Lord of the Manor of Buckland Monachorum, who lived almost within hearing distance of the excavating pick and shovel at Crapstone, already had tin interest, including two pitches he shared with Sir Richard Strode and others. The leat now gave him the chance to stream even more. He no doubt waited quietly behind the scenes while negotiations concerning the artificial waterway were going on, at the same time making exploratory delvings for tin wherever he thought water from the leat could be delivered. And deliver he did, using the 'the right of the tinner' backed by the strength of the Stannary Law and their notorious Court on the Tor.

In 1595 Sir Francis Drake was again out on the ocean attempting to plunder more Spanish treasure, but his once reliable Midas touch had gone and another expensive Elizabeth-sponsored expedition ended in failure. Along with disappointment came dysentery and Drake's death and burial at sea in the warm waters of the Caribbean, in 1596 at the age of 56.

With Sir Francis' death, the leat controversy with William Crymes landed in the lap of his brother Thomas, who inherited the famous old mariner's property. Like Francis, Thomas was a Member of the Plymouth Corporation and again like him enjoyed an agreeable contract for the mills. A member of the Corporation or not, Thomas had to do a great deal of thinking before he could contemplate tackling Mr Crymes, for it was not going to be plain sailing. But this was a dispute he had to fight, a reduced water supply to his mills, whatever next! The Drakes were not accustomed to having their noses put out of joint. Where they were concerned it was others who always aimed to please. Now the boot was on the other foot, it was their turn to tread cautiously, for Crymes was the one firmly placed in the proverbial driving seat. Thomas and the Corporation knew it, not least when the dispute reached the ear of Sir Walter Raleigh, Lord Warden of the Stannaries. The Court on the Tor and the Prison at Lydford was a fearsome nightmare for anyone's thoughts to dwell on for long.

With the dispute ongoing, several confrontations between workmen occurred. Many an author of Dartmoor tales has retold the story of one particular meeting of the parties concerned. The tinners had obviously had enough and lay in wait for the leat builders with the tools of their trade gleaming at their freshly-sharpened cutting edges. Merely in pursuit of their daily work, this was a frightening sight for the leat men to come across. Quickly overpowered, they were trussed up and on their way to Lydford and the dark dank hole of the prison before Thomas Drake fortunately arrived on the scene to persuade their captors to release them. What remuneration was paid to the tinners for the leat men's freedom perhaps only a more imaginative storyteller could relate.

Eventually after a few more aggravating years, the dispute was settled and an amicable agreement was reached, with William Crymes getting a forty-two year lease from the Corporation to tap water from the leat. Part of the bargain stipulated that the town's supply came first, at all times, and men from his employment were to aid the leat men in keeping the water to Plymouth flowing during times of ice and snow.

Well over two hundred years later, the leat man was still having the same problems, with others abusing the system. On 12 June 1821 Mr George Shillibeer, the Superintendent of the leat, wrote to Mr Batanbury of the Corporation, reporting a misdemeanour, saying,

Sir
You are desired to let Mr Hawker the Chairman of the Water Committee know that the Meavy Miller draws the hatch every day at 6 o clock in the morning and tourns out three parts out of the Leate 12 hours every day and some day all. I an under the nesasaty to follow him four times a day some days to keep him from taking the whole his perceedings seems to be very unlegal in every respect for the first place he suffers part of the water he takes out to flow in the Miners leate in the next place he let the water out of his leate at differn places for the inhabitants of Meavy village and the remaining part him takes himself which I suppose him has a right to.

I hope the Water Committee Gentlemen will take some steps in order to compel to the proper regulations so as to keep the water off so many hours also not to take off the water from out of the Plymouth leate for no other purpose then his own use not to draw out such quantity for the use of other individuals I am rather under some thought that the Miller at Mash Mills hath some interest in this concern but I can not say for truth as him is a person I never see.

When one reads of the Miller drawing the hatch, it seems to say, that at sometime down through the ages from Drake's time, concessions had been made to the Meavy Mills for tapping water off the leat. Mr Shillibeer goes on in the same letter to say:

Also I have one thing more to report to the Committee which is this as soon as the water is tourned off for any purpose the leat is immediately crowded with people of all ranks and descriptions killing and destroying all the fish and ripping and injuring the banks and budle places of the leate in a most imfamos and raskly manner the hope of hindering these perceedings originally used to be don by having notice papers from Plymouth town to whare head for £20 reward for any person seen tourning out the water or fishing in Mr Whitford is the person to refer too respecting these nototices.

> *I am Sir*
> *Yours Truly*
> *G Shillibeer*
>> *Shipstor June the 12th 1821.*

What wonderful tenacity and devotion to his employment this old gentleman had. He was no doubt an exemplary for a man nearing retirement age today, to care as he did for the Plymouth water supply, to police the leat in all winds and weathers, to play cat and mouse with the miller at Meavy, on occasions, as the man told the committee, four times a day.

Fifteen months later, in the days when time was not there to be rushed and stress related to work was not even on time's horizon, Mr Shillibeer, after further consultation with his employers at the Corporation, sent another letter on his action concerning the miller at Meavy.

> *Sir*
>
> *Agreeable to your request on Thursday last respecting the water being tourned off his course on Wednesday night at an unusual hour I called on the Miller at Meavy Mill and seen his son who superattend the business I then asked of him who tourned off the leate on Wednesday night after I tourned the stream home he then said it was wee don it I then asked him what his reason was for doing it at such unusual hour his reply was that they wanted the water for use of their Mills and that the right of taking this water extended to any hour whenever they wanted it either by night or day and that they should so continue this custome whenever they wanted the water for use of the Mills this is the result of his answer.*
>
> *I am Sir*
> *Your dutifull most*
> *Obedience servant*
> *G Shillibeer*
>> *September 21st 1822.*

George's life away from the leat was extremely busy and enterprising At the reasonably young age of thirty, along with his wife Sarah, he purchased Butter Tor House a very desirable property with walled gardens. He also owned Leeford in Sheepstor and two-thirds of Reedymead Meadows, and if that wasn't enough, he leased eight acres of land on Ringmoor Down called Holdichale. George was also a God-fearing man and his strong religious convictions took him to the appointment of Churchwarden at Sheepstor.

Meanwhile after several meanwhiles, letters to the miller from Mr Whitford of the Corporation made no difference at all to the situation. After visiting the miller for a response to his employer's endeavours on paper, Mr Shillibeer writes again to them.

How Sir
This is to inform you that the Meavy Millers son who superatends for his Father says that your sending to his father letters avails as nothing as him shall continue his usual practice in tourning the water out whenever him needs in his conversation with me I told him to particularly to he the right his Father had to this water he did not hesitate long before him gived me a candid answer that his Father had a right to take one stream out of the Plymouth Leate at any time whenever him wants it and to keep the same so long as he was in want of it...

No letter or document is available to tell us when and how the dispute was finally resolved, but enough was said in those that remain to give a clear insight into some of the problems the leat man had to face with the general public. They also displayed his ability as a mediator and diplomat and his utmost respect for his job and for those who paid his weekly wage.

For forty years George Shillibeer superintended the work on the leat, from Head Weir to Jump as Roborough was known in his day. By 1830, at the age of 72, his mind was telling him to slow down; life in general was beginning to tellingly tug at his years and weariness, prompting him to write and ask an obliging favour from his employers. In his neatest hand he wrote:

To the Mayor and Chareman and all other Gentlemen of the Water Committee.
I have now taken the liberty to address yo with these few particulars respecting the Office of which I am now serving under you and has for upwards of 36 Years which is a long servitude and as my years are now drawing on very fast to a conclusion God knows how soon therefore when this uncertain time comes or at any sooner period of time if I should be disabled or rendered uncapeable of the Office I am now serving under you will have the goodness to let my son fill the Office as him has been customd to the care and manigement of the leate from his youth up and can conduct the same as well as myself as him has had the super attention with me for this 30 years and him will feel himself happy to serve you in this situation as for his charitor of behavour and honest will bear the strictest examination if required therefore under these above mentoned sircumstances I hope you will do me the favor of granting this request in so doing you will greatly oblige your dutifull most oblidging servant who is now Gentlemen

Sheepstor Village.

Yours Truly
G Shillibeer Sheepstor August 25th 1830
(NB)
I shall be always happy to serve you for the welfare of your leate as long as life and strength will permitt.

As the nineteenth century dawned into being, George's son William at the tender age of twelve, went off to work with his father learning the skills of the leat man with plenty on the curriculum to absorb. He spent thirty-three years alongside his much-respected mentor, till the old fellow passed away in the closing days of Summer 1833. His headstone, beside the gravel path in the grounds of Sheepstor churchyard, tells of the appreciation of a grateful employer. When the low winter sun shines across the lichen encrusted letters, they read:

HERE

LIES THE BODY OF

GEORGE SHILLIBEER

A WORTHY AND RESPECTED

YEOMAN OF THIS PARISH

DIED THE 22ND OF AUGUST 1833

AGED 75 YEARS

THE TABLET IS ERECTED BY THE MAYOR

AND COMMONALTY OF THE BOROUGH OF

PLYMOUTH AS A TOKEN OF RESPECT TO THE

MEMORY OF THE DECEASED WHO FOR UPWARDS

OF 40 YEARS OF HIS LIFE HAD BEEN

THE FAITHFUL AND INDEFATICABLE AGENT AND

SUPERINTENDENT OF THEIR WATER LEAT

AND THE BANKS THEREOF FROM THE HEAD WEIR

SO FAR AS JUMP

Leat above Clearbrook.

Leat near Tyrwhitt's stables.

Amos and Emma Shillibeer.

The Corporation saw the value in George's wish and promoted William to Agent and Superintendent, the job which, when he died at the age of 82 in 1869, he had held for just four years less than his father. Altogether he had watched over the leat for an incredible sixty-nine years. William too, was commemorated with a headstone, which appropriately stands beside his fathers.

In the last few years of his life he would have been involved with a mile or two of the leat's improvements, with its stone-filled edging for the drainage of any dirty surface water and, of course, the leat's eventual granite-slab lining.

The 1850 census saw William filling his spare time working the farm at Redstone, a small acreage occupying the lower western slopes of Sheepstor. Here in the same year, Amos, the youngest of his five children was born. When William passed away, Amos was a young man of only nineteen, yet a mature one he must have been, for he was appointed by the Corporation to follow on from his father and grandfather to tend the leat in the same caring manner. Along with the leat's improvements came a fine cottage, built at the Head Weir for the Superintendent and his wife Emma Maria to move into. Here, opposite the rundown and much altered Longstone Manor, they lived for 27 years amidst fabulous scenery; the dwelling nestled beneath the heights of Yennadon and Peek Hill, sheltered from the scolding arctic winds whilst, all year round, the sun poured in to aid a healthy ambience for their sons George and Harold to grow up in.

It was here at the Head Weir, where the time-honoured Fishing Feast was held, to celebrate the delivery of the fresh running water to Plymouth. This yearly celebration was attended by the Water Engineer, the Lord Mayor, Councillors and other invited dignitaries.

Amos and Emma supplemented the income from the Corporation earnings, by working for the Brook family at Burrator House. Amos in his spare time cared for the gardens, and full-time Emma washed, scrubbed, cleaned and polished, before making her way back home to do more of the same in her own home.

The Brooks were formally the Rajah's of Sarawak, a British Protectorate in north-west Borneo, obtained from the Sultan of Brunei in 1842. Visible reminders of these Sheepstor days can be seen in the village graveyard. Up on the higher ground against the northern wall, the tomb of Sir James Brook the first Rajah is a rather lavish structure of polished red Aberdeen granite, whilst Charles the second Rajah, lies content with a largely uncut mass of grey Dartmoor granite. The memorial stones of those next-in-line of succession are considerably smaller and far less impressive.

The middle years of Amos' working life saw the initial plans for a reservoir that would drown their cottage and a vast majority of life as he knew it. Gone would be their home, their garden and the cosy Eden in which they lived.

Ironically it was after weather conditions disturbingly shoved the cosiness to one side for a while that plans for a major reservoir in the area was more seriously considered. Many a winter brought snow and ice to paint the valley prettily, and to toy with the patience of the leat man; but in 1891 the leat was swallowed by the same fearsome storm that slowed the Princetown train to a halt near Eggworthy and partially devoured the site of it.

Head Weir Cottage in the days of the leat.

The grandson of Amos, Mr William George Shillibeer of Bellever Farm near Postbridge, remembers his grandfather telling him of that winter, of how the Head Weir and the river beside it was frozen solid and how the freezing stemmed the dwindling water flow in the leat to Plymouth until all the storage reservoirs down through the system ran dry. In places on Roborough Down the snow lay an incredible fifteen-feet deep. Corporation workmen, pulled away from their usual occupations in the town, toiled alongside the leat repair men endeavouring to clear the waterway. All day and night they struggled but, with inadequate clothing, losing the fight to keep out the ever-dipping temperatures, morale eventually let the harsh elements win and cold and hungry men were forced to down tools in frustration and make their way home. A couple of days later, over three hundred men arrived on the Down dressed to suit what confronted them. Civilians and men from the army toiled side by side to clear nearly half the moor-travelling leat. Satisfied with the endeavours of their back breaking day all returned to their barracks and homes only for the snow-laden night skies to fill the leat again. The next couple of days saw nigh on double the numbers tackling the huge problem, and with the sky clear and blue and the biting wind abated to stillness they cleared the leat all the way to Weir Head, allowing the water to run again.

The same year, at the age of eighteen, after working for farmer Creber at Essworthy, Amos' eldest son George joined him on the leat. Within two years he was back on the farm again, this time assisting the clearing of the site for the foundations of the dam that was to flood his childhood home.

The dam may well have been constructed years earlier and Amos' purpose-built nest in the beautiful valley may never have existed if Plymouth had agreed to share its water from the Meavy with Devonport.

Drake's escapades with Spain were over and written into the great tome of history when, by the end of the seventeenth century, France became the aggressor for Britain to contend with. It was decided that the anchorage in the Cattewater was inadequate in the South West for the nation's warships. Facilities for the building and repair of ships, as well as places to house administration and barracks were required. The Devon shoreline in the mouth of the Tamar River was chosen as the site of the new dockyard and there developed the town of Dock. By the mid 1700s its rapidly growing population began to outnumber that of Plymouth and like its municipal neighbour it needed water, but when Dock, now Devonport, requested from Plymouth a certain number of gallons to supplement their now inadequate resource, their neighbour flatly refused a drop, begging the same reasons for withdrawing a supply to Stonehouse, nearly forty years before, namely that there was barely enough water to satisfy its own consumption.

In 1790 to supply the thirsty town with water, a flow from the very heart of the moor was looked at by an independent private concern, calling itself the Dock Water Company, aiming to obviously making a profit out of dry mouths with free water from the sky. But, who could question the merits when such a venture meant nearly thirty miles of contour-curving leat having to be excavated, starting high up on the West Dart before catching more from the Cowsic and the Blackbrook.

As well as the civilian population, the man-made stream would also supply the Dockyard and other naval establishments including the hospital. The idea was soon adopted by those it needed to impress and was put to Parliament who readily welcomed the proposals. However, Plymouth suddenly did not agree, informing the people of Dock that their supply was ample for both towns.

Beardown Man menhir.

Boulder moved by a flood.

The flow is born only a few hundred yards up the West Dart from the weather-stunted oak groves of ancient Wistman's Wood where the trees grow contorted and gnarled out from deep and hazardous crannies in a sea of large boulders, an amazing paradise for botanists where mosses and lichen are concerned. From the woods the leat can be seen on the opposite hill contouring Beardown for well over a mile before disappearing into the conifer plantation on the southern end of the Down. By the time it reaches here it is already nigh-on two hundred feet above the river. It passes under the darkness of the trees and enters full daylight again looking down on Beardown Farm. Now the leat has arrived in the Cowsic Valley and shortly after it flows beneath a bridge that takes the rambler down the farm track; the water runs out of sight through a pipeline. 1898 saw an aqueduct gradually stride across the Cowsic, a well-proportioned arched bridge finished in dressed granite, extravagantly built merely to hide the ugliness of the eighteen-inch steel conduit that carries the leat water across the valley by dropping a contour to ingeniously mushroom up into a stone-clad tank to unite with the flow from the Cowsic. The system made redundant the section of leat that ran for about a mile along the west flank of Beardown, where it discharged on to the Cowsic leat Head Weir. Etched on a stone, built into the aqueduct just above the arch, are the initials DWC - the 'D' does not denote the word 'Dock'; the organisation changed their name to include 'Devonport' about ten years before the structure was built, 55 years after the town itself changed its name from Dock to Devonport.

When the heavens open this narrow valley takes in a tremendous amount of rainwater, with its head high on the moor at about 1800 feet, it travels just over three miles before reaching the area of Beardown Farm. On its way it catches the volume of Conies Down water, all the steep eastern slopes of Holming Beam and the long elongated western side of Beardown. Flood waters gushing down this valley have in the past brought chaos and tossed stones and giant boulders over and over till they come to rest, alien to their original position. Just below the aqueduct, there is a stone with wording etched onto its face looking directly at the aqueduct. The wording tells of a flood that moved the stone, ending with the date uncompleted. On the other side the inscription, now partially buried, reads,

SWEET POESY FAIR FANCY'S CHILD
THY SMILES IMPARADISE THE WILD.

On an island farther down stream, there is another inscribed boulder that is approximately two feet high, six feet long and eight feet wide, has at some time been flipped over leaving the inscriptions upside down. What one sees if the light is right, when deciphered reads:

ADORE.THE.GODS.WITH.DAILY.PRAYER.
EACH.DEED.OF.EVIL.SHUN.WITH.CARE.
AND.LEARN.WITH.FORTTUDE.TO.BEAR.

Boulder and inscription.

Inscribed boulder.

The chiselled digits on the larger boulder behind are weathered to the extent of being almost unreadable, nevertheless with patience much of it can be distinguished and interpreted.

Whilst in the area following the leat, there are other inscribed stones for the interested to see. As one leaves the little wooded area that shades the two boulders a stone straddles the path. It bears the words 'YE NAIDS VENDERA'. On the way to the next set of inscribed stones, a neat little clapper will have to be crossed, then an arched bridge that again spans the river. In and around the flowing water, merely feet from the bridge, can be found etched on various boulders, the names of Shakespeare, Milton, Burns and Spencer; others that can be viewed are up in the field on the far side of the river, but to see these permission must be obtained from the present occupier of Beardown Down Farm. Like those in the river, all were chiselled at the behest of the Vicar of Tavistock, the Reverend Bray, the son of the farmer who enclosed the land in the 1800s. The stones or boulders in the fields are etched with the profound thoughts of Atticus, Cicero, Tasso, Theocritus, Gessner and Virgil. Virgil's lines, although a little matted with lichen, are still very sharply displayed on their granite setting.

After travelling the sometimes desolate quietness of the higher Cowsic Valley, the leat that one has come here to follow gradually weaves out into the open, high above the sad remains of once magnificent beech trees, blown down during a storm in the first year of the 1990s, leaving, after their timber had been taken away, only stumps with broken roots where foxgloves during their season now grow in profusion.

The leat leaves the moor and crosses under the Tavistock-Two Bridges road, wends its way through the fields of Waldron Farm, before converging with the water drawn from the Black Brook. This little river that starts its life on the north side of bare and windswept Black Dunghill, which very few people visit, was the first to contribute some of its sparkling flow to Dock/Devonport; the West Dart and Cowsic intakes followed later. Here also, during time of continual heavy rainfall, the gushing white frothing swell can be controlled to allow only what the leat can sufficiently take, the rest drops back into the brook. Just a little farther on the current almost cedes to the calm of stillness, allowing duckweed to gently wave in the retarded flow. Here in the warm summer evenings, tranquillity wraps itself around you, where swallows skim the water catching their last meal of the day before the dimpsy sets in and the twilight grey after sunset returns one's thoughts to more prosaic things.

Not far above, to the right-hand side of the leat, is Tyrwhitt's formidable grey granite prison, where convicted abusers of society are housed. Having escaped the clutches of the detaining gradient, the flow can be heard again as the gurgling ripples run towards the Princetown –Two Bridges road and the long curve around towards Tor Royal. Here the neatest bridge, incorporating a stile, spans the water giving access to Bull Park. The leat was thrust through this piece of land just as the young Tyrwhitt was in the advance stages of developing the acreage; an annoying disruption no doubt, right under the very windows of his newly-built home. Very little has changed here since his days except the beech, chestnut and sycamore have grown to full majestic maturity and now clothe the buildings with shade.

The leat has left the Black Brook and is well into the little Strain Valley, overlooked by the ample mound of Royal Hill; along here its neatness takes on the appearance of a small canal. Gone is the shaggy moorland-look, the hanging clumps of whortleberry, heather and ling, gone are the erosion-created inlets and trout-hiding overhangs. About a mile from Tor Royal finds the tiny moorland settlement of Peat Cot, nestling in a cleavage-like chink in the landscape. Here the leat turns away from its southern travel by veering sharply to the north-east. This tiny settlement of three dwellings and a chapel was established in the 1800s. The leat flows away from Peat Cot, still coursing the Strain Valley, until fully arcing a stone-clad hillside of comparatively good grazing and arriving in the great expanse of the Swincombe basin. Immediately below are the houses of the abandoned Whiteworks tin mine of which ample evidence of its not too distant past can be freely explored.

Cist and cairn near Devonport Leat, Swincombe Valley.

Just before the leat acutely zig zags between and around waste heaps and disused fenced-off shafts, the water flows under a clapper. Here controversy erupted when the water company found that the miners had bridged their leat, claiming that damage could well occur. However the miners took these objection to the construction lightly, for they had the Duchy, to whom they paid dues, on their side and who claimed the right by agreement to take water from the leat when negotiations for it to run through Duchy land first took place. The water company went contrarily through the motions of long verbal and written confrontations until eventually conceding to the miners having their way. Unlike the footbridge a little farther on, this structure is considerably more substantial, being made to take the heavy to-ing and fro-ing of horse and loaded wagons. From the bridge the much disturbed moorland spreads itself on both sides of the leat. Within a hundred yards or so the water flows beneath the Princetown-Whiteworks tarmac road then on to skirt the western edge of the much-revered and respected Foxtor Mire.

Devonport Leat's original cutting can be seen on the right of the flowing water.

One summer evening I brought a friend on a photo trip out to the spot where a sheep leap is available for crossing. This retired old fellow was during his working days a petrol tanker driver and always assumed after criss-crossing the moor for several years in his work that he had seen all there was to see of the moor, until the moment he arrived here. 'Well,' was his first utterance and, after a deep breath, 'well' was his second. He then went on to say 'Good God, I can see why you spend so much time out on the moor.' From then he went quiet, allowing me to explain how the mire below was taken into Conan Doyle's great story *The Hound of the Baskervilles*. After asking me if all the hills had names, I was delighted with total enthusiasm in telling him what could be seen from where we were stood.

On the left, just a few yards on from the sheep leap can be seen a kistvaen in good condition, set in its stone-circled cairn, the cover slab obviously robbed for use elsewhere. Running

Sluice gate on the Devonport Leat.

Tunnel exit.

Nun's Cross on the boundary of the forest.

in front of the cairn almost touching the circle, but paying enough respect not to, is what could well be an original cut of the leat before the water flow we see today was accepted as the required course. Around the curve towards Nun's Cross Farm is a dry leat bed running away from the right-hand side of our leat giving further evidence of an alteration. Still around the curve, the water flows beneath another cart track clapper, before reaching Nun's Cross tunnel. On the left, about midway between the two, the leat allows a little stream to add a few more gallons to its flow. Apparently this meagre trickle was the cause of the usual strife between the tinner and the water company. Deliberately channelled with a sluice gate, its loss in augmenting the catchment of the Whiteworks leat at the time of diversion supposedly put production at the mine in jeopardy. Although now in a little disrepair the diversion still drops into the leat, suggesting that the water company this time won the day.

As the water flows into the tunnel 'DANGER NO ENTRY are the initial capital lettered words on a sign fitted to the padlocked security gate, there to disallow access for the curious. The sign goes on to say, that a permit to work is required and another below reads 'controlled area radon gas refer to safe systems of work.' Here the entrance, like the exit 640 yards further on, is stone-lined for only about the first twelve feet. The flow travels in darkness in a north-west direction, for about two-thirds of the way, before flowing out into daylight again to the west. According to leat man Dougy Pigeon, there are two interesting features to be seen deep inside, by the lucky few who have the authority to enter. A waterfall apparently drops from high up on the interior's undressed face and, in another area on the walling, a cathedral appears fresco-like in the natural pattern of the smooth-weathered granite.

About midway along the tunnel, the leat leaves Duchy land by running beneath the Forest Boundary line. Siward's Cross, or Nun's Cross as it is more commonly known, was chosen as a boundmark when the Chase was mapped out in 1240 during the long reign of Henry III. This Siward, could well have been the Earl of Northumberland, who held several parcels of land around the country, including eight known substantial plots in Devon. But, the nearest of any of these to this cross were at Peter Tavy and Willsworthy, which after the Conquest, went to Alfred the Breton. The rest were way off the moor in North East and South East Devon, all of which went to Baldwin de Redvers after Harold lost to William at Hastings. The name Baldwin, made the first Earl of Devon in 1141, allows perhaps a peep into why Siward's name is etched on the cross, for on the face looking to the west, is the word Bocland; 'Bocheland' in the day of the Conqueror, Buckland today. In 1278 the land of Walkhampton Manor, together with Bickleigh and Buckland Monachorum, were given to the Cistercian Monks to found the Abbey of Buckland by Amice, the Widow of Baldwin. The family was granted the Manor from the king. Who held it before him the Domesday Book doesn't say. Perhaps the answer is inscribed on the eastern face of the ancient old cross, and the moorland travel of the leat from it, is through the land that once belonged to him.

Daylight at the Western end of the tunnel, brings the leat for the first time into the Meavy water catchment area. Here the ground immediately outside the tunnel is considerably higher than that of the entrance end, making the embankment on both sides of the leat a lot deeper. Often a pair of dippers build their comparatively large nest down in the almost unvisited seclusion of this fissure-like gully. The stonework of the tunnel's exit façade is for some reason neater than that of the entrance, also neatly finished by the mason just above the keystone, is a plaque, there perhaps to display the Water Company's initials or the date of the tunnel's completion, but for some reason its face staring at the departing water remained bare. On the right of the leat, almost adjacent to the gully, is the old tinner's house that is thought to have been refurbished and used by the builders of the tunnel. It is now in a bit of a sorry state with a beech tree and three shaggy-looking hawthorns peering down on to the few inches that remain of the fireplace chimney. Except for the occasional annoying broken bottle and the carelessly abandoned snack wrapper and, of course the trees, very little has changed in the remains appearance since I first visited the site at the start of the 1970s. From here, for about a mile and three quarters, the leat contours high above the Newlycombe Valley, as the water flows away from the gully in the seclusion of a divide in the hillside. Here a view opens to the eye like the drawing of curtains on a stage. Up on the right stands the comparatively modern Hutchinson's Cross, backdropped below by moorland scarred by tinners, small fields of forgotten farms, a conifer plantation and the impressive granite bulks of the Meavy Tors. Immediately below the cross, the leat calmly zig zags until arching around the hill and on towards Older Bridge.

Looking out from the tunnel.

Tinner's hut.

Leat below Hutchinson's Cross.

Older Bridge over the leat.

The leat running across a deep gert.

A disused valve beside the leat.

Sluice valve on the leat.

This bridge was the subject of amusement early one beautiful summer's morning. Whilst strolling up the Meavy towards the aqueduct that takes the leat water off Raddick Hill, I met up with a fellow whom I had seen from a distance, frequently stopping and looking around before lowering his head to what turned out to be his map. Thinking the man was in need of assistance, I asked if he had a problem I could help him with. 'No no,' he replied, almost haughtily. With that I carried on my way. Suddenly he called after me, asking with quite a cultured voice, if the aqueduct was Older Bridge, to which I replied 'You have got the slight problem of being in the wrong valley,' and went on to give a grateful man directions.

Older Bridge, a clapper, is there astride the leat and take a track on up over the hill to Peat Cot and Whiteworks from Norsworthy and Leather Tor Bridge. If the walker wishes to do so, there are seven other clappers to use between the tunnel and the river Meavy, nine if one counts the sluice gate spans. After leaving Older Bridge, the leat takes in a little more water from various tinners' gullies including the well-documented Drivage Bottom; it also spans others that are dry, the deepest with its bottom twenty feet below the running water. One can imagine the tonnage and effort to infill this huge man-made void, with none of today's mechanical excavators and dumpers available this was achieved with the sweating labour of man and his horse. On the left of the running water, not far from the fifth clapper is, rusting away, an abandoned sluice valve and its associated pipework; Nearby, still buried in its deposited place of employment is another, with its valve gate stem protruding at least six inches above the ground for the unwary to trip over. During a majority of its course, the slow moving water allows various aquatic weeds to grow and flourish, but from above Crazywell Pool, the gradient drops a little steeper encouraging the sounds of a faster flow, leaving no chance for any plant life to dig a heel in. A few yards on from the eighth and last bridge, one can see that another alteration was made to the original planned line of the leat running away to the left. Hidden from daylight here and there by gorse is a dry bed, it drops quite steeply down Raddick Hill for several yards until curving its travel along a course almost parallel to the stream of water that's been followed so far. Within a few yards it discontinues into the hillside's vast field of stones and boulders. The reason for its abandoned path is not known, but one can surmise that the steepness was at fault and the correction was made before water had chance to flow.

Walking the moors has taken me many times to this area, I have even captured on camera the hut circles near the Raddick Hill sluice gate, with the wonderful winter backdrop of brown and withered bracken and the mighty rock mounds on the sky line of Leather Tor and Sharptor. Yet I had never noticed, till being pointed out to me by my good friend, Sandy Gerrard, that the excavators took the water right through the centre of an outlying hut circle.

Within not too many strides from the ruined remains of the prehistoric little building, the leat water, but for its confining banking, cascades unchecked in a gleaming white torrent

Sluice gate on Raddick Hill.

Tumbling down Raddick Hill.

The leat aqueduct.

Water from the Hartor Brook.

The leat running towards Stanlake.

The leat above Stanlake.

down the hillside to the sudden confinement of an aqueduct that straddles the Meavy. The aqueduct that the fellow walker thought was Older Bridge. Just beyond the outflow of the aqueduct, the leat accepts a stream from a ten-inch iron pipe that arrives from a concrete sluice system that captures the water of the Hart Tor Brook as well as a certain flow from the Meavy. From the stone and timber water-carrying bridge, the leat drops in shallow steps so as to slow the torrent down a little while it curves around a sharp bend. From here to Stanlake plantation, there are five clappers to convenience livestock and the walker. Along this section of the leat, is a face of a doll cemented into the stonework. This tiny intriguing landmark is not the original, that was smashed by some brainless vandal in the early 1990s. It has always been believed by the romantic that the face, which was of porcelain, was placed there by a French prisoner of war, during the construction of the leat. Others say, it was introduced to the stonework by a mason during later renovation. The face we see today, is a replacement put there by a young moor-loving girl, who earned the privilege to do so when winning a competition run by the Dartmoor National Park Authority. Near the third bridge along, the leat begins to drop in steps again before it curves and spans the little Stanlake stream; always in this area one can hear and see the stonechat.

Below the south-western end of the curve, dating back to medieval times, are the sad ruins of Stanlake farmstead. Dating back still further are the remains above the leat, on the left-hand side of Stanlake stream; this area is a jumble of various periods in man's farming history, the fallen walls of field systems altered through the ages can be traced back to Bronze Age man. Their evidence is easily discerned even by the amateur enthusiast, especially in the winter months, when the bracken cover has disappeared.

No sooner the leat passes under the fifth clapper, it leaves the open moor and enters the plantation where it races downhill, tinkling over an uneven bed of rubble-size stones until the gradient quietens it to silence. Just a whisper here from the water allows the conifer-loving goldcrest to be heard, along with the chiffchaff and other more melodic warblers. The repeated call of the chaffinch, the song of the robin, the loud trill of the wren, all outdo the occasional laugh of the green woodpecker and screech of the jay. While under the trees the leat meanders for about a mile before arriving out into clear daylight again, above the ruins of Leather Tor Farm. It is always a delight to walk along here but beware of muddy pools where tree-felling equipment leaves long elongated ruts several inches deep in places. There are again five clappers to be counted along this stretch of the waterway route. Approaching the fourth, all the sounds of the plantation are drowned by the water gushing downhill; this is the only place, bar the cascade at Raddick Hill, where the excavator had little influence over the exact fashion and neatness of his work. Almost hidden among various species of fern and other plants tolerant to the wetness, the crescendo splashes and crashes, bubbles and gurgles in falls and spouts, till its tempest is calmed as it flow is sedated under the fifth

The fifth clapper bridge on the leat.

clapper at the bottom of the hill. The scene looking along the leat, especially using this rugged clapper, would surely fill any artist's canvas. The water flows away from the eye, between a thin collection of deciduous trees; at the end of this avenue the vista climbs to the sky via the splendid height of Sheepstor. Further on, breaks in the trees give away spectacular views of the Meavy hills and tors and above, in the distant haze, the cone-like Hen Tor on the Plym hides, camouflaged under the long line of the Langcombe Ridge. Only a few more yards and the leat runs under the Leather Tor Farm track.

A short stroll downhill will soon bring the inquisitive to the ruins of the farm buildings and its associated frost-free potato cave; a manmade grotto for storing his root crops. If a little ferreting around is had among the bracken cover on the bank to the right of the track, the stone circle of a cairn can be found, with its central kistvaen left open to the sky by the despoilers who years ago vandalised this Bronze Age monument. About a hundred yards or so from the cairn, the leat finds its first tarmac road for over five miles to run under. This is Cross Gate, a favourite spot for the elderly to sit in a deckchair and gaze out over the panorama, to see the changing light, to watch and listen. A heron floats gracefully on the air, gradually descending towards its next feeding place; a buzzard calls and circles, a raven using the thermals extends its flight across the valley and magpies, now in their plenty, flit on ungainly wings and chatter. A robin comes with friends from somewhere, hopeful for the crumbs of an enjoyed picnic.

The leat at Cross Gate.

On the left of the leat, a restored cross looks out over the same scene. Most of the crosses we see on the moor have been restored at one time or another, with the odd suitable piece of granite substituting for a missing head, arm or shaft. In nearly all cases the work was carried out with generous amounts of conscientious consideration for the end result, but not a lot it seems was afforded to this unfortunate specimen. A case of admirable thinking, latterly forgetting the original concept, the whole is an unlovely mix of various shapes, from square to octagonal. It would surely have been kinder to the original monument and its surrounding area to have merely allowed the socket, when it rains, to fill with water,

The leat leaves the beautiful area of Cross Gates with its water bubbling and gurgling as it runs along a slightly steeper gradient, passing beneath a small parapet bridge and sluice system, before arriving after about a quarter of a mile at Lowery.

The leat at Lowery Bridge.

Now sadly the dwellings are gone where generations of the Shillibeers lived, laid to waste almost without trace by the vandals in authority, who quite naturally thought they knew best. Just a few yards from here the water runs under the road again, through what appears to be a tiny picturesque arched construction, but on closer and rather difficult inspection, one can see that the entrance and exit are merely a pretty façade and the bridge turns out to be another simple little clapper. Just twenty-one inches reads on the tape when the height is measured from the gravel bed to the keystone of the arch.

Warning notice.

The leat nearing the Burrator–Walkhampton road.

Leat man Doug Pigeon told me that at one time he had the unenviable task of somehow manoeuvring himself along this tiny orifice beneath the road, to remove the problem of a blockage, 'after the water was turned away,' he hastily added. Merely a yard or two after leaving the road another clapper spans the leat, just before entering a wooded area of mainly oak. Under this deciduous canopy, the water flows through an elaborate but beautifully-constructed gauge-trough, its stonework likened very much to that at Burrator Reservoir. A little further on a cart track clapper spans the leat, here on the right of the now fenced-off flow is a notice, positioned in this idyllic glade of open greenery, to inform the reader not to pollute the water and that 'Bathing, Wading Paddling, Camping and Washing of Animals' is strictly forbidden. It goes on to warn the tempted offenders who do not take heed, that they will be prosecuted. Noticing the holes in each corner of the plaque fixed firmly to a post, it looks that at some time it must surely have been placed somewhere else.

Here also a locked gate bars the way, but steps in the stone walling allows the leat follower to progress farther. The path runs beneath conifers again, taking the walker slightly away from a much quieter flow until the tarmac Yennadon-Lowery road is crossed where the water is in full view again. Just over halfway along this stretch of the leat a small boulder can be seen right beside the path with the irons of the feather and tare still imbedded in it. Most times under the evergreen cover of conifer, without the full rays of sunshine, moss grows thick and hides what I think is the best example of the rock splitting method to be seen on the moor.

Within three hundred yards the leat runs under the Yennadon-Burrator road, then almost immediately under a clapper erected to carry an old field hedge that still stands on top of it, devoid of any vegetation below a canopy of conifer. Permission is required to view the next part of the leat. Where once more deciduous trees of mainly hazel drape their branches over the almost motionless water here, having covered less than half its original travel, the working leat nears its conclusion. A conglomeration of fine silt washed down from high up on the moor dressed in autumn fallen leaves often fills the waterway to overflowing, until men are employed in the area again to throw the clogging mass to one side. Half buried in the silt can be seen stones that could well have been fashioned by the feathers and tares left embedded in the small moss covered boulder, that was passed half a mile or so earlier under the conifers.

Looking down through the trees from high up on the leat embankment, one can see the roof and rear of the lodge built to replace Head Weir Cottage. A few yards on from here the water flows through an iron grating and divides into two streams, one runs under ground around Yennadon Down to the Dousland Treatment Works, the other cascades like a water-fall from a pipe, before tumbling steeply down the hillside under old oaks until running beneath the road to add a little drop more to the reservoir.

Before the reservoir.

The expanse of water that graces this part of the Meavy Valley, may not have been here if an earlier project had been adopted. Further up the river, below Black Tor, can be seen the evidence of a search for firm foundations to site a dam across the Meavy and Hart Tor Brook. Iron caps now seal the bore holes of the exploratory work. A pleasant few hours can be had here with the family searching for these objects, especially if a picnic is to hand. If the project had gone ahead, the prominence of Hart Tor, may well have appeared like an island, with Black Tor falls dwarfed or swallowed by the foot of the dam, along with two stone rows, many hut circles and the neat marker stones of the old firing range hidden, perhaps for ever beneath the water.

The reservoir and its immediate surroundings we see and enjoy today was the creation of the engineer Mr Edward Sandeman. He laid his ideas for the project on the table for the Plymouth City Water Committee to view not so long after the great freeze of 1891. By 1893 smiles crossed the faces of the gentlemen when the plans met with Royal Assent. Later the same summer, in the month of August, the first delvings into bedrock began. Dynamite was at times employed, not to oust the material into the sky, but merely to split it in a direction favourable for later masonry work. Mostly lines of feather and tare, sledgehammers and men with muscle and sinew straining to their limits, tearing a deep keyway out of the narrow valley bottom, taking just two years to excavate over 12,000 cubic yard of solid granite. Blister nurturing picks and shovels were used along with hand-winched cranes to load huge buckets and side-tip trucks which, when full, were raised from the gradually formed chasm by steam cranes, the material being placed to one side for use in later stages of the dam's construction, some shaped by the mason for the facing of the attractive cyclopean walling. Other stones, a few of very large proportions, were employed as infill never to be seen again, between the inner and outer walls, substituting and necessarily displacing vast amounts of hand-mixed concrete.

The dam under construction.

Looking at photographs of the project, thankfully locked away along with many other archives of local history, the site of the excavation is very reminiscent of a child's board game, with planks of wood worming in all directions, and ladders of all lengths propped here and there in all manner of positions.

For the period of excavation and until the workforce had fashioned an outlet through the eventual ever-rising masonry, the carpenters erected two wooden launders to carry water away from the project, one to convey the Drake's Leat, still feeding Plymouth, the other a huge construction dwarfing the former, took the river flow, even when the delivery was of flood proportions.

A crane on the dam wall.

Of the thousands of people who visit the reservoir and its surrounding area every year, very few realise that there is another dam holding the same expanse of water back. This construction can be found on the left, about a third of a mile from Burrator Dam, on the Dousland-Sheepstor road, it is nowhere near as spectacular in appearance as its counterpart already described, almost unnoticeable in fact to the casual visitor or the uninitiated regular day tripper to the fabulous beauty spot.

Invite to the fishing feast.

The dam appears as no more than a stone-lined bank, yet its construction caused far more geological headaches to Mr Sandeman than the far bigger Burrator Dam. Its building began about twelve months after its neighbour and took three years to complete, all that was thought to be needed was to dig a trench five feet wide and seven hundred long to find good solid foundations, but below the surface was found kaolinized granite (china clay) and springwater oozing in at one time at the rate of four hundred and fifty thousand gallons a day. The problem soon demanded the use of large pumps, capable of keeping conditions for the workmen more-or-less satisfactory. But it was still no place for the faint-hearted, for a hundred feet was met in depth before solid rock was found. One can not even begin to imagine what it was like to work down in that trench, with a maze of horizontal wooden props, wedged every few feet, to prevent the sides from falling in, and water running and dripping continuously and daylight limited to dimpsy at such a depth. It was planned for the trench to be filled with concrete. The estimated budget must have been well overspent by the time ten months was up and the workmen tamped the final mixes down, with thirty odd feet still remaining until top of the trench was reached. This area was packed with puddle clay, unlike china clay this material is water resistant and made an excellent embankment.

After five years of bustling construction work disturbing the rural peace, the valley here in the middle reaches of the river, again fell silent, but life for Amos Shillibeer, was never to be the same. His leat was now dry and sort of semi-redundant and the problems that went with it had disappeared. He had taken on the new job offered to him by the Water Committee as the first caretaker of the 650 million gallon reservoir, with able son, George, his assistant. With his previous home demolished and the foundation underwater, Amos had to reside for a while at Sheepstor, waiting for Burrator Lodge to be finished for him to move into.

1914 saw the beginning of the Great War, the so-called war to supposedly end all wars. It also saw the merging of Stonehouse and Devonport with Plymouth and the proposals of Burrator being raised to accommodate the anticipated increase in water consumption. The same year also saw the retirement of Amos, and George (elevated in position to replace him), with promotion for younger brother Harold to assist.

Fourteen years later the valley woke again to the bustling activity of construction work, when the proposals discussed during the Three Towns amalgamation came to fruition. The dam was being raised, but before work could begin a temporary suspension bridge, the buttresses of which can still be seen, was constructed across the water to carry the to-ing and fro-ing of Sheepstor traffic. Another task to fulfil before the raising could commence, was the dismantling of the road-carrying arches. This was made far easier, although much noisier, through the use of pneumatic drills. These vibrating machines operating in the valley must certainly have disturbed the peace, sounding very much like some demented mechanical woodpecker. The arches, five in all, came down for the duration of raising the overflow by ten feet, after which they were rebuilt, returned to carry on the job we still see them doing today.

The undertaking of the raising of the dam took four and half years, nearly as long as it did to build the original structure. Blame for this, can again be pointed at the Sheepstor end of the project. Keyways into the adjacent land on both sides of the original dam were excavated again to the fearsome depth of a hundred feet before sound bedrock foundations were found.

When finished, 376 million gallons were added to the reservoir, its greatest depth of 87 feet is from the overflow to the old river bed below. It is just over a mile and a quarter long, and is nearly half a mile in breadth at its widest point. The water, when the reservoir is full, spreads over an area of about one hundred and fifty acres, and a good eleven and half mile walk encircles the catchment area of 5,360. acres. This the Plymouth Corporation purchased from the Maristow Estate in 1916.

The following year saw the start of granite boundary posts being erected around the perimeter. If following their course takes the rambler's fancy, it is best to park the car near the public toilets and walk towards Sheepstor village via the Burrator dam, and along under a canopy of various deciduous trees, until two gates and a stile is reached on the left. Here is the Sheepstor dam, the dam that caused the problems during construction. Looking at it now one cannot imagine why. Walk along the path until a gate bars the way ahead, another stile here brings one to the water's perimeter road again. A look down whilst climbing the stile will find the first boundary post lying prostrate, with the date 1917 staring up at the trees.

Reservoir and suspension bridge.

The Sheepstor dam.

Overflow from Burrator dam.

Catchment area bound stone No.2.

Boundstone on the ridge dated 1919.

Boundstone on Yellowmead Down.

Turn right here and couple of hundred yards or so a rock strewn lane will find the moorland gate, here tucked away in the right-hand corner beside the gate post is the second marker carrying the same date.

In the shade of the tree-lined lane, it was cold but once through the gate and on to the open moor, the sky was full of intermittent cloud and the sun, on the occasions it shone through the clouds, was warm, bringing sweat beneath appropriate clothing for the time of year. The second marker on the moor can be found a few yards around to the right, standing against the same wall as the first. This stone again is dated 1917. With very little give in the ground, steps have to be chosen with care whilst ascending to the tor above because the previous night's freeze really did render the surface hard. The third boundary stone on the moor proper to come into view has the date 1919 etched upon it and, like all the rest, the letters and numbers are cut within a square frame. The third stone further up on a ridge displays the date of two years earlier; it stands just a few yards away from the huge bulk of Sheepstor, rising steeply to almost vertical. Expending a little more energy to reach the top will be rewarding, for the views of the reservoir below and the hills opposite stretching from the water's edge to the summits of Peak Hill, Leather Tor and Sharpitor, along with the panorama of the in-country, keeps one glued to the spot for a while.

On the other side of the rock mass the posts, four in all, all dated 1919, run in an east-north-easterly direction down the slope of Yellowmead Down, all in place from where the water runs off the hill towards the reservoir. Not many yards to the south from the third, one will see another beside a leat. This little waterway was running along the Down hundreds of years before the reservoir was even thought of. This is the Longstone Leat; it delivered water to the old manor house from the Drizzlecombe Brook in the Plym Valley. On the Down there are five markers, again dated 1919, set beside the leat's meandering course. Although they stand outside the catchment area, the water does eventually, after rounding the hillside, fall into the reservoir beside the Sheepstor dam. Searching out the markers along this part of the Down that feeds the Outcombe Brook can, if care is not heeded, give a bootful of soggy peat, for it is very wet and dotted with many tinners' pits and gullies and the odd pillow mound. It does pay to give the area the utmost respect.

Standing out quite clearly in the sheep-nibbled moorland grass, not far from the second marker, is the Yellowmead four-fold stone circle. Whenever one is in the area a visit to this monument is certainly worthwhile.

The following three markers are all set on the Yellowmead Farm side of the leat, with the last having a single clapper spanning the water beside it.

From here the leat is left behind as the walk to the next takes us to the foot of Leeden Hill where the digits on the marker say 1917. From the first, five more, all with the same date, ascend the hill where the tussocky terrain makes for awkward walking. The row as it rises gradually edges towards the Eylesbarrow Mine track, until the last stands beside it, near the junction that takes an often peat-sodden road, down to the ruins of the old Eylesbarrow smelting house. The markers now veer away from the track again and take a north-easterly direction. Six in all, all bearing the 1917 date, make their way up to the summit of Eylesbarrow, all looking out over the beautiful Deancombe Valley. Easy walking gets to the first two, with the second standing just on the edge of the track that led to where once turned the fifty-foot waterwheel. To find the third among a scattering of boulders on the hill, one passes through the almost unnoticeable line of stones employed to carry the flat rods, cranked to and fro, by the rotating fifty-foot giant. There is easier walking to reach the top of the hill, but to examine every marker, the feet must weave in and around and, sometimes for convenience, over stones and boulders of various proportions, with the eyes looking up now and again only for direction. The last marker stands between the two locally famous prehistoric barrows, which give the hill its name, it looks down on a Forest Boundary marker, wedged in a small squarish shaped uncut boulder. Crudely fashioned, this metal spike with a flattened head resembling an arrowhead, marks the bounds of the forest or, 'chase' of Dartmoor, first mapped out in the year 1240 as a designated hunting ground by Henry III. A closer look at the much deteriorated object will see on the left of its flattened face, the letter B, unfortunately rust has eaten away the right hand side, leaving nothing to indicate that it once displayed the letter F. Together they formed the initials of the Forest Bounds. When they were perambulated in 1609, one Hugh Elford of Longstone was employed along with others to perform the task, but by then the Forest had been in the hands of the Duchy since Edward III made the Black Prince the first Duke of Cornwall.

On the leat, beside a clapper bridge.

Walking up to this spot early one summer morning, the sound of music filtered through a light breeze. Whilst gradually getting closer, the sweet sounds began to make the familiar tune of Greensleeves being played on a flute by a young man sitting on the much disturbed stones of the eastern barrow. On meeting, not wanting to intrude on his chosen place of solitude, I merely passed the time of day and extended it only to say how much I enjoyed the pleasing results of his talent. I wondered a little while later if the lad knew he was sitting just inside the bounds of the land belonging to those descended from the man who wrote the delightful music he was playing.

Accompanying the water markers from here is the occasional unfashioned Duchy boundary stone. Taking a line more or less to the north-north-east, the ground drops down hill for a few yards before levelling to a gradient gentle enough to hold water in its fold, making for a mass of wetness when thawed, not hazardous nor unsafe, but good tread on footwear will help to keep feet from a slip down on to the soggy black peat. Until the bottom of the hill is reached, six markers can be counted, all with 1917 etched upon them. From the second, which has fallen with its face looking up at the sky, the ground gets worse for a while, for

Looking down the Deancombe Valley.

Markers between the barrows.

121

Looking towards the Swincombe.

Looking down at Nun's Cross Farm.

The first marker from Nun's Cross.

The third marker from Nun's Cross.

In front of South Hessary Tor.

The forest boundary marker on South Hessary Tor.

here the old shallow workings of the tinner come into play. From the fourth, the terrain drops steeply, letting wetness run free and walking just that little bit easier. Below here the rambler is in Swincombe country, where at one time in the late 1960s it was thought of flooding the valley to form a reservoir, where no doubt the Devonport Leat would have been terminated, leaving a disused tunnel and an empty watercourse to Burrator no more than a long curving trench in the landscape. Here Nun's Cross is met with its namesake dilapidated farm house just a stone's throw away looking out at the Dart feeding slopes of Hand Hill, Crane Hill, Down Ridge and Ter Hill. One can not imagine this valley and its famous Foxtor Mire under a six hundred acre sheet of water. Although it seems by scanning a map of the proposed high water level, that the kistvaens and monastic crosses may well have been safe on the water-lapping shoreline, the very thought of this exceptional expanse of true wilderness, with its magical impression of vastness and wonderful seasonal colouring, lost to the future, sends the senses reeling. How close the project came to fruition one can see by finding the capped trial bore holes above the river, where the throat of the Swincombe begins to steepen. It is unbelievable but true that whilst the strongest protests to the proposed flooding was boiling in the issues cauldron, one local newspaper reporter stupidly referred to the valley as 'merely a shallow saucer of grassland'.

Leaving Nun's Cross with its iron braces securing top to bottom, a track following a walk uphill to the north, will find near the brow, the first of ten markers, all dated 1917 and all more-or-less in a straight but undulating line until South Hessary Tor is met. It stands on the left of the track like the following two. From first to the second, which is only a couple of hundred yards away, the view is limited, the only points of any real interest, are the deep tinners' gullys of Drivage Bottom to the near left. By the time the third is reached, the view has opened to a beautiful panorama stretching from Gutter Tor fronting the great spread of Ringmoor Down to the rocky peaks of Leather and Sharpitor; then there is Combeshead and Down Tor with Sheepstor peering over them from behind, like some huge colossus giving a touch of drama to the scene. Adding tranquillity is Newlycombe Cross, standing on the closer horizon's brow, silhouetted against Burrator's shimmering water,

By the time the fourth marker is reached the picture is diminishing and fast losing its appeal; this stone stands just beyond the Norsworthy-Peat Cot track. The fifth, like the remainder until South Hessary is reached, stands on the right. It is noticeable, that the distance between this stone and the sixth, is far closer than any of the rest along this line, the pair are so close to one another, that either could well have been employed elsewhere. At the sixth, the boundary has run through a long line of tinners load-back pits with one beside it to the left being the largest and best example. The following four markers are stretched out, tucked alongside a newtake wall. By the time the second is reached the first real view of the middle moor and its distant hills on the horizon is so demanding to the eye, it is time to pause for a while and take it all in. The last stone stands in front of the twin rock piles of South Hessary Tor. Wedged into the summit of the easily scaled western portion, is another iron Forest bound marker of the same shape as the rusting object up on the higher ground of Eylesbarrow, only on the flattened head of this one, the F is the prominent letter.

Tracing the next five water-markers now takes one once again across an open tussocky moor until the Princetown road is met, the first tarmac surface since leaving the reservoir perimeter road six miles back. All six stones are dated 1917. From the first until the third is passed on the far side of the rise, the terrain drops its rainfall and springwater into the Hart Tor Brook. The fourth can be found at the head of a tinners' gully, looking down on to the fifth situated beside the western approach into Princetown, close to the southernmost of the two lodges built by Tyrwhitt that stand on opposite sides of the thoroughfare.

After crossing the road the following three markers, although of the same material and design, are dated fifteen years later, when the land was taken in from the Duchy. The three stones partly encompass the boggy ground of Meavy Head. If checking the dates is required, the first marker stands at the corner of a wall, just a few yards from the road. Following the same wall into the marsh will locate the other two, but could well give the unwary an uncomfortably wet sock or two; the stones stand just feet from one another, half hidden by fairly dense wetland plant life.

Getting out of here it is best to jump on to the nearby path that takes many a stroller, jogger and local dog walker to meet up with the old Princetown Railway track bed. Fifty yards or so along the path one will come across on the left the next dated marker (1917). This is the last evidence now of the boundary until a climb to North Hessary Tor is had. The way up is beside a small conifer plantation and a meander through a tinners' gully or two. Once beside the Tor beneath the steel giant of the television mast, a little look around one should come across, etched into the western side of the rock pile, at about head height, the date 1917. This is the only place on the perimeter where a natural feature has been employed to mark the limits. All the markers now, from here back to the reservoir, have 1917 chiselled into them.

Up here when I arrived on this particular perambulation, a mixture of snow and hail lay all around, making for standing on the summit a little risky; but the views from the Tor override the concern and encourage what is merely a step or two to the top. After soaking up the impressive panorama, the way now is more or less south-west. Finding the next three markers is not so easy, for all have fallen and are partly hidden by tussocky grass. The best way to locate them is to spot the twin markers beside the old railway track bed down in the valley below, and keep to a line between them and the mast. The first is found just a few feet from one of the mast's stay-wire's huge concrete bases. The second further down the hill beyond a scattering of various size boulders is unlike all the rest in that it is fashioned out of pink

Looking down on to Princetown.

One of three stones near the Princetown/Plymouth road.

Etched on North Hessary Tor.

Lying prostrate in the snow.

One of the A&T stones.

Hidden among the boulders.

granite. Still following the same line, will find the third a few yards after the hill has lost its steepness, by the time it's located, the row has passed through the Tavistock/Ashburton track, a trade route that also adopted markers to identify its course across the moor. The elongated stones are recognised by the letters A and T cut deeply into them.

The two markers that are stationed beside the disused railway, stand on the banks on either side of the cutting which the trains once passed through. From here the way forward to the next is to the south, aiming towards Black Tor on the Meavy. The terrain is tussock all the way for almost half a mile, until a crop of rocks on a rise partly hide the marker from view; it lies about a hundred walking strides from where the Princetown road is met again.

For some reason, from the railway track, until Yennadon down is arrived at two and three quarter miles away, the markers are far and few between. From the isolated post among the rocks, the catchment rim runs south-west for three parts of a mile across the Meavy/Walkham divide to Leedon Tor, with a great stretch of it through extremely wet ground. Although not necessarily hazardous, it can be uncomfortable to the uninitiated moor walker. From the hill where a number of rock piles protrude, the way is down through a sea of stones and boulders and an excellent photogenic group of hut circles. The next marker to be located can be seen from the circles up on the hill on the other side of the Meavy/Walkham saddle. Two stand as a pair just feet apart on either side of the Princetown road before it runs on over the brow and on down towards Dousland.

In this immediate area, if the interested are keen to find and investigate them, are stone rows of a totally different kind, laid out in prehistoric times and now more than partially dilapidated. Related to the rows is a ruinous kistvaen, all no doubt have been robbed for the building of the road just crossed. Up on the skyline to the south-east is the much-climbed rocks of Sharpitor to where the boundary runs. It then turns sharply to the south-west and on to Peak Hill where easy walking can be had along a broad ridge bearing garden-lawn like grass. Within a couple of hundred yards a neatly fashioned stone with the letters D.P.A. etched upon it stands guard in the middle of the route. The little stone was put there in 1982 by the Dartmoor Preservation Association when they purchased Sharpitor, thus saving it from the damaging effects from a mass influx of schoolchildren when Plymouth City Council wanted to use it as an adventure playground. Another four stones of the same fashion can be found if a walk around the tor is taken.

Looking up the gradual slope to Peak Hill from the D.P.A. stone, I can't imagine, a 260-foot steel mast standing on its very summit. On reaching where it once stood, one can gaze down six hundred feet, from directly above the ever-changing face of the water held back by the two dams of Sheepstor and Burrator.

At this vantage point, with its little pimple of a tor to sit on, one can take a look around at a great deal of the ground covered during the perambulation of the catchment area.

The twin markers beside the twelve-mile stone.

Majestically fronting the view to the north-east is Crossings 'Devonshire Alps' as he referred to Sharpitor and Leather Tor. Down below to the south-east the winter afternoon sun throws ever-lengthening shadows over land reluctantly abandoned by its farming community, when Plymouth purchased the whole of the catchment and wished for all the farms to be vacated.

I have had the privilege of several talks with Mr William George Shillibeer, the son of Harold, on the telephone and at his home at Bellever near Postbridge, where his wife Vera served up home-made buns and scones, along with strawberry jam and clotted cream and a cup of coffee. During one of our conversations he kindly listed on paper for me the last people to live on, or work, each individual farm. There was a Mr Gill at Stenlake, the Hamlyns at Lowery Farm and Vinny Lake, the Lillicraps at Leather Tor (where the potato cave can be entered), Mr Pearce was at Kingsett, who also worked the fields of Crazywell, Roundy and Norswothy Farms.

Mr Shillibeer remembers the dwelling and outbuildings at Norsworthy as being deserted but still very much intact. He also told me, that a fair acreage of the abandoned fields were, for the Second World War effort, planted out in potatoes. At Narrator, under the shadow of the great bulk of Sheepstor, lived the Watkins. The Williams' family worked Middleworth where not so long ago a beautiful granite trough was stolen. Who farmed at Deancombe he could not recall, but he remembers the Pengelly's at Combeshead; they were the last to leave the area, having been given permission to stay on for the remainder of Mr Pengelly's days. Mr Shillibeer remembers the funeral procession, with himself attending, following the horse and wagon that carried the coffin across the fields and through the lanes to Sheepstor Church, where he was buried just before Christmas, aged ninety one. He was known as 'Dicky Boy', to all who knew him well.

From the little Tor on Peak Hill, the rim of the catchment drops steeply to Peak Hill plantation, where a climb over a stile is needed to follow the line through an untidy conifer-shrouded area where branch loppings are left on the floor to hinder progress under the heavily scented canopy.

The next marker to be seen after leaving the twin pair beside the road a mile and a quarter back, is beside the road near Lowery Cross, built into the stone walling. Following the much fallen and repaired again and again wall, will find the second, again built into the stonework, under the shade of conifer. The third along this line can be seen from here out in the open, standing on the skyline, on the summit of Yennadon Down. The fourth, unlike the rest, has nothing to identify itself with, no prominence to sit on, no wall to sit in, it merely occupies

Built into the roadside bank.

On Yennadon Down.

a position in a clearing surrounded by gorse bushes. The fifth has the job of overlooking the disused section of the Devonport Leat, while the penultimate marker, is set beside the old Princetown Railway Track. The last, after a tiring and quite strenuous good eleven and half miles, can be found by crossing the Dousland-Burrator Road and steeply make one's way down through a maze of gorse, until the Drake's Leat is met. The marker is built on to the end of a wall, standing on the very edge of the leat, only yards from the tumbling overflow of the reservoir.

For several years after it fell out of use, Drake's Leat was cleaned and cared for, unlike today, for although still fairly sound in its structure it is to a certain extent neglected with gorse and brambles clogging the stonework, and mud in places spreads itself ankle deep. It can be followed around the lower slopes of Yennadon Down, but to avoid any further deterioration, it is best to leave walking on the bank to the surefooted grass-nibbling sheep, for there is, as most moor walkers know, only one Drake's Leat and total respect from the general public is needed for its wellbeing, and if the long term future of this important artefact is to be preserved.

A hundred yards or so towards the reservoir from the final marker we will find the track out on to the road. It was the aspect looking south from the foot of this slope that inspired the early nineteenth century painter Samuel Cook to simulate its dramatic features on canvas. Helping to stimulate the artists inspirations and towering over thirty feet with its foot almost in the leat is a vertical rock pile. Weathering over hundreds of years has made its appearance look decidedly unstable, but not an inch of the sections have moved since Cook made his way here and captured its likeness.

Aged documents hint to us that when the leat was first constructed a wooden launder carried the water across this precipitous area. Cook surmises in his painting that what we see today was masterminded and constructed in Drake's time, with the man himself conducting proceedings. Yet the real world tells us that the work was carried out during the middle years of the 1700s. Sweat must have poured profusely from the heaving and grunting men, for to carry the leat boulders of varying sizes in their thousands were tipped and manoeuvred into place to create an embankment with an average thirty-seven foot, sixty degree slope, for the waterway to run along. Adding still further to the scene's striking features is the steep nigh-on one hundred foot drop from the leat's edge, to the river below.

George Shillibeer, William George's uncle, was himself a very creative person. Just a little way along the reservoir's almost four-mile perimeter road, one will come across in early summer a magical mass of rhododendron colouring the area close to Burrator Lodge. These, along with other shrubs and trees, were planted by George during his time as caretaker of the reservoir. Another of his interests was the saving of local memorabilia, relics in stone that may well have been lost to the ravages of time or stolen to order by the unscrupulous. These

Standing on Drake's leat.

Mr George Shillibeer.

The Folly near Burrator Lodge.

can be seen again near the lodge, just above the water's edge. George built, or had built, folly-like arches to display his finds in; into one is the ancient gothic doorway from Longstone Manor, just above it cemented into the stonework, is a tablet displaying the letter E carved in relief, no doubt carefully placed in the position it held when the Elfords resided here. On either side of the doorway are other tablets, the one on the left reads, I E and A E with date 1637, what appears to be an 'I' in the first initials, is in fact a 'J' for John Elford, (it was the way letters were made in those days), and the 'A' in the second initials, is for Alexandra his wife. The tablet on the right of the arch, has the earlier date of 1633 along with the initials W E for Walter Elford. Below on the same tablet are two florets, one on either side of the initial B for Barbara, Walter's wife.

At the foot of the arch, if not covered in leaves, can be seen a tinners' mortar stone, no doubt brought from the Elford family's stamping mill. A little farther up the muddy old thoroughfare that once took the road over the Meavy to Sheepstor, is a neatly carved granite lectern, another relic from the Chapel of the Manor House. A few more yards of generally muddy walking brings one to another folly that George created, this one displaying the doorway carted all the way down off the moor from the tumbled ruins of Roundy Farm. This property is thought to have been in the ownership of Richard Crimes, for on the face of the doorway lintel stone, are the initials R.C. along with the date 1668. Richard was a member of the family that caused the Drakes so much bother with the Plymouth Leat. Also built into the second arch are two corn mill grinding stones, one on either side of the doorway, again relics brought from across the valley at Longstone.

In 1937 George retired, leaving his brother Harold, the father of William George, to carry on the Shillibeer way of caring for Plymouth's Water. However sadly for the family the mould was to break when Harold retired just eight years later in 1945. The Second World War took William George away from the valley and the reservoir, leaving the way open for others to apply for his father's position.

Born and brought up at Higher Lowery, just a few hundred yards from the reservoir, and with the industry flowing through his veins, this moulded William George into a real chip off the Shillibeer block. He followed his father into the profession at the age of seventeen, after first being employed as a gardener by the locally renowned naturalist, H.G. Hurell.

William George could see for himself after the war was over, that the working atmosphere at the reservoir was changing; there was a frostiness to touch, he no longer felt a part of it. His father was due to retire and a growing feeling of looking in from outside coincided with the grapevine rumours saying that the powers that be were considering the discontinuation of the on-going Shillibeer succession.

The saying goes, that there is no smoke without fire and, sure enough, a Mr Willcocks broke the 175-year-old mould when he replaced Harold as the Caretaker. William George was left with obvious disappointment; the chance to carry on the family tradition had eluded him, through no fault of his own, except five long years away doing duty for King and Country, where no one from the industry could value his worth.

Nevertheless, life had to go on and for another nine years he did his bit to bring home a wage, but his pastime that earned him a little more money, after reservoir hours gradually drew him away again. Farming a smallholding on a part-time basis, tending to a few cattle and an ever-growing interest in his Shetland Ponies, encouraged him to leave his full-time employment at the age of forty and take on the farm where he still lives with wife Vera and one of his two sons, tending to one hundred acres of good grazing and two hundred of rough moorland grazing.

A lectern near the Folly.

In William George's days with the Water Works, there were fourteen men under the supervision of the reservoir caretaker, there still was until 1984 when Mr Taylor, who a few years earlier had taken over from Mr Willcocks, found himself with just one, the other thirteen were found jobs elsewhere. The huge cut in numbers came about when the reservoir, having in 1974 come under the newly formed South West Water Authority, was being considered for sale, but the purchase didn't go through, neither did any of the redeployed come back. This situation left Mr Taylor and his assistant, with only a slightly depleted area of responsibility, to carry on the tree managing, ground clearing, walling, hedging, fence and stile repairs, as well as other essential reservoir husbandry work, such as the once-a-year Fishing Feast, held every June, when all other tasks are temporarily placed to one side. The lawns around the lodge are mowed, the flower beds are tended to, the paths are raked clean and a marquee erected along with a couple of tents; buntings is hung here and there to pretty the place. It was always the tradition for the workforce to trawl the leats for fish to eat at this function but it is clearly remembered by one member of staff that on one occasion, not too many years ago, an inquisitive Councillor, whilst returning from spending a penny, raised the lid of a bin that was hidden around a corner out of sight of the proceedings and found trout, packets of them, labelled 'Norway'.

Rhododendrons, Burrator Lawn.

In 1992, three years after the authority was privatised, Mr Taylor retired and left the Lodge to live in Sheepstor, at 'Moor View' cottage, where William George's uncle George lived.

As time goes by, so situations seem to change that much faster. No caretaker has occupied the Lodge from the time Mr Taylor and his wife vacated it, now his successor Mr Tim Edney has himself been deployed elsewhere since the Devon Lake Trust assumed responsibility for the reservoir's recreational activities and the welfare of its surroundings, on the first of April, in the year two thousand.

As the population of Plymouth and its surrounding areas rapidly increased, Burrator always faced the possibility of running dry during the summer months. Often now, with our

A full reservoir.

Planet supposedly warming up, and allowing the water table to almost dry out, before the rains come to save the day, our streams and rivers every year run low, resulting in the reservoir water levels receding to such an extent that it becomes the talk of the concerned visitor. Now with the larger Roadford Reservoir coming to the rescue, those with sweating brows can now relax.

CHAPTER 5
The Warrens

On the South-West slopes of Sheepstor, only a matter of a few hundred yards or so from the reservoir's lapping water, man made rectangular-shaped mounds of various lengths can be seen. Most visitors enter the area where the second water boundary stone is tucked just inside the gate, then expend their energy to merely reach the huge rock pile above. Rather than just passing them by, an inquisitive scan will see a slight depression in the ground immediately surrounding them, the more curious will eventually discover that this gully-like feature leads away from the lowest point of each mound and what the eye is looking at, is simply a drainage system that took rainwater away from an artificial rabbit burrow. There are nine in all, making this a small warren in comparison to some. Who built it and when, recorded history doesn't tell us yet. Their story perhaps, is still hidden among the charred and water-stained remains of the Maristow Estate archives that were sadly caught up in the old mansion's fire in 1982. Conclusions can be easily reached, that two of the burrows are of a more recent construction than the others.

Warren bound stone.

The warren could well have been a little extended income for a nearby farmer at the likes of Redstone or Narrator Farms; perhaps speculation can create its own narrative in one's mind. One thing is for sure, permission for their construction, would have had to have been provided by Maristow, with a little more rent per year likely to have gone into the estate's coffers.

A far more time-consuming exploration will find the remains of vermin traps, that were associated with the burrows or (pillow mounds) as the Ordnance Survey maps describe them. This ingenious apparatus was created out of stone, mostly granite of course. A couple of slates were necessary, along with some sort of thread and a couple of sticks. These traps were placed in certain areas where the warrener knew the martin, stoat or weasel, the rabbit takers, ran.

Old rabbit burrow on the slopes of Sheepstor.

Rabbit burrow not quite so old. Leather Tor and Sheepstor on the skyline.

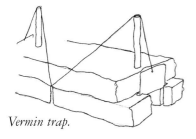

Vermin trap.

Remains of a vermin trap.

Drainage gully from a burrow.

The traps comprise two sides and a cover; the stones had to be fairly straight and even in form so as to create a small chamber, tunnel-like, into which the vermin would enter. Etched into both internal walls near each end, were two vertical grooves that the slate trap door slid into; the bait inside the chamber had to be heavy enough to hold the thread in position beneath it. The thread then came out through a slit like gap in one wall and on to the stick above that was set firmly into the holes on top of the cover. From the top of the stick the thread was then attached to the slate. Once the bait was taken, the thread was free for the slates to drop into the grooves leaving the poor unsuspecting victim trapped inside. Helping to lure the little poaching creature towards the trap and the bait were four low walls of no particular length or neatness, leading funnel-shaped right up to either entrance of the trap. The best example on this hill is to be found close to another more ruinous one, directly below the southern buttress of the Tor, where rock climbers practise their skills on a sheer face of salmon-coloured granite.

Here the x-shape appearance of the walls are intact, to view it with a camera it is best to climb the rock wall and look down from above. The walls of the tunnel are missing, used no doubt for some other purpose. The roof though, with its holes in its top, is lying to one side just a couple of feet away. The stone is three foot ten inches long by one foot four inches wide, each hole is about two inches in diameter and about the same deep, each are six inches from the end of the stone. Further up on the Tor's grassy rock-strewn area, at the inner foot of the western buttress, is another cover-stone of more-or-less the same proportions, unlike the earlier stone described that is buried to its upper surface, this stone's thickness can be clearly measured at seven inches.

There are several warrens dotted around the moor, all now abandoned for the purpose of rabbit farming. Up on the northern edge of Dartmoor, in the shadow of the huge mound of Cosdon Hill, Skaigh Warren spreads its many burrows above the southern banks of the River Taw. Headland Warren, overlooked by the more renowned prehistoric Grimspound enclosure, encompasses about six hundred acres of tinner-scarred landscape. A good few of its bound stones can be easily spotted beside the Moretonhampstead road between the Warren House Inn and Bennett's Cross, which was itself, utilised as a marker. More can be seen on both sides of the Widecombe road, above the farm that nestles in the valley near the infant waters of the West Webburn. Just a mile and half down the same road, squeezing between the hights of Challacombe and Hameldown, is the almost forgotten warren at Soussons, now mostly hidden beneath a canopy of conifer.

Below Rippon Tor on the Ashburton–Widecombe road, was the long-gone New House Warren. Rabbit burrows can be found on the West Dart among the clitter, above Wistman's Wood. A few more lie on the higher ground to the east of Crockern Farm, others can be seen on the Cowsic at Beardown Farm and beside the West Dart below the slopes of Round Hill.

On the left of the Double Dart below Dartmeet, scattered on the hillside and under the trees are the remains of Vag Hill Warren. Still on the northern moor, but only just, are the old rabbit burrows on the Walkham above Merrivale Bridge. Huntington Warren on the Avon, last worked by Mr Jan Waye, displays quite a dense scattering of burrows, all except a few occupy ground on the lower slope of the hill that is crowned by the so called Heap of Sinners, a prehistoric cairn. Nearly three miles down the Avon from Huntington, passing the reservoir on the way, is Yalland Warren, situated on private land tucked under the southern slopes of Shipley Tor.

The greatest concentration of warrens on the moor is undoubtedly in the Plym valley, where five border one another. Stretching its boundaries from Ringmoor Down to the line of the forest, makes Ditsworthy the largest. When this acreage first took to breeding rabbits isn't at all clear, there was no mention of them, or conies as they were sometimes called, when Thomas, Abbot of Buckland, leased the land to a Thomas Pooell, in the June of 1493. Mr Pooell took the tenancy, bringing his wife Joan and son, John, into the wild of the moor for seventy years, to a place named Derkysworthy, in the Parish of Schyttystor. It entitled the right to pasture his beasts on Rynnemore Down, it also meant a trek down the valley to Bickleigh when called upon to make repairs to the weirs and fisheries belonging to his landlord, and twice a year to Horrabridge to pay thirteen shillings and four pence rent.

Ditsworthy was originally, after the conquest, a piece of moorland held in the name of the king, until being granted to the Redvers family, whom Isabella de Fortibus, the Countess of Devon, was a descendant. It was merely a small parcel of land within the huge Manor of Walkhampton. It came down through the family to Isabella during the reign of Edward I after her father, the seventh Earl of Devon died. Isabella gave the Manor of Walkhampton, together with Buckland and Bickleigh and a part of Cullompton, to her mother Amicia. Isabella could afford to be generous, for she was a very rich widow, having already inherited the vast estates of her late husband the Earl of Albemarle.

1278 saw the gift from Isabella in the hands of holy men in white habits. Amicia had given it away to the Cistercian Monks so as to establish their House of Isolation and Worship. They came from Quarr Abbey on the Isle of Wight, the island granted to the Redvers along with their many lands in Devon, by William the Conqueror for services rendered.

But all may well have been different if Amicia's son, Isabella's brother had not died of poisoning in 1262, for he would have obviously inherited and the line of the Redvers would have lived on in his name. With that the monks may never have built their Abbey and Thomas, the Abbot of Buckland may not have been there to take Mr Pooell's, half yearly rent.

By the year 1552, the monks had gone, ousted by Henry the VIII, in 1539 after he fell out with the Church. By now the Slanning family owned the Manor of Walkhampton and an Elie Shullibear was living at Derkysworthy, with his wife Joan and son John, but there was still no mention of the word 'Warren' on the lease. Despite the years that had gone by and the estate belonging to John Slanning, Elie enjoyed more-or-less the same contract as Mr Pooell, paying only thirteen shillings and four pence per half year for the privilege of living out in the middle of the moor, near the upper reaches of the Plym overlooked only by Hentor and the great expanse of the Langcombe Ridge, with the hill crowned by the rocks of Eastern Tor.

Maristow came into Slanning ownership, when John who resided in London and was a Steward of the Inner Temple, purchased the estate from the Champernowns of Modbury. Nicholas Slanning, whose parents lived at Leye near Plympton was, along with Robert Foot and John Cance, one of the witnesses to Elie Shullibear's lease. Exactly what relation John Slanning was to young Nicholas documented history doesn't tell us, but John certainly favoured him, for he not only appointed him his executor but also delivered the Lordship of Walkhampton into his hands for him to become the first Nicholas of Maristow.

By the age of thirty-three Nicholas was the Member of Parliament for Plympton, seven years later he married, but by the time he died at the age of fifty-nine the marriage had not provided a male Slanning, leaving their daughter, Agnes, the only child and rightful heiress to her father's estate. By the time her middle teens had arrived she was already married and, for reasons that can only be conjectured at, she was left with no inheritance and Maristow went to her cousin Nicholas. Having already inherited his father John's estate at Leye, he became a very wealthy man and through his marriage to Margaret, the daughter of Henry Champernown, brought her family back into the fold of Maristow. Yet for all his wealth, his good fortune was not to last, for in 1599 he was provoked into getting himself killed in a duel with streetwise John Fitz, the son of the wealthy Tavistock landowner. Nicholas died leaving a widow and four children, a girl and three boys, with the eldest Gamaliel, still into the juvenile age of his teens, the heir of Maristow. Gamaliel married his second cousin Margaret, the daughter of Edward Marler and Agnes Slanning (the girl left with no inheritance), and from the short three year marriage (Gamaliel died aged only twenty six) came a girl Elizabeth and a son that father and grandfather would surely have been extremely proud of.

Named after his grandfather, he became the first Sir Nicholas of Maristow, appointed the Governor of Pendennis Castle, elected to Parliament for both Plympton St Maurice and Penryn. He married Gertrude Bagge, daughter of Sir James of Little Saltram situated on the shores of the Plym estuary. Being a devout Royalist, he involved himself totally with the second campaign of the Civil War, becoming a highly distinguished soldier. In 1643, from the cold winter month of January to near the end of July, he fought a number of battles, including the confrontations at Bradock Down, Sourton Down and at Stratton. At Landsdown he lead 300 musketeers to beat Sir William Waller's Reserves of Dragoons, but in the battle for Bristol, he and his men were driven back, with the loss of many lives. Sir Nicholas himself was fatally wounded and died from his injuries a couple of weeks later.

All appeared to be in vain, with Charles I his King being beheaded outside the Banqueting House of Whitehall; the Monarchy and the House of Lords were abolished and Oliver Cromwell, in victory, set up a protectorate, with himself as the Lord Protector. Yet within twelve years all that Cromwell had gained was lost. He died of pneumonia in the September of 1658 and, by April the following year, his son Richard, who succeeded him, dissolved his Parliament, allowing a Rump parliament to be restored and him to abdicate, leaving twelve months bar a few days to go by, before the Monarchy was restored with Charles II on the throne.

Not only was Sir Nicholas the owner of a large estate, a politician and a soldier, with fingers dabbling in various other time-consuming activities, he also found time to father four children, two girls, Margaret and Elizabeth, and two boys. The first son Nicholas sadly died when no more than a baby, the second to come along was oddly baptized with his dead brother's name; it seemed a generation could not go by without a Nicholas.

He grew up to more-or-less follow in his father's illustrious footsteps, in fact, except for his father's brave military escapades and his own honour of having a Baronetcy conferred upon himself, one could say it was almost carbon copy. Charles II just after coming to the throne touched him on the shoulder to dub him a knight. He was elected an MP and, in turn, became the Governor of Pendennis Castle.

But unlike his father, this Sir Nicholas married four times. He was into the third marriage when Edward Mead arrived at Dittisworthy in 1676 to be one of his tenants. The name of the place had changed considerably since the beginning of Elie Shullibear's time there, and the word 'warren' was now written on the lease to follow it.

Taking over from Mr Shepard, Edward Mead, Yeoman of Shittistor, with his wife Prudence and son Edward, signed to take on the task of working the acreage out on the moor. 'Ffour score and Five pounds of good and lawful money of England', had to be paid into the hand of Sir Nicholas, when the indenture was sealed on the 'Nyne and twentieth year of the raigne of the Sovraign and Lord Charles the second, by the grace of God of England, Scotland, France and Ireland Defender of the Faith anno domini.' But Edward could not really get his teeth into the work with any real enthusiasm until after the death of Susan, the doting widow sister of James Shepard, or on the determination of the estate of Martha, his wife.

The lease was for 'the terme and tyme of Ffour score and nyneteen years and the rent of Twenty shillings of Lawful Money of England had to be paid att the Ffourmost usual feast days in the year. That of the Feast of St Michaell Harchangel, the birth on the Lord, the annunciacon of our blessed Lady Mary the Virgin and the Nativity of John the Baptist. Also tied up in the agreement to sate Sir Nicholas requirements, for Christmas the wanting of either, the Warrens best capon or a gift to him of Twelve Pence. One journey a year to the Barton of Maristow was required, to assist with the harvest or pay the sum of Four Pence, again depending of the wish of the master.' Edward was also obliged to grind his corn along with Maristow's harvest at the mills belonging to Sir Nicholas at Bickleigh and Shaugh. He also had to find one sufficient and able labour man, one day yearly, to help repair and scour the head weirs and leats that delivered water to the mills.

All these conditions laid down allowed Edward 'to hund by Ferret and pitch netts and otherwise for his most benifitt and advantage'. They permitted him 'to cut sufficient timber for himself on the premises growing'; he could pasture so many beast and cattle on the waste of Sir Nicholas adjoining to the Forest of Dartmoor 'as may be re-interred in the fields of Dittisworthy. But, lff it happen the yearly rent or other dues as foresaid to be behind and unpaid in part or in all by the space of three months next after any of Feast aforesaid in which the same ought to be paid being lawfully demanded and not paid', Sir Nicholas would send in his Bailiffs and repossess the property. The same penalty would be meted out with the bailiffs appearing on Edward's doorstep, if a warning was not heeded to get intentional or accidental damage to the premises repaired within 6 months.

On the death of each in succession, Edward, Prudence and the son, a heriot (a thank you to the Landlord for allowing the Tenant to live and earn a living on his land) would have to be paid to Sir Nicholas or his heirs, of a beast, which would have to be the best or the sum of forty shillings.

Out of Sir Nicholas's four marriages, only one produced an heir, a boy, born to his second wife Mary; not a Nicholas but an Andrew, named after Mary's father. Andrew became the owner of the vast estate and of course Edward Meads, landlord on the death of his father in 1692. Andrew married his wife Elizabeth, up on the northern side of Dartmoor at South Tawton the same year. However only for eight years did Mr Meade take his rent to him, for Sir Andrew, drinking in a London tavern, maybe drowning the sorrowful thoughts of losing his wife only six months earlier, became engaged in a vicious confrontation with a fellow drinker and, like his Great-Great Grandfather almost a century before, came off second best.

With Andrew the Slanning name at Maristow came to a close, the marriage having produced no children and himself leaving no will, the estate by law went to his aunt Elizabeth, his father's widow sister, wife of Sir James Modiford the deputy to his brother, Thomas, the Governor of Jamaica.

The predominant name in the years of warrening in the Plym valley, is undoubtedly that of Nicholls. The name had throughout the years occupied all five Warrens and at one time, their energies simultaneously controlled the lot. The first of them to arrive and take up the challenge was William, he took over at Ditsworthy after the Meads' days were done. The man signed up to run the place and endeavour to eke a living out among the heather and the course blue grass of the moor. It must surely have been fairly lucrative for, in 1762, his son John replaced him; joining him was his brother Richard and sister Margaret. Like their father, they

A few of Legis Tor warren's rabbit burrows set within a prehistoric enclossure.

The vermin trap below Legis Tor.

also ran Legis Tor warren, they also took on the extra of working a six-acre plot of land on Ringmoor Down, paying three separate rents of three, six and ten pounds respectively.

Legis Tor Warren takes its name from the pink granite rock pile that sits on the southern slope of Ringmoor Down; it spreads its elongated artificial burrows along the hillside that slopes down to the Plym with a few situated within the prehistoric enclosures. Also here, if a time-consuming search is made, can be found the remains of vermin traps. The warrener here constructed them in various places, including the disused stream mining gullys and enclosure walls but, half hidden among the bracken and loose stones and boulders near the foot of the southern side of the tor, can be found a trap which is, apart from its cover-stone being slightly out of position, the best example to be seen on the moor.

John's lease tells of the threesomes right to employ 'dogs, guns, traps, netts and other engines and things for the destroying of foxes and other vermin for the protection of the warren of conies' (rabbits). The document also tells them to enjoy the privilege of pasturing their beast on all the moorland waste belonging to the estate, so far as where it borders the Forest. However, no trip to the Barton for harvesting is mentioned, nor the grinding of corn or scouring or repairing of the leats at Shaugh and Bickleigh, yet the same Heriot of their best beast was required on the death of the named party.

It is guessing time when one wants to try and determine the date of the vermin trap's development, indications can perhaps be seen when scanning the wording of the leases down

The way into the bait.

Looking down on to the walls.

Willings walls prehistoric reave.

The ruins of a small dwelling beneath a coating of vegetation.

through the ages. We can for instance, see that when Edward Mead senior signed his indenture, that no traps whatsoever were mentioned, yet when John Nicholls' indenture was written out, the word trap was there. This allows one at least to spend time in supposing it came into being during the years of Edward Mead or William Nicholls.

Dame Elizabeth was William's landlady for only a short five years until she died in 1724 at the ripe old age of 91. She left Mary and Grace, her two daughters, joint heirs. Her son, Thomas, who would have carried forward the Modiford name, died when still only a boy. Mary's husband John Dean, saw the end of his days well before Elizabeth, and Mary only out-lived her by ten years. Grace, after losing her first husband Edward Drake, married again to a Peter Heywood. It is with their son James that 260 years of Slannings and their heirs at Maristow finally came to a close for, after his death in1798, an altogether new family took over as landlords at Ditsworthy, purchasing Maristow and all its satellite Manors of Buckland, Walkhampton, Bickleigh and Shaugh and later Meavy.

Eight years after the trio of John, Richard and Margaret took on Ditsworthy and Legis Tor Warrens, a Richard Nicholls of Plymouth aged about thirty and his wife Sarah, aged about thirty three, took on the task of working Willings Walls Warren. What events took place in the Nicholls' family in the space of those eight years documented history does not tell us, or at least what remains of the fire and water ravaged archives does not. Nor do parish records, even the local graveyards, of Sheepstor, Meavy, Shaugh, Bickliegh or Walkhampton let us know of any sorrowful deaths in the family. The Christian names of Richard and John could be purely coincidental but when the Plymouth Richard, signed on the dotted line in 1770 to abide by the conditions set down in writing by John Parker, his new landlord, who later in 1784 became Lord Boringdon, the name Mary Frances Nicholls, aged about nine daughter of John Nicholls of Sheepstor was on the indenture, as in the care of Richard and his wife.

The warren which takes the full brunt of the winter's cold north easterly winds, utilises the left bank of the Plym for one of its boundary edges, another is the prehistoric reave of Willings Walls which lends the warren its name. The acreage is neatly parcelled together by the Plym's tributary streams of Hentor Brook and the Spanish Lake, that was at one time, called the East Tor Brook. It can only be surmised that the accommodation for the warrener was the fallen stonework now lying among the tumbled ruins of Willings Walls Reave, sheltering in the valley near the head of the Spanish Lake. Compared to its four neighbours, this warren was small with nearly all of the burrows being just yards from the tiny moorland abode.

It is a fascinating coincidence, that Ditsworthy's outgoing landlords' ancestors, had had associations with Jamaica like that of the incoming man's family. Mannaseh Massey Lopes was the descendant of Spanish settlers on the Caribbean island, who later came to England to settle in the Clapham area of what is now greater London. The family having certain wealth from the sugar industry, allowed Mannaseh to gradually rise in the ranks of English society, to be elected a Member of Parliament and to later, in 1805, to ascend even higher to become a Baronet. However, all in his doings throughout his lifetime was not achieved without a certain whiff of dishonesty. A spell in the cells of a prison came about, when he cheated, allowing himself to be returned to Parliament. Corruption with a capital C was the misdemeanour; the paying of monies to voters for the prolonged assurance of MP status. Yet ironically not so long after his release, with his chin still held loftily high, he was returned to the corridors of power, representing the Borough of Westbury in Wiltshire. He also became a magistrate of all things, sitting in judgement on others. Of course by this time he was well established at Maristow and landlord of the warren at Ditsworthy.

If the Nicholls family were the longstanding tenants of the Modiford era, the Ware's certainly were of the Lopes time, which is still ongoing. For over a century the Ware's worked the warren with Nicholas the first to take up the challenge, He arrived to take over from William, the last of the Nicholls at Ditsworthy. When exactly the transfer took place, the sorry state of the Maristow archives do not divulge, but we do know through the Sheepstor Parish records, that in 1834 Sarah Ware the wife of Nicholas the Warrener, died aged 36, her name shares the tombstone with his in the graveyard of Sheepstor.

From here lies the enigma of the Ware's local origins, for Nicholas lived for another forty two years until 1876. One wonders whether he lived the rest of his life as a lonely widower, or was he the same Nicholas Ware, Warrener of Ditsworthy, who married Margaret Creber, and shared the joy of producing seven children, between the years of 1837 and 1852. If so, why was he buried with his first wife and not with the woman who gave him such a considerable family, and seeing she was a Creber, a longstanding and well known local name, why is there no record of her death. Could it be that she left the warren with her husband for the County of Hampshire, where he died in the early years of the 1850s and where at the same time, they went their separate ways. Who was Mary, who died at Ditsworthy in 1839? Was she the daughter of Sarah and Nicholas? She certainly wasn't Margaret's. Was she the sister of Nicholas? There was a Mary born to parents William and Mary (a name quite frequently used in the Ware family) on 3 November 1797 in the County of Hampshire. According to the Devon Census Records of 1856, Nicholas has gone and William Ware is the warrener at Ditsworthy, He was born in 1820 but like Mary, there is no record or at least legible record of his birth; it is more than likely that they were brother and sister and both the children of Nicholas and Sarah who lie together under the soil of Sheepstor graveyard.

In 1846 Nicholas also signed to work at Ditsworthy, at both Willings Walls and Hentor warrens. The contract for his two extra parcels of land was for seven years, paying forty-five pounds a year for an estimated three hundred acres. This ample expanse allowed him to pasture his sheep and cattle over an even greater area. It opened up to him all the moorland waste belonging to the Earl of Morley, one Edmund Parker the second Earl, after inheriting

The ruins of Hen Tor House below Hen Tor.

Cupboard recess in the ruin.

Broken trough outside the house.

Remains of what could well be a quern.

Ditsworthy Warren House.

Dog kennel built into the 'kennel field' wall.

the title from his father, who was created Viscount Boringdon and the Earl of Morley in 1815.

The house of Hentor Warren, unlike that of Saltram which still stands magnificent, lies on the ground tumbled and scattered almost unrecognisable among the bracken, lying just out of reach of the cold early morning winter shadows of Hen Tor, the much fallen rock pile above, from which the Warren takes its name.

George Parker in 1712 purchased the original house at Saltram which was nowhere near the grand structure we see today, now in the hands of the National Trust. Built somewhere in the time of the Tudor period, it was at one time in the possession of the Bagge family, of which one member, Gertrude, married Nicholas the brave cavalier Slanning of Maristow. It was George Parker's son, John, who married Catherine, daughter of the Earl of Poulett, who first moved to Saltram from Boringdon and his grandson, again a John, who was created the first Baron Boringdon, and his son John who became the first Earl of Morley.

Back on the sunny side of the valley at Ditsworthy in 1856, with Nicholas having gone, William, when setting foot outside the warren house, master of all he could see, but for snippets of Trowlesworthy, he can freely drive his beasts to the edge of all horizons in view. As well as the Plym, his beasts can slake a thirst on the Spanish Lake, the Hentor, Shavercombe and Langcombe Brooks and the streamlets of Deadman's Bottom, Calves Lake, Crane Lake and Evil Combe, not to mention the Drizzlecombe and the boggy beginnings of the Sheepstor Brook and the higher moorland tributaries of the River Meavy. William firmly held the reins of the huge mass of land for nearly thirty years until age, and the losing of his wife in 1884, allowed the transfer of running things over to his eldest son Nicholas.

Two Burrows not far from the house.

Not so long after the death of his mother, Nicholas now aged thirty, married Emmeline Creber a local girl from down in the Meavy valley at Longstone, the Manor farm of the Elfords, that was soon to be drowned by Burrator Reservoir. Emmeline came to Ditsworthy and became something of a local legend in her own lifetime; she became known as the revered 'Granny Ware' of Ware's Warren. When the alternative name for Ditsworthy materialised isn't known, but it had already been established in Crossing's day when writing his renowned *Guide to Dartmoor*; it is still frequently employed today by the locals when conversation about the warren crops up. No doubt Emmeline's reputation furthered the Ware name throughout the valley and way beyond.

Nicholas died after only sixteen years of marriage, leaving Emmeline alone, way out on the moor to school her four children in the ways of life. She had to be strong and resilient, self-determination turned her stubborn as well as a little domineering, that meant the day had to go the way she wanted or look out for the consequences!

The only boy among her four children was Percy, although only eleven year old and keen to learn his father's trade, he was suddenly thrust even deeper into the hands-on working of

Percy and Elizabeth Ware.

Outside the bungalow at Burcombe Gate.

the place, not the childhood assisting of mother, but the actual carrying out of manly chores, that may well have frightened the less hardy away. Many a day while his sisters were at school, he would be absent, especially during rabbiting times. Nevertheless, it was in the long run to hold him in good stead, qualifying that life did not arrive on a plate but had to be gone out and got with graft and toil. It certainly nurtured the widening of his adroitness, yet with all his absorbed maturity and skills, his mother Emmeline was always there pulling the strings from somewhere behind the scenes, even when Percy eventually took over the running of the warren, she could be frequently heard having her say.

As he grew out of adolescence, Percy's working excursions out on the moor on horseback occasionally took him over the great hill of Eylesbarrow towards Nun's Cross Farm. Here he met and fell in love with Elizabeth Coaker; she lived there with her mum and dad who worked the small acreage, along with her five siblings. Before moving to Nun's Cross the family resided at Hexworthy, just above Gobbet Mine on the River Swincombe in John Bishop's house, from where Elizabeth went to school in the chapel of St Raphael's at Huccaby. The house, now in ruins, sits in a lovely tranquil area of the Swincombe valley, it is a place for a refreshment-stop and a look around. A ford and a delightful newly refurbished clam crosses the river to give access to where the house sits, shaded under a canopy of trees of mainly hawthorn and beech.

Like his father and grandfather before him, Percy took his bride back to Ditsworthy, where before three years were out, two children Priscilla (now Mrs Beer) and Wilfred were born to them, a third, John, came along ten years later. But harmony between the widow and the young mother was said never to run smooth, and the long days at the warren with two small children to attend to and the turmoil of Emmeline's interference, persuaded the family doctor to advise Percy, for the sake of his wife's sanity, to move away from Ditsworthy or, at least out of earshot of his mother's voice, suggesting the distance of at least a mile.

With permission from Maristow, Percy's handyman's skills came into their own by building a wooden bungalow at Burcombe Gate beside the Eylesbarrow mine track; from here not even the chimney pots of Ditsworthy could be seen, leaving life for the young couple to quietly flourish.

A great deal of the burrows to be seen on the warren today are in a sad state of repair, with their drainage channels overgrown; wet has got into them and reeds grow in plenty from their saturated mounds. Only a few that lie on the higher ground display their true shape and form. Likewise the vermin traps, of which there are several, all except for one, have had stones removed or disturbed for one reason or another, with some having just a few stones of its x-shaped walling to tell of its whereabouts.

Over the early years of rabbit farming, the warrener constructed the trap wherever he thought the troublesome pest made its usual daily run. Three vestige samples can be found among the rock debris below the buttress of Gutter Tor, another with only its tunnel side

Vermin trap, below the rocks of Gutter Tor.

A trap with no sides.

A trap on the left bank of the Sheepstor Brook.

A trap among the tinners' workings.

A redundant cover-stone utilised in the same trap.

145

A trap using an unusual design.

The same from a different angle.

stones missing can be located a little farther down the hill, not far from the higher end of a burrow. Down beside the Sheepstor brook, high up on the left bank, and now half hidden by typical moorland vegetation, is another good example. Across the brook sitting on a section of old walling another can be spotted, if the eye is keen. The cover of a trap belonging perhaps to the classic example of x-walling is situated a little further on among the tinners' workings, and here placed into one of the walls is what can only be an unwanted cover stone. A sample of which can be seen on page 145.

Another x-wall example, but nowhere near as good, is to be found in the huge tinners' gully that runs down to the Plym and Meavy Pool from the main Ditsworthy track. The best trap to be seen is to the west of this ruined specimen up on the slope of Ringmoor Down. Here the cover stone lies on the ground a yard or two away from the main proportions of the trap. Most traps differ from one another in their make up, all have the covers penetrated a couple of inches with two or three holes, and tunnels walls have slots that receive the incarcerating slates, yet this contraption is completely different from the rest in its mechanism. Three slates are employed in this trap, one at each end and a third in one of the sides; also employed, set in front of the side stone opposite the side slots, is a stone with a shallow hole designed to be deeper in its higher proportions than at the bottom. I can only surmise, without total confidence, that the third entrance was for easier access to the tunnel for the warrener, especially if he or she had large hands. However, what exact mechanical relationship the stone with the shallow hole had with the trap can only be open to the guessing game of conjecture.

By the time Percy worked the warren, the traps had been out of use for many a year but there is no doubt that with his handyman skills he would have been able to construct one and work it.

Running the warren meant long hours of work for the man, from sometimes before daybreak until long after darkness closed the day. Besides pony trekking across the grounds of the huge spread to lay snares and retrieve the entrapped prey, there were the burrows to keep in a state of favourable repair, vermin to check out and put to the gun, there was livestock to keep an eye on, fields and gardens to till, walls and fencing to mend and, on top of all these chores, he supplemented his warren earnings by toiling at his part-time landscape gardening business or, as his daughter, Priscilla, referred to it, his odd-jobbing.

Meanwhile out on the warren, Emmeline, by now known as Granny Ware to the locals and warren hands alike, kept her finger on the pulse of all that was going on around her, her continual frugal manner keeping the deep warren purse topped up enough to secure a way of life.

Priscilla, a small sprightly and energetic lady who was in her early eighties when I enjoyed a few conversations with her, remembers how Granny would charge her father for produce from the warren garden after he had bought the seed and tilled it, weeded and harvested it.

Granny also enjoyed adding to her purse the money she received after serving the occasional antiquarian, writer and strolling moor walker of the day, with her home-made bread and scones topped with home-churned butter and jam and cream. Priscilla remembers she didn't like Gran's bread, saying it was always lumpy as if the dough was in want of a little more kneading, the butter too often had a sour taste about it. She also remembers how the day's catch of rabbits hung from hooks on the warren house landing ceiling and how they were packed in braces in crates with their hind legs sticking up, before going off on the pony and trap to Dousland Station from where they were transported to the London markets. She remembers also the skin room at Ditsworthy, with pelts stacked high, dry and fresh alike stinking along with the odd fox and badger hides.

Wilfred's fond thoughts went back to his early mornings on Hentor meadows, where he and his father cut peat. He recalled how they could, on returning to the warren, if a breeze was in a favourable direction, smell the breakfast that was theirs to be had, frying in Granny Ware's kitchen. The thoughts prompted the memories of when the Plym was in flood that, on occasions, the clam would be washed away, making it difficult if not impossible to cross the torrent when business needed tending to on the other side. The clam would toss and turn along in the current until some obstacle prevented it from going any further, then after the flood subsided it was tethered to the horse, dragged back to its position and put back in use.

Granny Ware.

Fog was another hindrance to the warrener, unlike the farmer who has Venville Rights and only needs to tend his stock on occasions when it more-or-less takes his fancy. The warrener through the very nature of his trade needed to be out on the moor nearly every day. Wilfred, having arrived at Evil Combe on horseback, dismounted and left his mount to nibble its time away while he went about picking up his overnight catches and resetting the snares. During that time the dreaded moorland mist came down, thick and fast to the very tip of the reeds. Once out of the Combe on his way home, somewhere above Lower Hartor, he gave his horse a free rein thinking the animal knew its way back to the sanctuary of the warren house, but, within half an hour found himself back at Evil Combe!

Priscilla looked down to her hands on her lap and paused for a while from her normal flow of conversation before recalling the less likeable memories of her Gran. It was when her days by herself at Ditsworthy came sadly to a close, age and ailing health along with a concerning nudge from certain family members eventually persuaded her to vacate the warren house, where she had spent the best part of fifty years of her life, a majority of it without her husband Nicholas. Even then it was with reluctance that she eventually left her much-loved moorland domain.

After long and sometimes distasteful differences of opinion, it was decided, much to Percy's disapproval, that his mother was to go to his eldest sister's farm near Launceston. However all did not go well, for not so many months had gone by when Percy received a letter from his mother saying she was in a workhouse and badly wanted to come back to her home. Frailty of course could not allow a return to Ditsworthy, so the rather adroit Percy, along with sons Wilfred and John and Priscilla's husband James, quickly set about building a self contained annex to his Burcombe Gate bungalow so as to allow her a little independence. All went to everyone's satisfaction when she moved in, until one day while Percy was at work and wife Elizabeth was out shopping for the weekly groceries. Granny had been left in the very capable and caring hands of Priscilla, the day travelling along quietly with both women indulged in whatever was on their minds, when Priscilla suddenly became aware of a foreboding silence; out of sheer concerned curiosity she immediately went to investigate, but Granny's door could not be opened to allow entrance and from under it, came a trickle of blood. The only way in was through a window. Once inside, Priscilla found the old lady crumpled sorrowfully against the door. Granny being the person she was, had attempted to rearrange her curtains and standing on a chair, as a vast majority of eighty-plus year olds should not attempt to do, she fell.

The sad episode really did mean the end of Granny Emmeline Ware's long moorland life; from then on she was sadly in need of everyday professional care. After first trying unsuccessfully to place her in a local residential home, so visits could be frequent, her final days were spent at the Whitehouse, miles away at Bideford in North Devon, where she died at the age of eighty-four in 1945.

Not so long after his mother passed away, less than two years in fact, Percy lost his extremely busy life to cancer at the comparatively young age of fifty-seven. With Percy gone and daughter and eldest son settled away from Burcombe Gate with their own families, the situation left Elizabeth alone with just young John. In merely a couple of years, the once hive of family activity had mellowed quite substantially to comparative loneliness. She was left with just her memories of idyllic times gone by, where hard-working Percy made her a cosy home beside the infant water of the Sheepstor Brook; he had planted trees and shrubs for protection against the snow-clad winter winds that drift in over the moor. From her front gate he chose a landscape picture that the eye finds a joy to see, the view lies in the broad shallow cleavage between Leeden Hill and Yellowmead Down, where right in the V the Outcombe Brook rises before tumbling down into the Deancombe Valley. The spread of dramatic beauty encompasses nearly all the major Meavy tors as well at the Walkham's magnificent Great Mis Tor, the loftiest point on the skyline, where in comparison the Hessary rock piles (North and South) declare themselves as no more than little nubs of insignificance. From where Percy built the dwelling and placed the gate to his liking in 1933, the scene has changed very little, except television's great finger of lattice steelwork piercing the sky. Further to the rugged moorland scene, a glance to the left and a slight lift of the eyes will carry to the distant Cornish hills.

Priscilla, and eldest son Wilf, tell of how their mother, besides her household chores, always found time to play with and generally entertain them, but never were they allowed outside to play on a Sunday. They also tell of how she managed to find time to teach them the three Rs. With the local school at Sheepstor having closed down in 1923, and the nearest at Meavy being over three miles from Burcombe Gate, it was deemed by law that, without transport, it was too far for a child under the age of twelve to walk. So with her responsible and sensible head Elizabeth taught them herself. By the time John reached the age for school, transport was being provided.

The children's great aunt Celia was once the schoolmistress at Sheepstor. She was married to William, brother of Nicholas, whose wife was Granny Ware. Celia left the school in 1871 to have a baby, but died after giving birth to little girl Edith, a sister to her only other child Alice. Aged only twenty-six, she and William had been married for just four short years. She must surely have been held in high regard by the community of Sheepstor for a stained-glass window in honour of her memory can be see in the pretty hamlet's beautiful church.

No matter how palatable the memories are, time doesn't stand still and Elizabeth, without her beloved Percy had her work cut out to keep a financial head above water. Not only had she lost the handy income from her husband's part-time gardening, but the war years, when rabbit was frequently on many a working class dinner table, was over and with it came the gradual decline of warrening.

It seems odd, when life sometimes takes a ferocious double-handed swipe at those trying desperately to place the misery of misfortune behind them, that they simply carry on as if it was merely another of life's cruel episodes to strive through.

Not so long after the world had at last returned to peace, Elizabeth found she had a war of her own on her hands. She discovered that sheep from her flock were missing, not the usual few that may fall prey to the wild or age, but at least a third of her three hundred had disappeared. Out of sheer disbelief, making sure no miscounting was done during the first round up she, along with teenage son John, went out again, looking into every nook and cranny they knew of, every stream and tinners' gully, arriving home tired and dishevelled with ponies lathered white and dogs readily throwing themselves to the floor through exhaustion. But still the count was drastically and disturbingly down. Satisfied with the recount, Elizabeth immediately reported her findings to the local constabulary. It was then when it came to light that she wasn't the only one with stock missing, farmers from various parts of the moor were finding flock numbers down.

It wasn't long before word of the widow's plight reached the press and fanciful headlines in bold print came flooding out of the pages, even the London papers got to hear of it, with one finding the story satirically entertaining. The headline read 'Calamity Jane Rides the Dartmoor Range'. The writer went on to flippantly say, ' I want to tell you a story of a widow known as Calamity Jane, who lives alone with her son John, high on these moorland ranges, for their war with sheep rustlers is just about the bravest yarn I've run across outside a wild western.' His wordings still making light of the situation carried on to tell, how 'her cheeks whipped by the wind, are apple-red, her hands which grip a double-barrelled shotgun, are as strong as any man's.' 'I wouldn't ask questions,' she said ' I've handled a gun from a girl.' 'Yes sir, nice and polite as she is – this Calamity Jane is as hard and as natural as the wild moor where she's lived all her life.' The same paper produced a picture of Elizabeth on horseback, with young John holding a shotgun standing beside her, with sheep looking on and the moor blanketed in snow, when in fact, there was no snow at all.

The unscrupulous thieves, who turned out to be fellow farmers and lived just a couple of valley's away, were eventually caught after stealing literally hundreds of sheep; evidence of their dastardly escapades was merely a couple of the animals found in the back of their vehicle. Whereas years ago, they would have been hanged for the crime, in this supposedly more civilised age, just one went to prison.

As if the knock of having her sheep stolen wasn't enough for her dwindling income to contend with, just a few years later in 1955 along came a disease to wipe away what was remaining of the rabbit trade altogether. It spread like wildfire through the warrens, taking away even the occasional tasty dish for the warreners themselves. Myxomatosis, or 'mixy' as it was commonly called, was a man-made disease, developed in a laboratory by three scientists in New Zealand in 1953, as a pest control. The sight of an infected rabbit was not a pretty one, with its conjunctivitis-like swelling of the eyes, the bulging of the nose, muzzle, vulva and anus. The virus became less potent for those that survived and the animal became more resistant to the disease. Now, thankfully, very little is seen of it.

For a while life was kind to the residents of Burcombe Gate bungalow, with every day bringing the usual run-of-the-mill moorland highs and lows. John now in his mid-twenties had met Ellen and made her his bride, taking her back to the bungalow to live with mother. The following summer brought the delight of a baby, when their Jeremy was born, but by now John was becoming a little disenchanted with moorland life and, in 1961, the family of three left to set up home at Plympton. For the very first time Elizabeth was truly alone in the little oasis her Percy had built for her. With only her two dogs for company, when darkness fell and the oil lamps were extinguished, the world went black. The London paper said she was hardy, little did they know how hardy one can be. Christmas Day came and went quietly enough in 1963 with visits from family and friends, it was not until Boxing Day that the festive period became truly eventful.

It was early afternoon and the clouds began to turn a suspicious grey, it prompted the notion to John and Ellen who were paying their Christmas visit to leave a little earlier than was originally planned. By the time their car was heading down off the moor for home, snow was falling. Back at Burcombe Gate the sky had turned a menacing black and the wind had increased to complement the growing doom of an impending storm. By the time winter's early darkness fell, the bungalow was taking a severe battering from a howling gale, the wooden structure was groaning and creaking from the fearsome onslaught and the snow so fine was finding its way into even the tiniest opening.

Elizabeth, beginning to fear for her safety, picked up the telephone and with luck the line wasn't dead and she rang her neighbours, the Wakehams, a short but long, long mile away at Nattor Farm, to ask as to whether they could take her in for the night. 'Of course we can' came the reply, 'we'll come up and fetch you right away.' Before they got halfway there, Elizabeth with her dogs was spotted in their headlights, bowed against a blinding white-out.

She stayed with the Wakehams for a couple of nights until Wilfred could reach Nattor and take her home to his house. Another four days were to pass before Wilf and John could get a tractor up to her bungalow gate, even then the dwelling couldn't be seen, just the chimney pot stood above a drifted blanket of white. When they did eventually get in, the snow had found its way in under the eaves to such an extent that the weight had brought the ceiling in one room down to just a couple of feet from the furniture.

Sheepstor Church.

That was Elizabeth's last winter on the moor, for within a few weeks she said a sad goodbye to her well-loved home and followed the same route as John to Plympton where she lived until she died. A broken woman, I think not, a sensible one, yes.

She gave up the tenancy of Ditsworthy along with the rights to pasture on the land of the Lopes family (Lord Roborough) but still ran bullocks on the other side of the Plym, along and under the great stretch of Langcombe Hill. Elizabeth died aged eighty-three in April 1983, the same month as her dear Percy, and now shares a place with him in the grounds of Sheepstor Church.

Now what was described to me once as an old wooden shack, by a nice old gent who clearly did not know of its history, is gone and in its place stands a much sturdier structure of stone, used like the Warren House itself, as a training base for the armed forces. The Warren House, a mile from the tarmac road along the rough winding track, hasn't been lived in since a family from Kingsbridge occupied it for a couple of years during the Second World War. From then on it has been allowed to deteriorate into what we see today.

Trowlesworthy Warren House.

On the other hand, Trowlesworthy, on the opposite side of the Plym where the Cyril family now reside, is still in good habitable condition. The house lies about a mile and half downstream from Ditsworthy. Priscilla clearly remembers her strolls over the moor when in her teens to pay a visit to the Giles family who were then the tenants at Trowlesworthy. Always on a Sunday, neighbour called on neighbour, perhaps one week a walk down through the fields to the Mannings at Yellowmead, another along the road to the Legassicks at Colyton, or closer at hand to Nattor and the Wakehams, or vice versa. Someone would arrange to call at Burcombe Gate. The Pengellys down at Combshead being the exception, the friendship there was closer and visits were made whenever one felt like dropping in

Priscilla with amusement tickling her thoughts, remembers on one particular Sunday when she and her mother made their way to Trowlesworthy, way ahead of father and Wilfred after traversing around the the lower slopes of Ringmoor Down, they chose the usual place to cross the Plym and proceeded to jump and leap their way from boulder to boulder. Mother, as always, took the task confidently in her stride and was nearly on the other side when Priscilla slipped and fell down between the river-smoothed stones up to her armpits. But almost before she had time for the wet cold to take her breath away and gasp for air, mother had her out and on the way up through the hut circles and bracken to the house, where she was soon out of her clinging wet clothes and into something dry, quickly plucked from her friend Tryphena's wardrobe. Half an hour later, while snugly warming beside the kitchen range, father rattled on the door and walked in with Wilfred shivering, soaked through to the skin. 'He fell in the river,' explained father Percy, and with no exaggeration of course, went on to tell how Wilf was halfway to Cadover Bridge before he could fish him out. By the time a cup of tea and a bite to eat was had, the 'dimpsy' was setting in and a tilly lamp had to be borrowed when the four, this time together, made their way back to Burcombe Gate via the safe route over the clam below Ditsworthy house.

The first recorded mention of the land at Trowlesworthy comes from somewhere in the middle years of the thirteenth century, when the Earl of Devon, Baldwin de Redvers (who died in about 1263), granted four hundred and eighty nine acres of moorland to a Sampson de Traylysworthy. The boundaries utilise the natural features that encompass the acreage. The nub of land drains naturally from the peaks of its two salmon-red tors into five little streams that, in turn, empty their trickling water into the Plym. The boundaries, as the ancient document describes, extends from 'Pynekkes Lake to Blackabrook as far as Blackbrook falls into the Plym on the east part, through the middle of the turbary of Eastore to the well of Eastore Brook into the river Plym to the foot of Blackabrook, along with common pasture in Bickly Wood. The witnesses were Richard de Mewy, Robert De Spineto, Roger de Cadworth, Walter Pomerray de Goodameavy, Alexander de Hemerdon, Thomas de Challeswiche, Simon Ellewille.'

According to Henry Bedford Woollcombe (1834) of Hemerdon the property was worked for the Traylysworthy family till 1329, the second year of Edward III's reign, it was then let to Richard de Hokeston who lived at Lulleworthy, a farm once situated on Shaden Moor, between Dunston and Brag Lane, where now even the skeleton of its foundations are nowhere to be seen.

Seventy-four years later in 1403, there is controversy between John Hulle of Harston in the parish of Brixton and John Halswill, as to who has the right to utilise the land. Henry Woollcombe in his searching of the deeds, could not find how in 1404 it fell into

Mr Halswill's fortunate hands. Maybe it had something to do with him being married to Elenora the last in line to the Traylysworthy family.

Only four years later John Nicholl, his wife Joan and their son William, are living at Traylysworthy and paying a rent to the Halswills, it seems the Nicholl's family eked a toiling existence out of this wilderness for the next fifty-three years, until in 1464 a Walter Shcelybere volunteered his services to the soil when he signed or put his cross on a lease for the following fifty years. How long the land was actually farmed by his family isn't known, but what is available to see, although not too clearly, is the transfer from the Halswills to the Heles, a rather distinguished family, with its seat at Flete near Holberton. It is during this transaction when, I think, the ownership of the land finally left the Traylesworthy's.

The next to follow as the owners of the estate were the Crocker family. It had been supposed that it was at sometime in the hands of a Nicholas Harrys and that during the short reign of the boy King, Edward VI, Trowlesworthy became the property of John Crocker of Lyneham. Henry Woollcombe at first thought that it was granted to Crocker from the crown, in consequence of Nicholas Harrys of Shaugh, having to forfeit all his goods, chattel and personal estate to the King, through having been engaged in a rebellion that took place in Devon and Cornwall in 1549, which was suppressed by Lord Russell. Mr Woollcombe went on to say, that Harrys must have been killed in battle or executed, as in 1550 we find John Crocker granted all his land and chattels unto his widow Allys Harrys, in consideration of one hundred Marks. Mr Woollcombe, then throws the few lines of information up into the air by saying, 'I have been led into an error here, finding these instruments amongst the Trowlesworthy deeds, I imagined as my predecessors have done, that Harrys being of Shaugh, had something to do with the land of that estate, but it does not appear so by the deeds; Trowlesworthy is never mentioned.' Mr Woolcombe finishes by saying, 'I rather think I ought to have left all this out.'

The Crockers were reputed to be one of the oldest families in Devon. With hazy words of history telling how they stretch way back before the conquest. They arrived at Lyneham from mid Devon, where they lived not far north-east as the crow flies from Hatherleigh at Crockers Hele. Lyneham came into the Crockers' hands by John (born 1355) marrying the heiress of Giles Churchill, an ancestor of the Duke of Marlborough who was in his day the Lord of Yealmpton and Lyneham. The descending lineage of Masters of Lyneham includes from the first, seven consecutive Johns, till the parents of Hugh broke the sequence two hundred years later in 1555.

By the time the third John came along, the family was well rooted in the area, with his father having spread their ownership of land to include the Manors of Hemerdon and the estate of Bickfordtown above Sparkwell. During the middle years of Edward IV's reign, the Crockers really had arrived into the upper echelons of the establishment, with the fourth John becoming the Cup Bearer to His Majesty and to spread a little more elitism into the family, he was honoured with a knighthood after the Yorkists crushed the Lancastrians at the battle of Tewkesbury in 1471.

Sir John's grandson, the sixth John of Lyneham, was the man who acquired the moor land of Traylysworthy, in 1551, he leased it to a William Woollcombe, one of the witnesses to the signing was Richard Strode of Newnham, whose second daughter John Crocker married, with the union producing the huge family of fourteen children.

Nine years later, William Woollcombe bought Traylysworthy from the Crockers, for one hundred Marks. The family are known to have settled in the Plympton area in the time of Henry VI, they were then residing at Holland, a farm of modest acreage to the south of the Chaddlewood-to-Sparkwell road, now devoured by the Langage industrial estate. In 1584 the family moved to Challonsleigh near Lee mill, when John Woollcombe purchased it from a Hannibal Vivian of Cornwall. Four years later the family leased the (now spelt) Traylsworthy along with pasture on Leigh Moor and Bickley Wood to William Strode; tied up in this transaction could well have been the right to pitch for tin, for we see in 1625 that Sir Richard Strode, along with others, had men working the steams and hillsides of all three pieces of land rented.

1651 saw the end of the Strodes at Traylsworthy and a John Hamblin a skinner (spelt skyner on the lease) from Plymouth, paying William Woollcombe the rent of three pounds in 'Lawful Money of England to be paid Quarterly'. Henry Woollcombe writing in his accounts of Trowlesworthy, declares that Mr Hamblin was the person who first created the warren.

Burrows beside the Plym.

Seeing the name warren appears on the lease for the first time when Edward Mead signed on the dotted line, to take over from Elie Shullibear at Ditsworthy in 1676, then at the same time consider the wording in Henry Woolcombes' accounts of Trowlesworthy, it gives an idea as to when rabbits were first bred for commercial value on the moor.

The next tenant to arrive was Roger Phillips, a Maltster, in 1695. This man negotiated quite a good deal, paying the same rent as Mr Hamblin, along with a lease of ninety-nine years. For one reason or another he managed only 44 of them before Richard Lillicrap came along in 1742. This gent was not quite so fortunate, for his yearly rent shot up to a whopping great fifty pounds, to be paid quarterly, with the first payment of £12-10s, due on the four and twentieth day of June. It was around this time that today's pronunciation of the warren's name came into being, for on the indenture that John Warry put his monogram to in 1760, all three interpretations of Traylysworthy,

Traylsworthy and the new one of Trowlesworthy are written into the contract for all to see, making sure that all parties concerned were aware of the place in question.

John Warry came on the scene in 1760. He was a gentleman from New Inn in the county of Middlesex. He paid a nominal payment of just five shillings 'of Lawful Money on the fourth day of January in the thirty third year of the reign of George the Second, for one year only'. When the year was complete and expired and ended, he had to pay the rent of 'one Grain of Wheat'. One of the witnesses was Richard Lillicrap, another signatory was a Tristrum Avent.

John Warry's appearance on the scene is uncertain. It may well have been that Richard Lillicrap Senior had died, leaving his son Richard, who did not actually live at Trowlesworthy, to live in hope of running the warren. The Woollcombe family not wanting to tie the land up to any one person for too long, brought in John Warry as a straw man, a someone and a no one to act out the part of a temporary lessee, thus breaking the sequence between father and son. As Mr Jeffrey Hackney of Wadham Collage Oxford explained, 'Common Recovery was a pantomime way of conveying land, very ingenious and admirable, given the constraints of the day.' After Warry's association with Trowlesworthy, Richard Lillicrap junior of Shaugh, took over the warren, paying the same rent as his father, but with a vastly reduced lease of only seven years.

1790 saw the Woollcombe's arrive at Hemerdon after Thomas Woollcombe purchased the property along with Bickfordtown from his second cousin Maria, granddaughter of Tristrum Avent, who in 1725 married Elizabeth, sister to William Woollcombe grandfather of Thomas.

The Avents along with Peter Ryder bought the properties from the Crocker family in 1632. It was divided one moiety (portion) of Hemerdon to Ryder, the other with Bickfordtown to Nicholas and Tristrum Avent, the latter, the probable grandfather of the signatory to the Warry Indenture.

Research by the National Trust places Peter Nicholls at Trowlesworthy when the house we see today was built. However doubt crosses the trail when they find that the land tax assessment covering 1786 to 1830 sees a Richard, William and Thomas but no Peter there. The house was no doubt built during the very earliest years of the nineteenth century, a major clue to this could be seen when researching the old tin operations in the area. In 1825 a trespass was made on Trowlesworthy when the excavation of the Bottle Hill mine leat was cut through the warren's pot water stream; a letter of complaint delved out from the Woollcombe archives, tells of how the illegally excavated waterway had cut off the pot water, which has for the last twenty years run and supplied the home of William the Warrener, having been brought there by his father the former tenant. Along with the letter is a rough graph of the present house, displaying the original pot water route, and the new one directed from the mine leat. This reveals that the warren drinking water was brought to the premises in about 1805, without doubt to the Warren's newly constructed dwelling.

A natural boulder for a bound stone designated No 1.

Above Hen Tor marker No. 3.

Recumbant marker No. 4.

After the cramped conditions of the longhouse, this new dwelling must have been wonderful, built with the local moorstone of various shades, sizes and colours, it offered the ample space of five rooms upstairs and four down with access to the peat house through a small doorway in the kitchen. Across the courtyard was the pelt house and annexed to this was the toilet with its wooden seat pitched above the pot water leat.

A Peter Nicholls did work the warren adjoining Trowlesworthy. In 1807 Lord Boringdon granted a lease for Peter to farm the rabbits of Hentor Warren. The boundaries, as the indenture states, are from a certain row or heap of stones joining Trowlesworthy Warren and Spanish Lake (formally the Eastor Lake) about forty land yards above the same, to a large rock marked with the initials H W B 1 up near its left hand loaf-like shoulder. From there straight on in an easterly direction to another stone marked H W B 2, this marker is shaft-like, similar to the following two; the third can be found after crossing the sopping wet head waters of Hentor Brook (sometimes called the Walla Brook) the stone occupies the loftiest position of them all situated at about fifty yards South of Hentor itself. From here the indenture tells us to proceed to the head of the delightful Shavercombe Brook, where No.4 can be found. This stone has laid prostrate face down for I don't know how many years, with various interested parties looking for it. I found it for myself in the early 1990s, nowhere near the actual head of the stream but a few hundred yards down in fact. Being alien in shape to the rest of the rocks and boulders lying around it gave itself away. Being considerably stronger back then, the long elongated object didn't take that much turning to pleasingly expose the inscription H W B 4 but reversing the task to hide its face again, wasn't so easy, thus leaving the disturbance for others to see. The direction from here is to Coles Mill on the Plym, Mill Corner on the Ordinance Survey Map, where No.5 can be found no more. From here the warren is bounded by the tenement, of Willings Walls.

When asking Wilfred Ware if he knew the whereabouts of No.5 he told me the story of how a particular Ditsworthy Warren Hand bragged to his grandfather, Nicholas, of how he heaved it in the river.

Back at Trowlesworthy in 1825 not only did the Bottle Hill Mine Company encroach on private land but they also drowned many rabbits when valuable burrows became waterlogged and ruined. When the leat whilst still under construction overflowed into them, some of the burrows, according to William Nicholls, were of the very best. After all the agitation and uncomfortable friction endured the situation was eventually resolved with the Mine Company paying compensation to William. Out of it all, the warrener gained a little more income by receiving five pounds a year for maintaining the waterway that flowed through Trowlesworthy land.

The 1839 census saw the end of the Nicholls' era as Warreners on the moor. The new family at Trowlesworthy were the Lavers, the first mention of them at the Warren was when

Courtney and Anna the two daughters of Henry and Elizabeth were Baptised at Shaugh, on the first day of September of that same year. This acreage within the warren boundaries, was well established by the time Henry came along and entered the name of Lavers into the Trowlesworthy history.

After transferring some of his energies from the warren of Legistor, 1856 saw John Lavers as head of the household at Trowlesworthy. He no doubt crossed the Plym just below where it takes in the water from the Spanish Lake, where a clam sat across the water. Nothing can be seen now of the little bridge but for three large bolts imbedded in three moss-covered boulders lying in the middle of the river.

According to census records, John's time at Trowlesworthy was over by the early years of the 1870s. Nothing very much is known of the man, one can only surmise that he may well have been the brother of Henry, and like Henry his origins lie somewhere away in the misty yesterdays beyond our knowledge. Likewise Jane of Trowlesworthy, who found the end of her days at the age of 77 in 1870, could well have been his wife, with Richard the renowned Lavers of Trowlesworthy, who found himself sitting in the warreners chair after Jane passed away, their son.

It was during the Lavers' occupation of the warren when a little more land was enclosed; a plot to the East of Clover Field was walled to create two small fields, the family also spent considerable energy gathering stone to erect the boundaries of square field and the little triangular enclosure near the Plym, to the north-west of the main complex.

Bolts that once held the Clam to the riverbed.

PLAN OF TROWLESWORTHY FIELDS 1842

1. BUILDINGS & GARDEN
2. POTATO FIELD
3. CLOVER FIELD
4. POND FIELD
5. CARRION FIELD
6. LOWER GARDEN
7. GREAT MEADOW
8. LITTLE DO

The fields of Trowlesworthy Warren.

Rabbit Bridges.

Cylindrical carved block, lying between the Trowlesworthy Tors.

The troublesome mine leat of 1825 that split the warren in two, no doubt caused problems for access to the higher slopes with either having to precariously leap the water or, span it where wanted, by a fairly sturdy plank, which would obviously rot, and quite quickly, in the damp conditions out on the moor. It was Richard Lavers whose initiative spanned it with the aptly named Rabbit Bridges. There are twenty-one in all on Trowlesworthy land, mostly of cut stone, split by the tare and feather; others are of natural slabs of granite of various dimensions, with just the one collapsed, being washed top and bottom by the flowing water. It is thought that not all the little clappers, for that's what they are, were erected by Richard, and seven is the number credited to him. It can only be assumed that the china clay people laid the rest, for they were the parties who adopted the valuable source of water when the Bottle Hill Mine closed and it was, and still is, in their interest to have access to both sides for the little matter of dredging and repairs. It is noticeable that some have been refurbished and added too, and even strengthened with concrete. This bridge though, is the odd one out, for it is a lot wider than the rest and most probably the first to span the flowing obstacle and the one to trigger the whole idea into Richard's head.

The bridge originally carried a cart track to the granite quarry at Little Trowlesworthy Tor, run by a John Freeman and son. At one time, the two comparatively moderate size masses of rock protruding through the hillside's surface had the name of Trowlesworthy Tor and Eastor, the latter now Great Trowlesworthy Tor, for some reason known for certain only to history, was almost untouched. The raven was nearly always allowed to nest there in piece. On the other hand, Trowleworthy Tor, now quite appropriately with the word 'Little' placed before it, had its very heart torn out, blasted for the mason to skilfully ply his trade. What wasn't carted away for his use can be seen as waste in two elongated heaps, one pointing to the Plym, the other to the outlet of the Spanish Lake.

After being abandoned a little over hundred and thirty years ago, the plinth with its centre pivot hole that carried the quarry crane, is still in remarkably good condition. Shaped from stone out of this quarry, was the beautifully polished mantel surrounding the fireplace in the library at Hemerdon House. Out on the hilltop encircling the tor, dozens of huge boulders have been cut, some into twos and threes and hewn roughly into a shape of appropriate proportions, some square and cube-like, others rectangular and varying in length. A few can be seen to be trigged up, still waiting for the masons' finishing touches, the most conspicuous of all being one of cylindrical fashion, poised like some huge granite kettledrum waiting to be struck, with scars of the tare and feather still as sharp as the day they were first bored. It is my belief, that like all the other partially worked material lying around on this hill, it was abandoned when Mr Freeman for one reason or another decided to leave. The company whose head offices were in London, at Great College Street, Westminster, was at one time the premier quarry employer in the South West, with depots in Plymouth and Cornwall, and the main office at Penryn.

Back down on the leat the weathered remains of vermin traps can be discovered for the interested to see, unlike the conventional x-shape these display just a V with its tapering neck ending on the brink of a drop into the water, it appears to be designed to drown its victim, in the similar manner to the trap already mentioned on the left bank of the Double Dart. When one takes a closer look at the stonework of these traps, one in particular tells us that its victim may not have fallen into the leat, for here, right on the very edge of the bank blocking the way into water, is a substantial boulder. Something here hints that it was moved into this position to accommodate the flow of water along its channel. Added to this theory, is that the crude but supposedly successful contraptions were obsolete and so much already part of history that even Richard Lavers in his long life span, knew nothing about them.

The early married life of Richard Lavers was spent off the moor, it was not until 1853 that he, with his wife Eveline, came back to Trowlesworthy to share the house with Jane until she died. The marriage produced seven children, three of whom died in infancy, the last to be born was Henry, in 1862, the same year that his mother at the young age of thirty-seven passed away. Five years were to elapse before Richard saw fit to begin again and start another family. The marriage to Sarah brought along three more children, two of whom the couple sadly lost, Thomas, at the age of three, and Eveline aged seven.

There was a Thomas living with Richard and Sarah when the old warrener passed away in 1914 at the ripe old age of ninety-four. During Sarah's time of holding the warren reins, two young china clay workers from Plympton, who were half-brothers, supplemented their earn-

Remains of trap in a prehistoric enclosure wall.

The trap running to the leat.

Another trap utilising an enclosure wall.

A trap beside the Plym.

ings by working part-time for her, one brother was a Sorton the other a Giles. The first mentioned took the challenge of working the rabbit breeding acreage full time when Sarah died in1926 in her eighty-ninth year; just eight months earlier Thomas died at the age of sixty-nine, born in 1856. This man must have been Eveline's son, Sarah's stepson. The reason Thomas' existence brings a frown to my brow, is because I find it curious as to why there is no record of his birth slotted between that of James born 1853, and Eli in 1857, and if Thomas, Richard's son by his first marriage, why christen another boy with the same name in his second marriage, when the first Thomas is still alive?

Whilst Alfred Sorton was settling in at Trowlesworthy, Robert Giles got himself a wife called Minnie. He also purchased a milk round at Plympton, delivering by horse and cart from where he ladled the milk out of churns into whatever container the housewife had for him to fill, the horse clip-clopping and stopping, clip-clopping and stopping through Underwood and its neighbouring narrow streets, until the round was done.

The thirteen years Alfred Sorton lived at Trowlesworthy were not so pleasing for his wife, Isabella, as they were for him; the loneliness and the solitude out on the moor wasn't a bit to her liking. The throngs of people enjoying the moorland Plym for recreation today, hadn't arrived and hikers rambling past the warren door, were far and few between. Her thoughts were forever over the hill and the in-country where a neighbour was less than a stone's throw away. In the end she could take no more and persuaded Alfred to leave the rabbits where they were and get away from her seemingly everlasting torment away to the village of Shaugh.

Minnie and Robert Giles.

Meanwhile down at Plympton, Minnie Giles is thinking of the moor, for Robert, has over the years, adopted a liking for a little tipple, too many, too often, in the local hostelries, enough in 1937 to encourage her into nudging him in the direction of selling the milk round and taking over the tenancy of Trowlesworthy from Alfred.

Minnie, a local girl from Lutton near Cornwood, was no stranger to the warren area, at one time she lived with her Aunt and Uncle, Mr and Mrs Skidmoor at the Counting House, the green-coloured bungalow situated just above Cadover Bridge. Mr Skidmoor was the Captain at Shaugh China Clay Works only a matter of yards away, on the other side of the Plym.

The Giles' three children, all well within their teens and more, were familiar with a society that included the usual steady flow of everyday facilities that life in general brought along with it, the normal amenities that were taken for granted, like local shops, cafés, chemists and hairdressers. The public transport of buses and trains, no more than a few minutes' walk away to enable a short trip to Plymouth and theatrical entertainment, the school and church was at the bottom of the hill and the chapel along the road. There were people, cars and lorries going past their door, neighbours within earshot, nattering, laughing even perhaps arguing. There was gas street-lighting, mantles to illuminate rooms in the home and a flush to take the toilet contents away. Unlike the many earlier children born to the warren, for

Tryphena, Charley and Bob, this was their first sight of it and its pure isolation. Four miles into the moor, with the last three parts of a mile over a clapper bridge and a meandering rough stone strewn cart track.

One of the first jobs Robert Giles did when he arrived at Trowlesworthy was to knock down the old longhouse and utilise the fallen masonry to construct the yard walling. Admirable intuition for its time may be, but it could well have been derelict and in his thinking beyond repair. Whatever, he obviously saw no use for it and did what he thought needed doing. Today a preservation order would have been placed on such a building, and rightly so, not one stone would they allow to be removed. No doubt Charley assisted in the task of demolishing the old structure, but his warren days were short-lived and instead of nets for the rabbits and shotgun for the vermin, he was given a uniform and a rifle when he was called up to join the rest of the lads going to war. Whilst his elder brother was away risking life and limb, young Bob enjoyed the quiet life, tending the rabbits and caring for the revenue supplement stock of sheep and bullocks. Cutting peat for the fire was another matter, before he would venture anywhere near the old fibre for fuel, someone else would have to clear the vegetation just in case the viper was lurking in its midst. His sister, Tryphena, who was the eldest, passed her working day employed by Miss Walling who lived in the bungalow situated along the lane among the outer fields of Brisworthy Farm. Triff, as she was so affectionately called, reached her work by crossing the Plym below square field, assisted by young Bob who would lay planks from boulder-to-boulder for her to cross, doing the same for her return home.

Adder below the warren.

As far away as Robert may have been from the wicked tipple, he never quite deserted his fondness for the taste, often using it to quench a thirst on Monday Market Days at Plympton. He would leave home astride his horse with a brace of rabbits or two to sell. Stabling his mount at Lee Moor House, where the Skelly family lived, then catch the bus the rest of the way. The memories of days gone by, floating verbally in banter fashion from man to man whilst keeping an eye on the stock for sale, then off to the Hele Arms to quench a dryness, leaving eventually to catch the bus back to Lee Moor, with an occasional uncontrolled wandering of his legs and a hint of a slurred Lee Moor please when the conductor came his way. Triff amusingly remembered on one occasion, when he arrived home without his horse, he had somehow made his way home forgetting it was still tethered at Lee Moor House.

By the time Robert took over at Trowleworthy, the mainstay of the Warren's income was from sheep and bullocks, the consumption of rabbit had been reduced tremendously. The thirties slump was practically over and people's affordable preferences went to other more desirable cuts of meat. But by now, what with the Second World War being established, and the money belt having to be tightened by most, rabbit was back regularly on the meal table.

Life was never easy for anyone living in the depth of the moor, it was tough going. One had to be resilient, there was no flick-of-a-switch apparatus to be had, no water on tap, no electricity, no fire in the range to cook, until it was cleaned, reset and relit. Pans and buckets of water were heated for a tin bath beside the fire; to be filled the water was brought into the house from the lip stone of the pot water leat outside. The toilet sat over a branch of a stream from the same supply. It could be found across the yard annexed to the inside of the smelly old pelt house, lighting to it was a candle or the old tilly lamp, and death for the old and young alike came nearly always in the year's later months.

When the sun is getting lower,
And the cold is on its way,
When shadows grow at their longest
Before darkness ends the day.
When in the stillness of the nights,
Before the North-Easterlies blow
Reflections on the ponds will freeze,
And long curtains of icicles will grow.

Making a rick at Trowlesworthy.

Tryphena at Trowlesworthy.

Len and Tryphena at the Counting House.

If proof was needed that winters on the moor could be worrying, 1947 snowed the warren in for six whole weeks. It was always plain commonsense that told moorland folk that during the long cold months, it was imperative to keep the larder well-stocked to overflowing. Also the plentiful store of other essential provisions was necessary to have in reserve if the problems of cold, wasn't to gradually creep in to give cause for concern.

The luxury of electricity was the Giles' contribution to Trowlesworthy. In 1955 the family purchased a generator and had the house wired to take its power, but the first thoughts towards the employment of its energy wasn't for lighting, that was of secondary consideration, it was for television that the expense was originally envisaged. There was apparently, an exploratory attempt at generating electricity at the warren, said to be the effort of Richard Lavers. It apparently lit up the courtyard and nothing more and was controlled only by tuning the water flow in and out, which is behind the outbuildings bordering the moor. Here can be seen an elongated stone-lined pit where a junction off the pot water flow turned a wheel. It looks very much as if areas of an older pit was at sometime refurbished and altered to complement a wheel of certain other proportions.

Thirty years as a warrener, saw the end of Robert Giles' days at Trowlesworthy the last of the rabbit breeding people on the moor past away in 1969. He lived his last eight years without the companionship of Minnie, the warmth she gave his home, the jollity she exuded into every corner, her cooking that sated the appetite with a prolonged resounding 'Aahh!' All had gone from his life leaving a void he could never accept. Before the same year was out, younger son Bob, who was now on his own, vacated Trowlesworthy for the Counting House above Cadover Bridge, where his sister Tryphena and her husband Len had set up home, and where his father spent his last few weeks.

After the Giles' departure from Trowlesworthy, the property was gifted by the Woollcombe family to the National Trust. Since then the house has been in the hands of Mr and Mrs Cyril who, after purchasing a much bigger generator and endured its continual drone for several years, now enjoy the introduction of mains electricity. Water is no longer caught at the lip stone but is delivered on tap, pumped from a well out on the moor, and rabbit warrening to them is purely an occupation that existed some time in the not too distant past.

CHAPTER 6
China Clay

China clay pit.

Leonard Vincent was smitten when he first saw Triff, he fell for her cheekiness and her happy-go-lucky manner encouraged him to visit to Trowlesworthy a little more often; he was introduced to her by his brother Harold who regularly frequented the Warren.

If today's world was to drift back through time to Len's childhood, the young couple may never have met and he may never have matured into the man everyone loves. Authorities would have taken him into care, somewhere far from the world he knew and loved. Len was born at Heathdown near Elfordleigh, the youngest of six children, five boys and a girl. Still as an infant, Len and the family moved to Collard Farm, where the outlying field hedges border the moor. By the age of four, he had lost his mother to illness, leaving him to be raised as best the family could manage, without the caring arm of a loving mum. With father at work on the mica dams at Dartmoor China Clays earning to supplement the inadequate income that the Collard acreage brought in, Len was pulled along in life by his considerably older siblings, but gradually one-by-one they left the farm by day to work wherever their chosen employment took them, leaving the young boy to fend for himself as best any child could.

Len was by his own admission a scallywag, a rascal, artful but not cunning, hardened but not harmful. His days were full from getting out of bed to reluctantly going back to it. Often he would be late for school, his Wotter friends calling up to his bedroom window, 'come on Vinny,' he would jump out of bed and throw a quick breakfast together of kettle broth, milk or tea sops, and up across the fields to be met by the teacher and a ruler over the hand for being well behind the bell.

With his head full of what he wanted it to be, very little of his academic schooling sunk in to any great depth; his young mind's eyes were always looking at life in general, learning the trade of taking in all he felt he needed to perceive. He loved weekends and school holidays when he could be with his father down on the mica dam, or at home harvesting, reaping all that his elders knew about living in the cocooned world around him. He left Shaugh School at fourteen. Academic qualifications? He never knew there was such a thing (he once told me), and went home to work for his keep on the farm, until going out to work proper, as he put it, at the age of fifteen on the clay works with father and the white world of Dartmoor China Clay.

Len was now fully integrated in a man's world, expanding his knowledge of life outside the closetted boundaries of Collard Farm. Life now was altogether different, unlike at school, here he had to keep up, or be out on his ear. But he loved it, being where he wanted to be, where to him all real men worked. But sooner than anyone could have imagined, life was to change and fashion him into manhood considerably quicker than even Leonard could have ever dreamt in his wildest nightmare. For no sooner had he began courting Tryphena (Triff), war was with us, pulling Len from her presence and into khaki, first at the Citadel in Plymouth, then on to Shoeburyness in Essex for further training before going over the Channel to France and the Belgian border.

Engaging the far more heavily armed Germans, meant his regiment was driven back, until reaching the sea, then home again on a ship named *Daffodil*, an old converted train ferry that was eventually sunk off Dieppe in 1945. Whilst in France, Len's only vivid memory of a close encounter was when he dived into a huge spread of stinging nettles after hearing the whistle of a shell that passed over head. He now tells with a chuckle, of how his Sergeant explained after seeing his Private covered in the resulting rash, that at the time he dived into the nettles the projectile had already gone past.

In 1942, while he was home on leave, Leonard married his Tryphena, spending a little time with her before going off again, this time to India and Burma, and confrontation with the Japanese, where he drove support vehicles delivering ammunition to the men on the front line.

Apart from the well-etched mental scars from five long years of war experience, Len and his brother-in-law Charley, arrived home unscathed. Yet with life having to go on as if as normal, it wasn't long before they were looking for work. Howard Skidmoor took the pair on at Shaugh Lake; Howard took over the position of Captain when his father, John, retired. It was customary for the china clay companies to employ father and son, uncle and nephew, brothers and cousins, the system supposedly nurturing good working relationships and ensured no slacking, with the youngsters respectfully pulling their weight in front of their elders. It was also an unwritten code of practice that men from certain areas around the periphery of the works would not usually work for certain other companies The close-knit communities kept their lives and workplace to themselves, with rivalry unquestionably controlled by a silent, wordless theme of patriotism.

The working atmosphere wasn't at all pleasurable for the outsider, as Len was known; he was ignorantly looked upon and treated with suspicion until well into his years of employment with the company. This truly unhealthy practice gradually died out as companies began to recruit managerial staff from outside the industry.

China clay, that Westcountry geological phenomenon, owes its discovery here in our midst to William Cookworthy. William was born into a Quaker family in the South Hams town of Kingsbridge, in 1705, the eldest of seven. When first into his teens the household lost its breadwinner. His father, a weaver, died at the comparatively young age of forty, leaving his wife to nurture their plentiful issue as best she could. 1720 saw a Silvanus Bevan, an apothecary from London, who was also a Quaker, visiting Kingsbridge. Whilst in the town he got to know William, no doubt becoming acquainted through the Quaker Friendly Society. Before the gentleman left for his return to his travels he invited the boy, when the time was convenient, to the great metropolis to study under him.

Although there is no record of William ever attending the old Kingsbridge Grammar School, he must surely have had some sort of formal education, for his intelligence obviously impressed Mr Bevan for the man to have offered him an apprenticeship. The school was built with the generous donation from a Mr Thomas Crispin, a local man who made something of himself, yet never forgot his home-town roots. The school was built for the needy with a desire for learning. It is now used as a museum and dedicated to William's name.

At the age of just fifteen William said goodbye to his mother and his younger siblings and made his way apparently on foot to his future with Mr Bevan, spending his time in London learning to become a pharmaceutical and mineralogical chemist. Six years later saw a fully qualified twenty-one-year-old arriving in Plymouth, where he set up in business with the son of his London benefactor.

When nearing his middle years, William became a Minister of the Friendly Society and travelled extensively around the Westcountry. Being a mineralogist, he became enthusiastically interested in porcelain, fostering his knowledge of the subject by reading the papers of the Frenchman, Baron Reamur, who had written down and published his experiments with kaolin, a valuable commodity, yet unknown to the scholars of the day to be lying beneath the soil of Britain. Of course the mineral had been known to locals in various places in the Westcountry for who knows how many years, but they were obviously oblivious of its commercial value. It was during one of his ecclesiastical travels that William first discovered it. Through his acquaintance with a tin mining captain, he inadvertently found it deep in the peninsula of Cornwall, on Tregonning Hill, an elevation overlooking the long spread of Praa Sands. The miner employed it to repair the mine's furnaces, most probably without the slightest thought towards its geological make-up and the value of the kaolin within. William later went on to discover kaolin of a far more rewarding quality at St Stephens near St Austell.

So, through this eminent chemist, the china clay industry in Britain was born. Up until then the country imported the material from China, in the province of Jiangxi. It was first discovered there on a hill called Kao-ling, hence the English term of kaolin, meaning white hill.

It is thought that Mr Cookworthy made the odd excursion up on to Dartmoor during his Friendly Society days, and took home samples of clay from around the present clay producing areas of the moor, but with always the same disappointing results regarding its quality. Where exactly these samples were supposedly taken isn't known, but it could be guessed that they may have been scooped from any stream where the old tinners had turned the surface of the moor over; the Tory and Piall Brooks being good examples.

Unlike Mr Cookworthy, whose interest in kaolin was to manufacture fine porcelain, the person to actually locate the material on Dartmoor was a manufacturer of earthenware, a much cruder version of more-or-less the same thing. The gent was a Mr John Dickens from Plymouth. He found clay on Lee Moor in 1827, yet for one reason or another three years were to pass before he began production there. He was no novice where china clay was concerned, for he already had an interest in a pit at Trethosa in Cornwall, from where the material for his earthenware business came. Unlike Mr Cookworthy, John Dickens had the good fortune of finding what he was looking for on his doorstep, close enough in fact to persuade him to sell his share at Trethosa to a Spencer Rogers, a man on his business travels from Watlands, near Newcastle in Staffordshire.

So the first china clay pit on Dartmoor began to take shape, with kaolin the principal prize of the excavation. The mineral is a component part of the granite structure, the decomposition of the felspar crystals through chemical action over millions of years. The other parts are quartz (sand) and mica. Granite is an igneous rock, *ignis* in Latin meaning fire. It spewed violently up through the earth's crust, according to the geologists, about 300 million years ago, and from then on hydrothermal activity has altered it, kaolinising the felspars into a soft powdery texture, commonly known as china clay.

Excavation of the material gave Mr Dickens far more problems than merely what the notorious Dartmoor weather could throw at him. He had to contend with local labour from within the surrounding area knowing nothing about clay workin; yet employ it he had to, meaning his presence was warranted on site a great deal, at least until some level of competence was sufficiently instilled. Another more crucial hurdle, and by far the most surmountable, was age; he was a man nudging towards seventy. As time is the judge of all man's limits, within two years age was the rein that gradually pulled him off the moor and back to his Plymouth workshop. Along with that decision, he gave up his share in the project to the partner he set out with; but this gentleman was merely the financial aid and knew no more about clay production than when the digging first began. He, no doubt, was very rarely on the moor for he was a seaman of rank and merely looked upon his association with Mr Dickens as an investment. He took in another partner, a brewer, who knew even less about the industry than he did himself. And with a workforce of limited experience, it soon became clear that it was best to cut his losses and leave the burden on the moor to someone else.

1833 saw a William Phillips, a glassmaker from Sunderland visiting the Westcountry. Somehow the three men's paths crossed, money changed hands and the pit on the moor had a new man at the head of production. It was from here on that the industry on Dartmoor was set to become firmly established.

It seems incredible how quickly William, who supposedly had no association or hands-on knowledge of the industry, realised he was on to a good thing. He knew that the sub-let contract he had agreed to wasn't appropriate to his plans towards the pit's future. William was a man who, after getting a foot in the door, must surely have done his research to the last detail. Like the tinner before him, he was a true adventurer, with no chance of contemplating any grass maturing beneath his feet. In less than two years he was rid of the seaman and the brewer and their insufficient twenty-one year lease, and negotiated a new one for ninety-nine years with Lord Morley of Saltram, his landlord.

At first, the obvious water supply to the pit would have been the infant and inadequate flow of the Tory Brook, the same stream William's predecessors would have used. There is an uncanny coincidence about this little stream being employed on the outset of clay washing on Dartmoor; it rose on White Hill Yeo, White Hill being translated from Kao-ling, the very place where clay was first discovered in China.

William must have either been down into Cornwall to acquire all he needed to know concerning clay production, or perhaps he employed the necessary expertise. Not that there was a tremendous amount to know in those early days, the industry was still very much in its infancy, the methods and procedures used were still pretty crude, employing of course the only ways then developed. To start a new clay pit from scratch in William's day would have been the same as it is today, apart from the mechanism used. Today there is massive mobile plant and powerful water pumps. William would have had to start his pit where a stream of water could flow. With the site determined, the initial stage of operation is to clear the area of overburden (burden meaning in this case material that has to be removed before production can begin, the likes of vegetation, peat and soil and any other material that may be detrimental to the colour and quality of clay). This costly inconvenience was taken away and merely dumped somewhere clear of the working area. All this sheer graft would have been carried out by men using dubbers (picks) with one wide blade and one narrow, and shovels, loading the burden into carts for horses to haul away. Two leats were then introduced to the site; one from the source of the water supply, the other away from it. Once the site (called a strake) was established, the workforce would then roughly dig the white surface and pummel the lumps of clay-bearing material as the water ran down through it. This operation crushed the soft kaolinised felspar crystals into powder, leaving the three components of kaolin, quartz and mica, as separate entities to float in suspension out of the worked area along the existing leat to the next place in the production line.

Once established, William, in 1839, brought a greater flow of water to Lee Moor, bringing it around the hillsides from the River Plym, well over four miles away. The leat took its water out of the river just a few yards downstream from where the little Calves Lake runs into

Clapper bridge over Phillips' Leat near the Langcombe Brook.

Depth of the leat not far from the clapper.

it. The easily recognisable artificial watercourse runs alongside the river, above old tinners' workings, before curving south, around the hillside where it gradually degenerates, eroded into nothing, on the gentler sloping terrain. A little further on it would have turned to the right, where it once ran through the ample spread of tinners' spoil heaps, before crossing a weir and collecting a little more flow from the Langcombe Brook. From here it arches around the great sweep of Giant's Hill, where there is today enough of the leat surviving to actually walk in. I say walk in, because by doing so we help save the banking.

Just around the curve where the Plym can be looked down into again, a neat one-stone clapper bridge spans the course from bank to bank and beyond, as it traverses the steepest part of the hill it is in places nigh on four-feet deep, until the steepness of the ground lessens and the way forward begins to veer to the south. From a cairn just a few yards above, the Plym, after it escapes from the narrow confines of the abyss below, can be seen meandering down along the edge of the Drizzlecombe valley. From below the cairn there is very little to see of the leat for a while, the ground from above has over the years (with the help of livestock), issued its soil into it, leaving just a hint of its right-hand banking to follow. But as it passes above a prehistoric settlement, it can be spotted before again disguising its run for several yards into a mere trace on the ground.

While strolling along here during a photo shoot, I had the good fortune of discovering for myself two unrecorded kistvaens, just a few yards downhill from my intended direction, one bearing its four stone cist to the wild Dartmoor elements, the other hiding, with one stone missing from its chamber, beneath its incomplete vegetation-shrouded capstone.

Back up on the leat walking is easy, but not for long. Sooner than one would like, the tussocks take command and progress starts to get a little uncomfortable with a regular stride pattern becoming increasingly difficult to enjoy. The leat can still be traced beneath the great grassy mounds for a few yards, when it turns south-south-west, but thereafter the going gets really tough and the leat in places disappears altogether. There is a tinners' gully that runs down the hillside, but it is of no great depth at this elevation, and William Phillips would no doubt have bridged it with a launder. There is an area of moss with water, shining in the sunlight, trickling slowly through it. It is best not to dawdle, for the side of the hill here drains into the Shavercombe, and is saturated. Walking through the bracken and reed one's boots sink to the ankles and above. Yet worse is to come, even with the welcoming sound of the delightful Shavercombe Waterfall dropping into its crystal clear pool, it can make you wonder what the hell you are doing here. The leat has been eaten completely by tussocks of huge proportions, the only way forward is to place your feet between them where soggy brown liquid squelches into your boots. For about twenty yards you are grateful for a free hand that prevents an embarrassing stumble on to all fours, especially when laden with rucksack and camera, and with a dictaphone occupying one hand.

Thankful relief to the sweating brow gets closer, when the ground drops sharply to the banking of the brook. From here until the little stream is reached, the leat can at intervals be seen again. For a few yards, reed in a straight line give its route away, and it then skirts around a small area of tinners' heaps where the old mine waste has been utilised to secure the water's flow. Suddenly the brook's very edge is there and the leat, which now has the appearance of no more than an elongated bench clinging to the almost vertical banking, turns acutely to the south, eventually running on into the pool below the falls.

Nearly every year a pair of crows nest in the tree that throws its shadow across the pool, but one nesting season I came across a mallard's nest on the banking, and a noisy wren made its home just a yard or so from where I sat to have my refreshment. From this beautiful idyllic spot, the leat once followed the brook for some forty to fifty yards, but a tremendous amount of erosion must have occurred here since the leat was abandoned, for there is no sign of it or its banking until out of the little ravine and on to the open moor again. Here the direction curves around to the south-west, below the small rock pile of Shavercombe Tor where the terrain is far more agreeable underfoot. For about half a mile, while traversing around the hillside, through the long-forgotten medieval fields of Hentor Warren, the leat, although of no great shape, is clearly definable, running under several little clappers, while reeds line the route like some protracted municipal flowerbed, with grass on both sides nibbled almost to its roots.

The leat crossing the Shavercombe Brook.

Reeds still line the way when the leat turns gradually to the south, heading more-or-less towards Hen Tor itself. Now the ruins of the Hentor Farm buildings are in full view, that is those that can be seen above the summer bracken. From here the freedom of being able to view all around while casually strolling is now over, at least for a few hundred yards, as the leat passes through a gully and on around the tumbled farm buildings. Here it is full of water, seeped from the wet ground above it.

Within a few yards it is dry underfoot again but the going gets no easier; hidden beneath dense bracken are boulders and clappers, some fallen while others are still in their horizontal position, allowing easy access to either side of the leat. After about four hundred yards, open ground is met again, here William Phillips must surely have been happy at not having to excavate his leat a contour or two higher, for this is an area where the thawing of the Ice Age sent a great deal of Hen Tor tumbling down the hillside where it lies scattered today covering several acres of ground. By the time William surveyed the contours for his leat, a considerable amount of the debris would have been harvested by prehistoric man for his enclosures and round-house dwellings, just yards away on the same hill. Also the developers of Hentor Warren would have helped themselves to a certain tonnage, for the warren buildings and field walling.

Shavercombe waterfall.

Just a few yards from a neat little clapper that barely leaves the floor today, the leat zigzags through a tinners' gully, while doing so it meets a huge boulder right in its way, and rather

The leat ran under this boulder.

Meadow pipit on its nest.

than move the great object from its path, the constructer ran his water beneath it. A few strides further on the Hentor Brook is crossed where a weir would have encouraged a little more water along the leat. The way now is fairly easy walking again, with just a series of rocks to avoid and the odd patch of bracken to walk through.

Soon the Spanish Lake valley is arrived at and the Trowlesworthy Tors are in full view; the leat is clear to see and is again lined at its deepest with reed. While strolling along this section of the leat, I saw a pipit staring at me from its nest that was tucked into the foot of a tussock, right on the edge of the leat. I have found many a nest during walks on the moor, but never as late as 22 July.

Halfway along what is almost a straight line the reeds give way to bracken, until the leat disappears into squelching wet tussocky ground where it once arced around the rises of Spanish Lake. It appears again as it falls into another artificial watercourse of much larger proportions, excavated by ECLP when they diverted the Sell Top Brook into the Spanish Lake in 1972. The work was carried out to prevent a considerable volume of water, especially during times of heavy rain, from eroding their contour flood leat below. William Phillips' leat carries on from here for another few yards with little alteration from the modern day, until a barrier constructed of moorstone and concrete holds any water that may collect there, encouraging it back into the Spanish Lake. Now from the barrier, the leat has only half a mile downhill travel to go before being devoured by the modern-day works. Along this stretch, on the sides of the leat's banking, I have picked many a succulent whortleberry, 'urts' or 'hurts' as the long-established moorland dwellers call them, getting my fingers and mouth stained purple from the tiny fruit's ample juices.

Five years before the watercourse was excavated, William in his wisdom knew that having men traipse all the way up on to the moor to do a hard day's graft would have its problems, at times being cold and wet and miserably fatigued by the time they reached their place of work. Housing he thought was the answer, close at hand, just minutes from their area of toil. So within two years of his china clay adventures beginning, cottages were being built, some of moorstone others of cob. One terrace out on White Hill Corner was perhaps for sentimental reasons named Sunderland Cottages, after his home town. Most probably being diplomatic, he called the second terrace, Boringdon, after the family name of his landlord.

Twelve months later in 1836, William's son, John, was born in Shaugh Prior, at about the same time that he was having a house built on the moor where he and his wife brought up John and their two daughters. When the house was finished is not known to me, the abode which was quite substantial with seven bedrooms, became known as Lee Moor House. It sat in just over thirteen acres of rough moorland ground that was gradually over the years to become a beautiful fertile oasis, surrounded by huge white pits and sky high conical tips. In behind its walls and hedges there were pine trees of various species planted to break the severity of the north-east and south-westerly winds. There was a walled garden and greenhouses where grew the family fruit and vegetables, and a summer house and lawns were laid out for croquet. There were stables for riding ponies and three small dwellings to accommodate the staff who served the family. Rhododendrons and azaleas of wonderful colour shrouded areas right down to the edge of two small lakes, one being the first delvings for clay on the moor, its water fed from out on the moor, overflowing into the second pond which had steps descending into it. This was the family swimming pool. From this pool a small stream was delivered out of the oasis on to the working strake of William's Lee Moor clay pit, the pit we see today, that has grown to become one of the largest in the world.

Boringdon Cottages at Lee Moor.

When John was old enough he joined his father in the business, soon proving his worth when he was made a full partner. William already had a friend who had put money into the venture in the shape of a Mr Featherstonehaugh who hoped to make a profit from his investment. He came from the same town as William and obviously knew him very well to entrust a lump sum of his finance in a hole in the ground high up on the bleak terrain of Dartmoor. The trio operated under the name of W. Phillips & Co.

As the years went by and the pit became larger so the waste heaps grew. Surely something could be done with the troublesome materials that there was little market for? Being a man of 'get up and go', his industrious brain ticked over and over, allowing thoughts to run continually through his mind he eventually came up with the solution: it was the brick. After experimenting with a number of mixtures, he found the formula, a blend of his dirtiest unsaleable clay, and some of that troublesome sand and mica suddenly became a most valuable by-product.

A Phillips brick.

By now, as well as Lee Moor House, seventeen cottages including Shade Terrace, settling pans and drying sheds, a half-mile adit driven through solid rock, a pug mill and its furnace, were all built and put into operation, with more men to pay. No sooner had William gained from one venture, he was pouring it into another; revenue never seemed to stay in his pocket for long. Although the man was extremely enterprising, his financial capabilities let him down; in fact at one time it brought real trouble for him. The situation had been looming for some time and it dropped him in hot water with his landlord. Although relations with the Earl were never very congenial they did, in 1846, turn most decidedly sour.

During research for an essay concerning the relationship between the Lee Moor Methodist Church and the china clay industry, the late Mr Eric E. Lambourne, former preacher at Lee Moor, unearthed evidence telling of how the Earl submitted a case to Mr Green of Lincoln's Inn, London, for a judgement on the possibility of the bankruptcy and imprisonment of

Phillips' Adit.

Mr William Phillips. This totally unsavoury predicament was brought about because William owed the Earl rent money to the tune of £1250. the record of how he pulled himself out of this hole has yet to be found, but pull himself out he did.

The distasteful hiccup didn't hold him up for long for he was soon developing the works even further. With the adit nearing completion he began building extensively, developing clay drying, brick making and earthenware products down in the Torycombe Valley, where, when eventually finished, the adit would deliver the contents of the clay stream into drags (catchment pits). In William's day the pits would have been hollowed out of the ground and drystone lined of dimensions to suit the individual clay producer. The sand and rough mica being the heavier of the constituents they dropped immediately out of the stream and remained in the drag, whilst the clay particles overflowed and carried on in suspension to what was called mica runs. These were shallow troughs, several yards in length by about twenty-four inches wide; the number of troughs again varied according to a producer's wishes. These elongated systems trapped the finer micas, allowing the clay particles to again run on into tanks where it was allowed to settle before the resulting clear water drained off.

The clay when reaching a dryness of a pliable consistency, was cut into manageable 'cubs' and stacked several high under a shelter which allowed the air to circulate around them; hence the name of the structure, air 'dries'. However, the development down in the valley again drained William's income. Finding finance was always an obstacle, yet it never dampened his enthusiasm, and progress generally aided progress; but unlike Wesley the man he followed with his religious convictions, William was always in haste, always in a hurry. Money, money, money; the lack of it nearly always held him back, and it often played on his mind.

After nearly twenty years, the man from Sunderland again began to feel his ambitions for Lee Moor were faltering. Something had to be done to steer them back on course. William was undoubtedly a brave entrepreneur, working with the odds stacked highly against him, yet his time to reap any reward for his enterprise was running out. His only chance of survival, he thought, after laying all the initial foundation work, was to dissolve the company and create another by bringing in a few extra shareholders in order to raise the finance needed, and thus to stabilise and push forward towards his goals. His wishes materialised when the Earl and four Plymouth bankers united with William and his partners to form the Lee Moor Porcelain Clay Company. With £100 000 raised, the sweat on William's brow was now reduced to just a slight dampening; but, it was never to disappear altogether, for this meant that although he held the reins where production was concerned, he had harnessed himself to those who knew little or nothing about the nitty-gritty end of the industry, yet, because of their financial input, would occasionally want to pull a few interfering strings.

Having developed his production system to his liking, it was now time to look at ways of getting the product off the moor to the customer a great deal quicker. Horse and wagon over the rough highways of the day was slow going, and a railway of sorts from the moor to the in-country was the answer. Because of the colossal expenditure it could only have been a dream in the mind of William, yet the idea must have been in someone's head for it was put forward in 1851 by Lord Morley, round about the time he and his banker friends became directors at Lee Moor.

The Earl obviously knew that a line to Tavistock from Marsh Mills was being considered, after all it was designed to run through some of his land. It was to be known as the South Devon & Tavistock Railway, a branch of Brunel's line that would eventually run into Cornwall. The men behind the Tavistock scheme were a Mr Toogood along with Messrs Bampton, Frean and Dabb.

When William first met Mr Toogood, the gentleman agreed to William's plans for a branch tramway to be laid to Lee Moor provided he had the support of the Earl and the rest of the clay company's directors. A question mark must hang over whether William's plans were actually used, for in a letter to his fellow directors, Mr Bampton states that the course and arrangement of the line was determined by the Earl himself along with a Mr Hawkshaw, an engineer engaged by his Lordship to oversee the project. Nevertheless, whosoever's plans were used, they were approved by the man himself, Isambard Kingdom Brunel, on 3 July 1852. Once negotiations were completed, the line to the clay works on the moor was to be up and running by March 1853, with the work being carried out by Messrs Hutchinson & Co. But the venture was to give William even more headaches.

According to a much-disappointed William, things didn't run anywhere near to expectations, while all engagements had been performed as was agreed by him and his fellow Lee Moor Directors, the South Devon & Tavistock Railway Company had repudiated their end of the bargain. Bampton had not had the branch ready for traffic or, if not ready (according to their ideas of railway making and working), would not permit the road to be used until 20 March 1855 (two years behind the time agreed), and refused to put it in working condition. In a summary of proceedings, William goes on to say that Bampton insisted that the work was completed in July 1853, with the exception of some details at the Drum Pits. In the April of 1854 the work was inspected by Lord Morley's engineer Mr Hawkshaw, the same Hawkshaw that after Brunel's death completed the construction of the 245-foot high Clifton Suspension Bridge that spans the river Avon at Bristol. This gentleman wrote to Mr Bampton on the 22nd of the same month, saying he was happy with the work done, apart from a problem with unsound timber. However, Hutchinson & Co solemnly denied that any timber of unsatisfactory condition was put in by them, yet argued that the passing of two years may have affected portions of it, and were prepared to examine the problem areas for themselves. But when Mr Hutchinson and Mr Bampton arrived on site, they found that William had already taken possession of the system.

William was an angry and frustrated man and he was extremely critical of the grossly inflated cost of the railway. He explains in his summary of the situation, dated 21 November 1855, that 'our business being suspended for more than two years had cost the company £22 000 in lost revenue'. He went on to say that:

> ...shutting our clay out of the market at a time when trade was good and our clay in good request, postponing our getting into the market until commercial prosperity passed, extreme depression took place and we are driven to further sacrifice by a reduction of 2 shillings per ton which will affect all our future sales of clay. This would not have taken place had we got into the market in 1853 or the spring of 1854. The loss of two years brick trade and other sacrifices and actual losses consequent upon the act of the railway party far beyond £3000, all this is the consequent upon Bampton obstinately determining upon a bad line and making it without proper regard to the cost of construction.

The lookout at the top of the Torycombe incline.

Incline and the Wotter branch.

Apart from the mechanisms at the inclines, the tramway trucks were horse drawn, the great hoofed steeds pulling them along from Lee Moor itself to the summit of the Torycombe incline situated near the rocks of Alder Tor. From the foot of this incline all the way to the summit of Cann Wood incline, and from the foot of this descent, the line ran all the way to the docks at Laira. After the various deficiencies were corrected, the line began to deliver Lee Moor's production down to the boats at Laira Wharf, but, not without the occasional mishap. The camber apparently was too steep on the curve at the foot of the Torycombe incline and on a number of occasions it deposited the trucks and their valuable contents on to the side of the track.

The line from the summit was very steep, dropping three hundred feet from the 725 contour down to the 425 in less than six hundred and fifty yards. The curve at the bottom was far too acute where safety was concerned. Using a double track, the system was operated by cables one-and-a-half inches thick connected to two winding drums, each revolving in opposite directions. Gravity was employed, using the heavier load going down to pull the lighter load up. The drums and their housing are now filled in, supposedly for safety reasons, buried not to be seen again when it really should have been allowed to stay open to display a part of our industrial heritage, our history, a view of our past for the future to see. Surely with all the profit taken from the industry, profit that has lined the pockets of so many, it is sad that not a penny has been put into a fund to save, maintain and protect this small piece of our past.

It was not until 1858 that the system became totally reliable. That was when the incline was laid where we see it today, dropping the more comfortable gradient of three hundred feet in seven hundred and fifteen yards. Also altered was the course of the line over the Wotter Brook; here the wooden viaduct was made redundant and a route taken further along the

425-foot contour before crossing a small bridge that was built to span the brook further upstream. From here the line travelled through various little fields until reaching Coldstone; here it curved as it entered a cutting. Before this feature was created, a tunnel was envisaged to run below the length of the acreage. As the end of the cutting approaches Truelove Bridge a span carries the road that allows access to Coldstone and Truelove Farms before carrying on up towards Collard Farm and Wotter Village. From the bridge it is just over a third of a mile to Whitegates, where, when the line was in operation, a level-crossing interrupted the road transport of its day on the Plympton to Shaugh Prior road. Once this road is crossed, the track then weaves its way through the loftier acreage of Brixton Barton Farm before entering beneath the pine-clad trees of Cann Woods. A length of a few hundred yards below this canopy brings the track to the summit of the second incline, but not before the drum housing is passed over.

Drum wheel at Cann Woods.

Unlike the scene at Lee Moor, here a small section of one drum can be seen; planks of wood positioned across the inside of the right-hand doorway to hold the infill in place have either rotted or been pulled out, allowing just a glimpse for the interested to savour. The building next door once housed a set of drums that were found to be wanting when an increase in tonnage was needed. Down beside the right-hand banking can be seen a length of the drum's rusting cable and, to the right of the drum house, there are the ruins of a small building that was most probably the drum controller's crib house.

Merely by picking up a fallen brick or two from those lying around, one can see by the name Martin moulded into them that the building was not constructed in the Phillips' era at Lee Moor. After leaving this site to descend the incline, a small viaduct was crossed, the structure constructed of three stone buttresses spanned by a wooden base for the track to run on. Although only the buttresses remain today, it is still an interesting and well-built feature to look at. Unlike the Lee Moor/Torycombe incline, this descent drops in various gradients and, although the drop is twenty feet more, the steepness is lessened by the one-and-a-quarter miles to the bottom. Part way down the track bed, one can see discarded granite sleeper sets and the rotting remains of wooden ones. Also on the left-hand side of the track, half hidden among tree branches and thick undergrowth, is a tall post. This item of wood-work along with others long since gone, carried a wire for the bell warning signals situated at both ends of the gradient. These allowed the top and bottom men to signal to one another when their wagons were ready to roll.

A Martins brick.

Farther on the track bed widens; this was the midway passing point where the track was double. Here set into the right-hand bank can be seen still standing the rusting remains of a small corrugated iron hut. The man stationed here was there to make sure that all was well as the trucks passed one another, and if not he could also activate the warning bell to the brakesman up at the drum house.

At midway, the bellman's shelter.

If those interested are really keen enough, they can with some searching spot a roller almost completely submerged by soil and leaves that have been washed down from further up the incline during heavy rain. Not far from where the track bed narrows again, a forest road is crossed, and just beyond this can be seen a twisted yard or two of rusting cable wire. The track bed now descends through a quagmire of dank and musty wetness in a cutting of almost gorge-like proportions. Wellington boots are recommended for a majority of this section for one wrong step can sink a foot out of sight. However, it is a beautiful place where sunlight rarely gets through a canopy of beech. There are various types of fern dotted everywhere, and fallen trees lying at different angles, some to climb over, others to squeeze under. Ivy cascades down the steep sides of the cutting and pendulates from nearly every convenient branch. Where this lovely feature peters out can be seen an unruly pile of granite sets.

The next point of interest which is only a few yards away, is the viaduct spanning the Plympton–to–Roborough road at Plymbridge. To view it, it is best to walk down to the road via a path opposite the granite sets. The viaduct when first constructed was of the trestle type with the wooden props standing on granite plinths of about five feet high. It can only be assumed that the trestles were done away with and the stonework built up to the top when the high-sided road vehicles came this way on a regular basis, when the angled stays of the woodwork would have been at risk of being damaged.

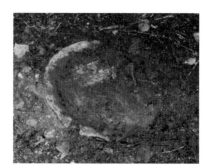

Tramway guide roller buried in the grounds of the tramway bed.

From the viaduct, the foot of the incline is only yards away, and here the track bed widens. This, like the section at the drum house and the midway point, was to accommodate a double track. It is while the track bed is at this width, that it crosses the Cann Quarry Canal for the first time. This little waterway, now looking in a sorry state, carried slate away from the quarry before the quarry's tramline was built.

Just a little further on, on the left, under a canopy mostly of oak, is the dilapidated remains of the stables where the tramway horses on this section of the line lodged at the end of a hard day's work. After leaving the stables the following morning a pair would take the strain on a set of (normally) four loaded trucks and begin their first pull of the day, the linked convoy re-crossing the canal to join the track of the Cann Quarry line. Placed to one side along here can be seen old slate sleepers discarded when they were replaced by the long wooden ones. It is along here that the line met up with Mr Bampton's South Devon & Tavistock Railway, running along on its left-hand side, until crossing it to run on its right. Here the tramway remained for just under a mile until turning right for Weighbridge Cottage and Girder Bridge that spans the tidal Plym. The line then followed the river for a few yards to where the Longbridge carried the old A38.

If a tram driver from William's time on his way to the wharf arrived at this spot today, he would stare in disbelief with mouth agape at the scene in front of him and slip back into yester-

The deep cutting near Plym Bridge.

What remains of the stables at Plym Bridge.

year with severe traumatic shock. Today's architects have created giants from the drawing board, with office blocks, hotels, huge flyovers, roundabouts of huge proportions, superstores, and automobiles in tremendous volumes going where traffic lights send them.

Moving away from Longbridge, the tram would have run in a straight line until it reached the area where the Marsh Mills Hotel now stands. It was round about here that it junctioned with the Plymouth Dartmoor Tramway that arrived from the Forder Valley direction. After crossing the little Shallaford Brook (a stream now hidden from view by various buildings and road projects) it turned left for a few hundred yards until nearing the Plym estuary where it turned right and met Mr Brunel's line after his bridge over the river Tamar was completed, to run into Cornwall. The tramway ran along on the right-hand side of the distinguished man's iron thoroughfare, until crossing it near the entrance to today's Laira Junction. From here it followed a straight path, running parallel to what is now the long stretch of the Embankment. Nearing the end of the straight, the horses hauled the trucks round a long left-hand curve before a right turn took them on to Laira Wharf and the end of their outward journey.

William Phillips enjoyed only a couple of years of seeing production being delivered refreshingly easily down to the wharf for shipment, before living life on the very edge caught up with him. A duodenal ulcer eating away at his health eventually took him to his maker and he passed away in the summer of 1861. Sadly his epitaph, for establishing a manufacturing giant on the bleak south-western edge of Dartmoor that has supported thousands of lives, and lined many a pocket, remains unwritten. All we see today for his effort is the state of what remains of the tramway, his adit or level, still being utilised, and a few bricks lying around with his name moulded into them. A very sad memorial for such an adventurous man.

If life for William was uncomfortable with some of his fellow directors, it was double the trouble for his son, John, when he stepped into his shoes to manage the company. John was only twenty-five when he took the reins, and although he absorbed the working knowledge his father passed on to him, he never inherited his spirit, his boldness or the mettle for confrontation. Before William was cold in his grave, John was being dictated to, criticised in the way he was running things, even though he never swayed from his father's production methods. Why should he when they were so successful? Successful enough for others to invest their money in the project, yet those who could not have their own way with his father, were certainly going to with John. William's death left the young man in an extremely vulnerable position, for although he and his mother still held shares in the company, he was now totally at the mercy of those who were not fond of his father, as John's name was not included on William's 99-year lease when signed in 1835. The land was now back in the hands of the Morley family, leaving John merely to be employed as the manager. The directors who knew little about clay production, looked upon him as inadequate and interfered with his everyday working of the place; their ultimate aim was to be rid of him and get their own man in to run things.

By the end of November, only a few months after William had passed away, the directors were looking to Cornwall for advice. They found it in the shape of a Mr Pease, who was encouraged to come to Lee Moor and cast an eye over the production and working methods used there. His first criticism was of the Torycombe complex, thinking it extravagant and many of the buildings a waste of good money. He was so critical of production methods that he advised a Mr Clements, a director who often had his judgemental finger up to the knuckle in meddling, to send young Phillips to Cornwall to see how production should be carried out.

Whatever John took in on his visit still didn't satisfy his directors and they soon requested that Mr Pease should return to Lee Moor and judge the worth of what Phillips had learned. In their eyes he had taken in nothing, and letters from one director to another describing John's shortcomings kept the mailman busy. 'There was too much mica in the finished product, and lack of detailed reports of the workings,' they said.

In another letter John was described 'as being willful and obstinate, and would not be surprised if those working under him took any notice of his instructions,' and the letter went on to criticise John's 'objections at the outset of piecework.' Another letter read, 'I begin to be afraid that it is hopeless to expect to get any good out of him.'

Poor John must have wondered what sort of hell he had landed himself in. This most uncomfortable situation did eventually get to him, and in a letter dated 11 January 1862, one of his adversaries portrayed John's distressing circumstances to the Earl, an extract reading: 'about ten days ago he was too unwell to do his work, after being absent for two or three days, he then went missing and did not return home one night, a search was made and he was found the next day at the inn at Ivybridge, where he stayed the night. The doctor recommended a complete change, he was in fact nearly out of his mind.' By 23 June, just twelve months after his father passed away, John, along with his mother and two sisters, had left the moor and were living at No.1 Matlock Terrace, Torquay.

The directors of the Lee Moor Porcelain Clay Company had wished for Mr Pease to take over as the manager, but he no doubt thought of being treated in the same fashion as John and turned the job down. Yet he did recommend a Mr Harris who accepted the position, along with the responsibility of being the Secretary, all for a salary of £120 a year, a saving for the company of £180, for young John Phillips drew £300. The directors hadn't changed, they still treated the new man with total disrespect in not thinking his position important enough for him to reside in the spacious house and grounds of Lee Moor House.

John Phillips did not dwell on the nightmarish experience for long and was soon looking along various avenues where making a living was concerned. Up until now, clay had been his life and he set up business as a clay merchant in the ball clay country of Newton Abbot. After a while, like most businessmen, this wasn't enough to sate his ambitions and, in his search to expand, he signed a lease to become the proprietor of the Aller Vale Pottery. Here he produced similar products to those that he and his father had produced at Lee Moor, in the shape of bricks, clome pipes chimney pots and tiles. This he occupied himself with until advancing to finer terracotta art ware, some of which can be seen at the Royal Albert Memorial Museum in Exeter, and his eventual expertise in this field gave him licence to lecture on the subject. The man that Lee Moor cast aside became a prominent member of local society, a local historian and anti-quarian and a leading member of the Devonshire Association.

Meanwhile back at Lee Moor, Mr Harris' reports tell of disappointing yields of kaolin. In fact the results were so bad that the men who knew very little about what they had invested their money in, quickly put the lease up for tender. Had they, in their utter blindness, pushed John out to leave the works at the mercy of someone who knew very little more than they, or, was there something a little more crafty going on? Did the Cornish pull the wool over someone's eyes? After all, if the yield at Lee Moor was so low, how come William Phillips was so happy with it, and why did three prominent Cornish clay producers nigh on trample over one another for the right to work it and, within four years, had almost doubled the Phillips' output.

John Lovering and Edward Stocker were beaten to it by the Martin family, Rebecca and her three sons, William Langdon, Edward and Thomas, from St Austell. Lee Moor Clay Works had its name changed again and the name of Martin appeared on the sign at the entrance of the works. William Martin being the eldest son ran the organisation with his mother, still fragilely holding the reins until she died just twelve months after the Lee Moor complex came under her control.

After Rebecca passed away, William Martin posted himself at Lee Moor House to run the Devonshire side of the business, leaving his two siblings to handle the pits in Cornwall. His intention of living at Lee Moor House is confirmed when the Methodists of the little settlement voiced concern as to whether a room at the big house would still be available for worship, as it was while the Phillips' family resided there. A letter from the Reverend Edwin Blake of St Austell, written before Rebecca passed away, and sent to a J. Loutit, a fellow Minister who preached at Lee Moor, assured him that his congregation had nothing to fear from Mr Martin. Part of the letter reads:

> *The family has been Methodistically trained and Mr Martin's mother is a member of our society. The family usually worship with us, so that I have no doubt of your being allowed to continue your stated services at Morley Works. William Martin visits the works twice every week and will do so throughout the winter, but in spring and summer it is his intention to reside there. I will speak to Mrs Martin whose wish the sons will properly obey.*

Once William Martin stamped his mark on that which William Phillips had established, he began to upgrade and within a couple of years smoke and steam from coal-fired dries rose from the Torycombe Valley. All the buildings Mr Pease thought too extravagant were being utilised. The kilns, were pan-like in fashion, and those that Martins' first introduced to the Torycome would have been about forty-feet long by ten wide and eighteen inches deep, with a firebrick and tile floor. Below the full length was a flue of more-or-less the same dimensions, at one end was situated the furnace and at the other, a chimney. The clay to be dried would have been settled to a consistency of a thick sloppy gravy in a stone-lined pit adjacent to the kiln. The clay would have been let on to the floor of the kiln, by opening the hatchway of the pit, and the material was then spread over the floor of the pan using 'shivers' until the desired depth of usually a few inches was reached. Once the furnace was roaring away, the clay began to progressively dry over a period of about a week, with the material nearest the immediate source of heat obviously ready to be shovelled out first.

Unlike the old air dries of William Phillips' day, this system reduced drying times from months to mere days, thus increasing production by huge margins. If there were any doubts as to whether the Morley family was doing well out of the Martins' venture at Lee Moor, 1867 tells us quite categorically that they were, for this was the year that the Earl purchased the land of Cholwich Town for £10 000 from the Parkers of Delamore at Cornwood and leased it to the Martins to enable the Saltram coffers to swell that little bit more from the extra dues from further sales.

Like William Phillips before him William Martin certainly did not allow the grass to grow under his feet, for it was around this time that he began developing the area of Whitehill Yeo for the purpose of clay extraction, but unlike poor William Phillips, this family could extend their boundaries with the backing of their Cornish profits. To the layman it must have looked as if the Martins had the midas touch; even the demise of the Bottle Hill Mine was to be to their advantage. The mine's closure in 1877 allowed the clay

Bottle Hill mine leat meeting the Spanish Lake.

The Torycombe Valley in full production.

company to adopt all the water from the tinners' leat that ran around the contours from the Plym below Ditsworthy Warren House. When the water along the Phillips' leat ceased to flow is not known, one could surmise that it could well have been about this time, for why hang on to a four-mile waterway with the regular maintenance it warranted to ensure a constant flow, when the one adopted is half its length and delivers a greater volume? The clay works, had tapped the mine leat from the early days of William Phillips' time: a sketch dated 1837 showing a leat flowing from Great Hill above Cholwich Town to Small Hanger China Clay Works also clearly shows the flow from the mine leat to the works at lower Lee Moor.

For twenty-three years William Martin had been in control at Lee Moor before he died leaving a legacy that William Phillips must have always dreamt of: three pits in full production and the brick, tile and pipeworks expanded considerably. Added to the Phillips' cottages at Sunderland, Boringdon, Shade and Chapel Terrace, were the rows of Blackalder, Hillside, Broadoaks and the old Phillips' air dries converted into dwellings. Within twelve months of William Langdon passing away, his brother Edward died leaving Thomas in full control.

It was getting on towards the 1880s when Thomas had thoughts of developing a works a little to the north-east of the prehistoric stone rows on Wotter Common. The idea took fruition only for it to be the Martins' one-and-only failure on the moor. Half-a-mile of branch line was laid to it from the summit of the Torycombe incline, but the pit was extremely difficult to work. There were seams of good quality, but these were outnumbered by those of unacceptable grades. The method of washing at the time was ideal, it was easy to be selective, steering to and running a stream of water down over the quality wanted was simple, but very little could be done to prevent its deterioration when rainwater came in from all angles. Thomas gave the pit plenty of time to prove itself economically viable but eventually surrendered to its problems and closed it down after almost ten years of perseverence. Another of Thomas' innovations, was, in the early months of 1899, to introduce to the Lee Moor Tramway two steam locomotives. One worked the line at Lee Moor above the Torycombe incline, the other below it to the summit of the Cann Wood incline, leaving horses still employed between Plymbridge and Laira Wharf.

Thomas had lived thirteen years into the twentieth century when he died at the age of 79. Seven years before he met his maker he came to the conclusion that Lee Moor pit was in need of another adit; he thought that the pit was far too deep to be operating as it was, so he made the calculated decision to terminate the employment of the waterwheel and flat rod system of elevating the clay stream one hundred or so feet up to the old Phillips' adit. The new one was nowhere near as steep as that of the one being made redundant, in fact it arrived out into the Torycombe almost beside it. The adits were normally cut to a height of about five feet with the width more-or-less the same, but this could vary by several inches throughout its length. Depending on its gradient, the floor was stepped every so many yards by using lengths of timber laid across the floor with their ends wedged into the sides, these spaces were filled naturally by a conglomeration of materials dropping out of the clay stream as it ran down through and out into the open. This simple idea that not only retarded the speed of the flow but also prevented it from gouging out the floor. In more recent times the 'new' adit has collapsed and once again the stream delivered up to the Phillips' adit, but these days by pump, on its journey to the ultra-modern processing plants in the Torycombe Valley.

The last of the Martins to have control at Lee Moor was Thomas's son Reginald; his other son Claude joined the armed forces and was killed in action during the First World War. In 1919, six years after Reginald took control, the Martins' name disappeared from the sign at the works' entrance, when the amalgamation of the Martins, the West of England China Stone & Clay Co, the Great Beam Clay Company under Medland Stocker, and Walter Sessions North Cornwall China Clays, created a single company English China Clay. Thirteen years later, in 1913, the company ECLP was born when English China Clay united with Lovering China Clays Ltd and H.D. Pochin & Co Ltd.

Mr A.D. Selleck whose father C.R.M. Selleck, was a well-respected Captain at Lee Moor, tells of his time living in the village near and after the end of the 1800s.

Situated as it was, three miles respectively from Cornwood to the East and Shaugh Prior to the east, five miles from Plympton to the south with the wide open spaces of Dartmoor to the north, it will be realised how complete was Lee Moor's isolation in the days when the only means of transport were horse drawn vehicles. All food supplies had to be brought by road. Martins traded with the employees for a time, but eventually a Co-operative store was opened, sponsored by the men themselves and run by a committee of men, whose names are remembered today. The Plymouth Co-operative Society ran the business.

Lee Moor was a wonderful place to live in those days; well over a hundred children attended the Wesleyan Sunday School with a staff of over twenty teachers taking bi-weekly turns 10 to 11 a.m. and 2.30 to 4 p.m. Over sixty men could be seen at the morning service at 11 o'clock and at the evening service often 150 people crowded into the little chapel to hear the preacher who was usually a 'local'. We had a regular Minister about once a month. The choir stalls were always filled, and did they sing! There was eight in the bass section, four tenors, dear old Simon Lavers with his violin, and all those wonderful girl trebles. I was privileged at a very early age to sing in the alto section with Maud Manhire, Bessie Loram and others, all joyously egged along by Mr

Bettes the choirmaster and Mrs Bettes the organist. Sunday School Anniversary services were a real festival of praises with the chapel packed to capacity: aisles, pulpits steps, choir steps, every inch of space occupied and often an overflow of scores of people too late to get inside. What a day! All the little 'tackers', boys and girls, the older lads and lassies and the courting couples, parents and friends from the surrounding villages, all united to swell the glad song. Most of the parents contrived to fit us little ones out in new suits and dresses for that day. What a show: picture hats for the girls and usually a wide stiff collar stuck under our chins for the boys. I remember we sang, 'Brightly gleam our banner pointing to the sky.'

Anniversary Monday and June Tay (tea) was the great social event of the year. The chidren paraded through the village. Sitting after sitting of people would satisfy their appetites and tell their tales. Then the younger ones would go down to the green just above Torycombe Gate to indulge in games – 'kiss in the ring' and 'two's and three's' were the first favourites, and many a romance had a beginning in the twilight of June Tay day.

We youngsters would strain our eyes to see the various arrivals [of entertainments]. Somebody from Torycombe would report that they had seen cheapjack, penny dip, coconut shies, Oliver's Sweet Stall outfit, or Lions with his fruit stall, billy dip in later years, someone else with the hobby-horse, another with what was called 'ladies' teasers' (tubes made of lead filled with water) with which the more adventurous 'roughs' of about nine would bombard the 'kiss in the ring', needless to say obstructing kissing operations.

Sad to say, it was a much-depleted choir that gathered for the Monday evening service, especially in the soprano and alto section (I learned why as the years rolled on). These village Methodist tea drinks had to be experienced to be appreciated. How we looked forward to the time when we were old enough to be appointed by the Sunday School Committee to carry the hot water in those tin kettles around to the various tea tables at which the women presided. These scenes were repeated in a lesser measure at Whitsun and Easter, Band of Hope and Mission Band teas, then Harvest Festival tea, What a glorious time this was. Saturday afternoon and evening, the fruit and vegetables, flowers etc., would be received by the ladies who had just the knack of arranging so beautifully those gifts of our Heavenly Father. I still retain the memory of the aroma from the apples, pears and the other fruit and flowers.

As we have already stated, Lee Moor was then an isolated and self-contained community, most of the workmen who lived in the twin villages of Lee Moor and Torycombe had their garden and allotments. Almost every householder kept pigs and poultry, many others kept a cow. The Dartmoor pony was also bred and kept in quite large numbers. Nearly everybody possessed a quite smart pony and turned out in either dog cart or jingle. In the old days it was quite an occasion when the farmers, led by farmer Tom Selleck, drove the pony 'drift' off Shaugh Moor to Neil Gate, and then corralled them in one of the fields where identification by the various owners took place. Many scores of these animals were then driven by the Lee Moor owners back to the village for the brand-

ing mark to be applied to those which were turned out on to the moor again for breeding, some being retained for sale to dealers who came to buy them for use in the coal mines etc.

August Bank Holiday for many years was a great day for Lee Moor. The local pony show took place in a field known as Company Park. Classes for trotting, riding or driving, would be well filled and competition keen, and some outstanding animals were always to be seen despite, of course, the fact that a fair proportion were something like Modbury Dancing, not very neat but strong. The musical programme on these occasions was provided by Tinker Bray's Band. The Bombardon, as we were told it was called, the big bass, was blown by Tinker himself, his son George, the cornet, his son Ned the trombone. These were all outstanding performers. Tinker could always be depended on to produce that deep resonant bass note from the bowels of that weird instrument which had been bruised and dented over most of its surface, making any attempt at polishing impossible. Although some of his Lee Moor critics insisted that he was sometimes scat behind the rest. One of the most fascinating things to me, was to watch Ned Bray blowing the trombone. How marvellously his cheeks would stretch, he seemed to distend his facial features to such an extent that we small boys would wonder when he would burst, but he would go on serenely producing those notes. George Bray was a great hero because every small boy wanted to blow the cornet and, as we listened to him, he always seemed to come in at the right time to save an awkward situation, and to us he was only second to Gabriel. There were of course, quite a range of other players filling in the unity. There is a story told that on one of the very rare occasions the band was engaged away from home to supply music at the celebrations at Plympton, of the local Friendly Society. The big drum was played by Bill MacBean who was small of stature. He went on flogging the drum for quite a distance towards Plympton St Mary Bridge while the rest of the band turned left at Dark Street Lane, but I could not vouch for the varacity of this report. However, Tinker Brays Band was quite an institution and the Band of the Royal Marines could not have been more important to us.

After completing his training at Lee Moor and working alongside other members of his family, including his father-in-law, Captain John Diamond Cobbledick, C.R.H. Selleck's interest in his work soon took him through the management structure to second-in-command. Seeming contented and satisfied with his lot, he courageously took on a tremendous challenge.

At the turn of the century, there was a greatly increased demand for China Clay and investors were keen to acquire 'Setts'. The Lee Moor group was producing ever-increasing quantities. The main Lee Moor Pit, Cholwichtown Pit and the new Whitehill Yeo Pit was in full production, but Wotter Pit had been abandoned.

In September 1901, my father re-opened Wotter which caused rather more than a 'nine day wonder' that he should have the audacity to re-start a works declared uneconomic, redundant and worked-out by his former employers; they said he was heading for disaster and they were nearly right.

The epic struggle began. Father, Chris, C.R.H. or Cap'n Crissy as he was variously known, packed his belongings on the carts behind Shamrock, the old grey mare, and Tommy's horse, Tommy being a family friend for many years after, and trundled over Highboro Hill together with nine of us six boys and three girls. Mother who was the most wonderful homemaker soon settled us in at Wotter House, for a time we shared the house with the Elliot family who went to Perks Farm, Shaugh Prior. My father, who soon found his slender capital stretched to capacity, acquired a second-hand traction engine and trucks from a local firm of brickmakers to haul the clay to the railway station.

A few other oddments of equipment came, then with about four or five men and his own family, he got down to the job. Then trouble came on trouble. As already indicated, china clay production depends on adequate supplies of water. The water for the group of Cholwichtown, Whitehill Yeo Lee Moor and Wotter was drawn from the upper reaches of the Cad (Plym) near Trowlesworthy. We found the lifeline was cut, the stream had been diverted at Lee Moor. Means were then devised to collect water on our own limited watershed, ponds had to be constructed to try to meet the situation. Our next problem was difficulties of transport; the roads over Dartmoor in those days were little more than bridle paths and to drive a traction engine laden with ten ton trucks of clay was asking too much, and we were thus landed into trouble with Plympton RDC. Our local neighbours also. In seeking alternative routes we tried the roads to Bickleigh, Cornwood and Plympton railway stations (the law required us to employ a man with a red flag to walk in front). I remember one memorable morning going out to play from school at Lee Moor, when we all rushed out to the road to see our engine complete with guard and red flag coming down the road toward Torycombe. Quite an impressive crowd had gathered when 'Cap'n' Bray of Martins, under orders, forbade the driver, my brother Chris, to proceed any further over that section of the road; but necessity called for desperate measures and after what was mostly unintelligible conversation, Chris, naughty boy, after opening the cylinder drains which enveloped the 'Cap'n' in a cloud of steam, drove on his desperate journey.

'Cap'n', when forced to retire, was heard to remark, 'they do'in it in defiance', and needless to say the name of that engine from that time, was Defiance. However, a few years afterwards the two families celebrated the marriage of my brother Chris to 'Cap'n' Bray's daughter, Mabel, so time healed the breach. We then stuck to the Cornwood road, but what a shambles! My father now had to face a hostile District Council, and when challenged as to what he proposed to do about this four-to-five miles of road, he promptly replied that he proposed to repair it. To say the least, this seemed an impossible task, but we tackled it and literally thousands of tons of stone, stent as it is locally called, were raised by us, hauled and rolled in by our engines over this section from Wotter to Cornwood free of charge to the RDC.

With such teriffic strain on our traction engines, breakdowns were frequent and it seemed as if the limit must soon be reached. One evening on his way home through Lee Moor my father was led to go and see bedridden Jack Quest. Jack had not been able to meet at the Sunday morning 8 o'clock prayer meeting for some time, so father felt it his duty to see him. Jack relates the conversation:

'Well Chris, how is it with you?'

'Not too good Jack, bit of a headache. Engine broke down today.'

'You're going through it Chris, wish I could help. Never mind Chris – (reaching for his bible) – read the 37th psalm.'

So he read as far as verse 25, 'I have been young, and now I am old, yet have I not seen the righteous forsaken nor his seed begging bread.'

Said Chris to me some time after – 'I don't know exactly why but he seemed to have a lump in his throat and couldn't read on for a little while.'

I knew and we all knew, that things had become so tight that we had not the power to stave off poverty much longer. Frugality and thrift had been the order for five long years – but he read on, prayed on and worked on he was not forsaken and those who knew him well, know that his seed are not begging bread. But, how dark was that hour before the dawn, only those who went through it, will ever know. We, the members of the family, were variously employed on jobs where we could contribute most to the common good. My brother, John, trained at Lee Moor in all branches of the smith's trade in addition to making necessary ironworks for the development of the works, continued to earn something extra by making and repairing implements and shoeing horses for local farmers; there was no eight hour limit to our days. Chris had to spend most of his time as a mechanical engineer, repairing engines, designing gadgets to make things run more smoothly on the works. Will, at fifteen years of age, went on the traction as driver. I have known him work the twenty-four hours round the clock if it happen we had a cargo boat waiting.

Our problems piled up as we proceeded. One of our particular problems at this time was how best to use the water at our disposal. The old Cornish way was to let the water trickle over the top of the stope (clay bed), having broken the surface with dubbers, at an angle of about 45 degrees from the bottom of the pit to the top edge of the stope. One man would break a strake of, say, ten to fifteen feet in width. We found at Wotter that our stope was getting very thin, and the clay touch not friable, so the water would run clear instead of taking away the clay in solution.

My father, by this time had been elected to Plympton Council, came home from Plympton having made a few observations on the pressure needed to send water from a fire hose to the top of a burning house, expressed the opinion to my brothers that water pressure was the answer to our washing problems.

C.R.H. Selleck's son, Chris, the engineer of the family, soon got to work on the idea using the same stream in gravity but feeding it through a two-and-a-half-inch pipeline. The experiment was successful and the Selleck family had developed a new way of washing clay. Within two years, instead of gravity they employed pumps to increase the pressure even further. Within the first five years the Sellecks had pioneered a method of clay washing still in use today, in the twenty-first century, although the company, now Sellecks & Sons Ltd, was still struggling to make ends meet:

Martins' old works at Wotter.

Clay tanks, now filled in for safety reasons.

Then suddenly on a Sunday morning, came the answer to our prayers. For some unaccountable reason to us 'Cap'n' Chrissy was called out from the Sunday Morning Service at Lee Moor. Was someone ill? What had happened?

It happened on this wise: Messers, Punchard, Stewart and Vivien, three successful speculators in Malayan rubber, were looking for a china clay sett and wished to do business with my father on the spot. He respectfully but firmly refused to do this on the Lord's Day, but arranged to meet them on the morrow. They met, the die was cast, the deal was made, and the new era for Wotter began in 1906: Selleck & Sons Ltd went into voluntary liquidation and the Dartmoor China Clay Co, was formed.

This marked the beginning of a great advancement. China clay was found to have much wider potential uses than merely as a filling agent in cotton manufacturing, papermaking, or the actual making of china or pottery. Chemical research proved the possibility of the production of colloidal clays which were in ready demand. Wotter was soon producing this particular brand in this field known as 'Catalpo'.

C.R.H. Selleck & Sons were installed as managers for the newly-formed company. Suddenly, using A.D. Selleck's words, 'there was a great burst of activity'. As the pit extended production, so it became necessary to streamline the effort and energy put into it, by getting the product nearer to the main roads and docks for shipping. By 1910 plans were in hand for a letter to be sent to Lord Morley's Agent, asking for a meeting to explain their idea of laying a pipeline from Wotter Works to somewhere nearer to sea level. Their thinking was for their clay to run in suspension for about six miles whilst descending around eight-hundred feet to the kilns the company hoped to build somewhere near Cann Quarry. The plan came to fruition and the clay ran along the pipes, but just that little bit further, to Marsh Mills, where clay drying is still carried out today. Although the pipeline venture was successful, money was, however, also readily invested in a little more modern form of transport, for some clay still had to be hauled along the lanes to Cornwood station.

Such was the increase in production, the company felt obliged to build cottages to house and nurture a stable workforce; with this development the village of Wotter was born, all through the courage of a man who had tremendous faith in himself.

Turning off the road into the eastern end of Wotter, the scant remains of old workings can be seen directly in front of the observer's view. The surviving granite stonework is all that is left of settling tanks, and kiln, most of the upper structure of the buildings have been demolished for safety reasons, leaving very little for the inquisitive eye to ponder over. Although the buildings were used by the Selleck's, they really are a sad epitaph of Thomas Martin's exploits at Wotter. Nearly all the tanks are partly filled with clay waste and an almost impregnable density of gorse. The clay pit itself is hidden behind the conical waste heaps of its working era, and now giant machines from our modern age are creating a waste heap to more than dwarf them, gradually tipping and pushing the developing monstrous pile from a northerly direction to infill the pit which is now only a quarter of its proportions when abandoned.

Water from the flooded, shrinking expanse flows over a weir which more-or-less reforms the Wotter Brook, and following the little stream down its steep descent, one has to cross the road near the eastern entrance to the village. No sign of any old clay workings can be seen under the oaks of North Wood, until crossing the brook at a convenient spot about fifty yards downstream and climbing the even steeper banking on the other side.

When on the top, one sees what appears to be a secret hidden from the world, except from the meandering walker who happens to come across it in their wanderings. The scene is very much reminiscent of a scaled-down industrial version of Machu Picchu, the lost City of the Incas of Peru. Here is the true remains of the Selleck's time in the clay industry. Here can be found the adit that once arrived from the pit. Water still trickles from it, but only from somewhere within its pitch black interior. There are mica runs now shrouded in moss and grass, and rusting broken sections of their plug mechanism still lying in their operating positions. The runs lead to three cone-shaped tanks lined in a row, sunk in the ground. These are the primary tanks of the complex, shaped like nothing else on the moor, they are about thirty feet in diameter across their tops and taper to a depth of about twelve feet. In these, the clay was allowed to settle to a certain density. Whilst doing so the water was run off through a series of pin holes running down one side of the cone. These holes would have had plugs placed in them and taken out again to let the water off as the clay dropped out of its liquid suspension and settled to a soupy consistency. From here the water ran into another tank where it was pumped back up to a reservoir ready for its rotation in the clay washing system again. Once the clay in the cones reached the desired density, it was let out of the bottom to run into much larger tanks. Again there were three but differing in shape; they are about the same depth as the cones but are oblong. Again they have the sloping sides making for easy dispensing from these tanks. The white slurry, that was never allowed to anywhere near solidify, ran down through its six-mile pipeline to the kilns at Marsh Mills, and there dried ready for easier delivery to the dock and the customer.

Up on the south-eastern slopes of Crownhill Down can be found what remains of Small Hanger China Clay Works. Worked for eighty-three years by the Olver family until its closure in 1952, the two pits and their related waste heaps are now losing their whiteness, as all around gradually steals back to nature. A winding lane takes the interested to all of its production areas. A starting point in the search for what can be seen is best taken at Drakeland, a small hamlet a mile or so above the village of Hemerdon. Just before crossing a little streamlet, turn up an unkempt lane to the right, and a little way up, again on the right, a boundary hedge topped with wire netting runs uphill beneath a canopy of trees.

Wotter pit adit exit.

Mica plug lever system.

Primary tanks, the first of three.

Primary tank's pin-holes.

The third settling tank.

After ducking and weaving to avoid thorns and brambles, scratched and pricked, one comes across a chimney stack still in remarkably good condition. This old marvel of masonry is the remains of a worn-out kiln that finance could not be found to repair. To the left, as the walk up to the stack is in progress, are the almost unrecognisable, even to the most enthusiastic of field researchers, sparse remains of settling tanks and pans hidden beneath a conglomeration of ground-hugging bushes and trees. The air dries, that took the place of the kiln, were situated a little further uphill and, like the kiln, are now merely in the memories or photographs of those that knew of them when they were standing.

Back down in the lane, and a few more yards on, a T-junction is met, and the way forward to the next point of interest is straight on. Almost opposite a house on the left, again hidden from view by clothes-tearing brambles and thorns, as well as nasty stinging nettles, are the much more substantial remains of another set of settling tanks and pans. The lane from here carries on for another couple of hundred yards before a gate and open ground comes into view. On the right, set in its own grounds is Clay Moor House, built by the Olver family for themselves in 1881. The pit that earned them the revenue to afford such accommodation can be found among a wild labyrinth of gorse bushes, but anyone expecting to see the old dwelling house of Small Hanger Farm, will be disappointed, its dilapidated and apparently dangerous state persuaded the present owners of the complex to raise it to the ground, leaving only the sorrowful state of the barn still standing.

Would-be visitors should always take care to ensure that private property is not invaded and permission must always be sought.

Chimney and air dries where nubs of clay stacked high can be seen.

According to the sketch already referred to of Crownhill Down dated 1837, someone had already begun prospecting for clay at Small Hanger. Who it was, delving into the ground there I do not know, but I am aware that fifteen years later, Edward Blake, a ball clay merchant from Newton Abbot was dispensing with his interest in the place. An indenture dated 17 November 1852, tells of how he is ridding himself of the eighty-two acres, one rood and twenty eight perches or, thereabouts, of Small Hanger.

Seventeen years later, almost to the day, a 'Fredric Bishop of the Mount in the Parish of Stoke upon Trent in the County of Stafford' got rid of it to John Olver of St Austell.

During John's early days at Small Hanger, more than a third of the 38 people who worked for him were casual labour, there when they were needed, eager to earn that little extra to supplement a meagre living standard. They were there with a foot in the door, waiting hopefully for the chance to be taken on permanently when an old hand's lifespan came to a close. Such evidence can be found when the wage record book is carefully perused.

Position of Small Hangar works on Crownhill Down.

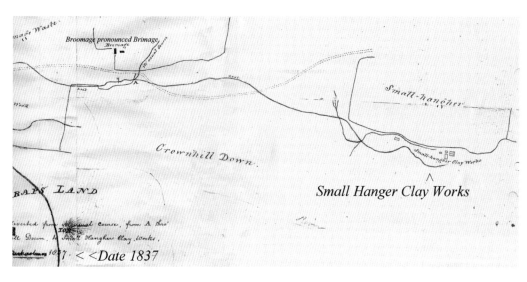

Broomage pronounced Brimage

Small-hanger

Crownhill Down.

RABIT LAND

Small Hanger Clay Works

<<Date 1837

JOHN OLVER & SONS
China Clay Merchants.
PLYMPTON.
WORKS. DEVON.
HEADON.
HEMERDON AND
SMALLHANGER.

John Olver's business card.

John Olver's pay records book.

John and his wife, Mary, produced a family of three girls and four boys. All the boys when their academic years were over, were employed at the works. John (junior) the eldest, who died in 1882 at the age of twenty-five in Denver, Colorado, started first, followed by Fred and Arnold. All three worked alongside the labourers in all winds and weather, earning the same money and arriving home with the same dirt ground into their hands. Another son, Wilcie, wanted nothing to do with the trade and opted to find his own way in life.

It is hard to believe that children were on the payroll of the clay producers at such a young age; even John Olver's own sons began working at least a couple of years before their teens were reached. But this was during the reign of Victoria and not so long after Dickens wrote about the perils of child labour.

The first mention of Arnold, John's youngest son, in the list of labour, is in 1883. Being born in 1872 means he was only eleven years old when he started work. Looking at the amount of labour John Olver employed makes one wonder where they all earned their wages. Compared to the Lee Moor complex, Small Hanger was small, still only in its infant stages of development. However it can be seen where their labour was spent when one finds Headon as well as Hemerdon printed, along with Small Hanger, on John's business card of the day. His wage record books, clearly confirms his involvement with Hemerdon, for there he operated the mica kiln at Galva between February 1881 and March 1883.

John Olver.

The men were also employed to do tasks other than those that were of the norm for a clay worker. Here they could bargain with the boss over a price for the job to be done. For instance a John Mumford, who was a Jack of all trades, negotiated a price of one shilling a perch for wall building in the month of March 1880, earning himself fifteen shillings on top of his clay work job for which he did nineteen days at two shillings and eight pence a day. He also did a bit of paving work for three shillings and six pence, earning himself a total of three pounds nine shillings and four pence for the month. Another example, in the July of the same year, Ned Collings went home with a smile on his face, for he had earned a whopping great eleven pounds six shillings and eight pence, for twelve days clay working. He negotiated three separate prices for taking off three different types of burden. He priced a seven-fathom section at two shillings and eight pence per fathom, another section of forty-six-and-a-half fathoms at three shillings a fathom, and a ten and a quarter stretch at three shillings and six pence per fathom.

Other tasks undertaken for extra pay included breaking waste (rough ground) in order to provide better pasture, and harvesting stone from off the moor for walling. The building of Claymoor House and the extension to tiny Small Hanger Farm House made use of this material, with men assisting in both projects. Small Hanger, with its outbuildings and fields were let by John Olver to Arnold for thirty pounds a year.

Fred left home sometime in the 1890s, hoping to start his own business back in Cornwall where the family came from. He found a deposit of clay to excavate, only to find his capital was a little short of that needed. He was a married man with a wife and children to find for, and with his research done on the cost of production, sales, transport and expected profit he wrote with a little trepidation to his father for a financial leg-up. When he opened the pages of his father's reply, he was more than a little disappointed; his chin must have dropped to the floor with a thud. After settling down to gather his thoughts, he wrote in reply:

> *Dear Father*
> *I thank you for your letter, I told my wife when I wrote it what the answer would be, I only asked you to become security for me for £100 for about eighteen months, I didn't ask you for any money, but never mind I shall try some of my friends. One thing I shall not have to thank you for it, I daresay I shall manage to pull through somehow...*
>
> *...Yours is a peculiar letter in the first part you go on to say that clay works are no good nobody will lend money on them and advise me not to touch mine here, in the second part you say you intend opening a new works on Small Hanger, if clay works are such poor speculation, why do you want to open a new one or be it to any one else to work. You know and I know that at present time it is one of the best speculations in the County...*
>
> *...You offer me 30/- a week to come home with you and a chance of doubling it if I am up to the mark, a remarkable good offer I must admit, you would hardly think me up to the mark if I did accept, I am a bit of a fool but hardly as bad as that...*
>
> *...I have a duty to my wife and children, I could not accept it, to give up my business here by which I can make 30/- per week, I can live here as well on 30/- as I can at Plympton on 35/- per week, to spend perhaps £10 or £15 in moving my goods and be at your mercy, to give me the sack when ever you liked and me with a wife and family, where should I go, my business gone no money, nothing. No father it is not good enough, I am quite prepared to do anything I possibly can for you but if I come home and give up my business here it must be under conditions that you can not turn me out whenever you like.*

Whatever the lack of harmony was all about between the father and son, didn't prevent Fred from eventually returning to Small Hanger, to become a shareholder.

Until the motor lorry became the established mode of transport, horse and cart was the only way to convey the Olver's products; it was drawn either to the railway sidings at Hemerdon or to Plympton station. Boats were also used, with the men employed at Small Hanger loading vessels with names such as *Duchess, Thistle, Romola, Snowflake, Trevallas and Stirling.*

But first the clays had to be carted all the way down through the lanes to Sutton harbour, this task very often done by a local man who may well have been supplementing his earnings from elsewhere.

From 1907 to 1911 a record book shows that nearly ten-and-a-half-thousand tons of clay and mica material went out to customers by sea. In 1907 every month saw boats with Olver's material in their holds sail out of Sutton harbour, fourteen in fact, carrying an average of a hundred-and-forty-five tons. The following year a dozen boats sailed away with an average cargo of a hundred-fifty-six tons on board, but one for reason or another the winter months of January, November and December saw no sailings at all. The circumstances could well have been caused by the problem of the freezing of the water flow to Small Hanger for washing the strake, thus creating a shortage of stock. Yet in 1909 every month was occupied, with the men loading fifteen boats each carrying an average of a hundred-and-sixty-seven tons. Then in 1910 January, November and December missed out again and only eleven boats left the harbour laden with an average of a hundred-and-forty-eight tons. In 1911, the last year logged in the record book, only the month of December was left wanting a sailing and an average of a hundred-and-fifty-one tons was loaded into each of the sixteen boats that sailed.

On 1 January 1911 John Olver and his three sons got together at Claymoor to form a new Company, to be called Olver & Co, for the working of the clay works at Small Hanger.

Resolved 1st that we the under signed do form ourselves into a Company to carry on the Small Hanger Clay Works and that the Works be divided into 64 Parts or Shares to be held as follows viz:

Arnold Olver to hold 40 Shares

Wilcie Olver to hold 10 Shares

John Olver to hold 10 Shares

Fred Olver to hold 14 Shares

Resolved 2nd that neither of the Shareholders shall be able to sell his right in the Small Hanger Clay Works, but if either one of the Shareholders whose names are mentioned wish to relinquish his Share he will receive his share of the Money belonging to the Book Debts and also his share of the money lying in the bank to the credit of the Small Hanger Clay Works by giving up his share in the Works and all the Material also Plant and Machinery.

As was usual, the majority of the firm's customers were from the pottery country of Stoke-on-Trent, but some were from farther afield, even Europe, whilst others manufactured their wares just up the road at Bovey Tracey. Also there was on the odd occasion the request for clay from a neighbour who, for some reason, was in need of a few tons of a particular grade. Indeed, Olvers stock of their best clay at one time was low and they were in need of help themselves. In 1916, John Olver in a letter to his friend and fellow clay producer, C.D. Blake of Watts Blake & Bearne, tells of his embarrassing predicament of not having sufficient stocks to satisfy his customers, a reply came back to John on 15 January, which read,

Dear Mr Olver

I received your letter on the 8th, in reply to mine of the 6th inst, and I am very pleased to learn that you will come here before long and have dinner with me. You are one of my oldest friends, and it always does me good to have a chat with you. I am full of engagements for the whole of next week – therefore please do not come until after that time. You say you have more orders than you can supply - therefore I write to say that Watts Blake and Bearne & Co will be much pleased to supply you with one or two hundred tons of their best clay (which is now of extra good quality) at a moderate price, which will leave you a nice profit and prevent your customers from going elsewhere, and perhaps not coming back to you again, you can be made both the Consignor and the Consignee of the clay so that W.B.B & Co will not know who your customers are – so you need not be afraid to get some clay from them.

Mr Body is again writing to us for information about clay rents and royalties – and no doubt he will try to raise the assessments of all the clay merchants including your worthy self, he is nearly as bad as the Kaiser, has he written to you – I mean Mr Body, not the Kaiser.

Please send me a few lines to say that you have received this letter, I am very glad that you your sons and daughters are quite well, my kind regards to you all.

Yours Faithfully,
Charles. D. Blake

Fred Olver's pit at Small Hangar.

Arnold Olver's pit at Small Hangar.

Three years later the man who put Small Hanger on the china clay industrial map was dead, his life had allowed him to reach comfortably into his nineties. When their father passed away, Fred and Arnold took complete control of the reins of the company, but not without a little controversy, for disharmony raised its ugly head again. The brothers were just not compatible, even in life in general their thinking took them in separate directions, likewise their ideas of clay working were different, so much so that the situation led to the pair working separate pits. Arnold carried on mining for clay in the original Small Hanger hole in the ground, whilst Fred opted to have his men toil in the pit spoken of in his father's much displeasing letter, while still trying desperately to establish his own business in Cornwall. Fred also took the drastic measure of demolishing his chosen half of their father's processing system and building his own to his own specifications, whilst Arnold kept his half intact and worked it for 33 years, until he retired. Fifteen of those years he had the satisfaction of providing clay to the world famous Wedgwood Potteries in Staffordshire. The brothers' companies each had different logos, Fred changed to F.N. Olver where as Arnold favoured and retained Olver & Co.

Although the two boys inherited the business, they had to pay royalties to all three girls, even when on the odd occasion a loss was made.

George Prout of Lee Moor was one of Arnold's men. He remembers the two brothers being like chalk and cheese, with Arnold liking a laugh and a joke and a few drinks with the locals in the Treby Arms, whereas Fred was more serious-minded and was often overheard referring to his brother as 'Old Beer Belly'. George's job was drawing sand out of the pit up to the tip, using a horse and a small truck on rails. Nearing his ninetieth year, he recalled fondly how his horse heaved and snorted pulling a full load up the incline, but he would, on the return journey, gallop all the way back down by himself with reins draped loose over his withers, stopping at the bottom ahead of his master and waiting patiently for the next trip up.

George began working for Arnold Olver on the farm at fourteen; after a couple of years he became a little discontented with his farm labourer's wage and eventually plucked up the courage to ask his boss for more money. George was told that if he wanted more money he would have to leave the farm and work for it down in the pit, his first fortnightly pay packet held £2.18s.4d, less deductions of course. He had worked eighty hours for eight pence and three farthings per hour! The rest of the workforce, of which there was now merely five men, and grown men compared to George, were on one shilling an hour. Within two years, young George was on the same money as the others, eleven pence an hour. It was 1931 and recession had taken a strong hold on world trade, and with Arnold having a fight on his hands to sell his products it gave the men no other alternative but to take a penny an hour pay cut. It was during the depression that Arnold lost his closest competitor, his brother Fred died in 1932, leaving his son Frank to run F.N.Olver, which he did until the Second World War came along and disrupted the world again.

With the dwindling demand for china clay during the war, the Board of Trade opted to close down a majority of the Cornish and Devon pits. A concerned Arnold Olver, wondering about his chances of remaining open, wrote to the British China Clay Federation for more information about the unhealthy situation regarding his business. The reply that came back without too much delay is illustrated here.

With these conditions laid down, Olvers & Co could not possibly qualify, yet they were found to be so financially economical in their production methods that they were permitted to carry on as usual on the recommendation of a Professor Jones from the Board of Trade, who was employed to assess each individual case.

The only person unprotected by the circumstances was George Prout. He was the only employee among the five to be under the age of thirty, and as Arnold's business didn't come under the Governments protection scheme, he was obliged to go to war. George remembered this as a time of great uncertainty;, it seems that the situation (without appearing too condescending) wasn't made at all clear to him, and a cloud remained hanging over the whole

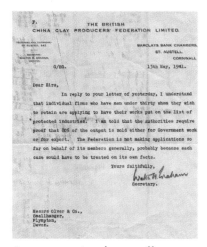

Letter concerning the war effort.

affair. With a frown deeply furrowing his brow, he recalled how a week before he was due to leave his home for the first time, he decided to take some time off work, but just for devilment he never informed Arnold. When his boss called on him to enquire about his absence, he merely said he needed some time to himself to think before going off to war.

During the hostilities, with his pit closed down, Frank took employment just a stone's throw away at the wolfram mine on the hill above his settling tanks, leaving his Uncle Arnold to keep an eye on things, which was mainly preventing his pit from flooding during heavy downpours of rain.

After the lengthy hostilities were eventually over, Frank left his job at the mine to reopen his pit and begin trading again. Not that his business was left totally without income, for while it was closed down, Uncle Arnold on a few occasions bought off him the material that was left drying on his air dry shelving to sell on to his own customers. Those purchases earned Frank a nice £255.25s. Meanwhile George Prout, having survived at first hand the frightening experience of war, was back in civvy street working at Lee Moor.

Arnold Olver.

In 1946, Arnold, at the age of seventy four, attempted to get modern when he splashed out £93.6s. on a hose monitor and pipes for washing a clay face down in the pit, doing away with the strake system that had held Small Hanger in good stead from the beginning of its conception. With no water pumping facilities available to him, Arnold had to rely on the monitor being gravity fed; it was here where his plans sadly fell apart. The source of water in the pond above the pit was not high enough, leaving the gradient below that needed to generate the pressure warranted at the hose. After twice attempting to secure the system Arnold wished to implement, he gave in and returned to the time-honoured strake to produce his clay.

Eight years later, with Frank having ongoing health problems and Arnold in his eightieth year, the pair reluctantly agreed to scale down production in anticipation of closing down. 1952 saw Small Hanger sold to ECLP, and the place gradually degenerated into the state we see it today.

Just a glance to the north, from the edge of the Small Hanger pits, one can see a conical shaped heap of china clay waste. This material was brought to the surface from the pit it overlooks, known to the locals as Stocker's. This hole in the ground, now partially filled with water, was once the clay workings of the Nicholls family.

The inspiration at the start of the delvings here was John Nicholls. He was, like William Cookworthy, an industrial chemist, with workshops in St Austell, producing among other things, gunpowder, for sale to the numerous mines in Cornwall. In 1855 John Nicholls decided to broaden, his horizons and venture into the china clay business, but, by this time, most of the china clay bearing land in his native county, was taken by those who got there before him. With this situation in mind, he felt his only option was to look to Dartmoor, where William Phillips had found success.

It was just as well that John's entreprenuerial instincts took him into the clay industry, because twelve or so years after his Dartmoor exploits began, Alfred Nobel would have blown his gunpowder operations in St Austell into oblivion, with the Swedish engineer's discovery of the much safer explosive, dynamite. John's choice of site was never going to be the cosiest of places, it sits on a saddle between Crownhill and Headon Downs, catching the winds from all directions, with the north-easterly that often froze the strake to ice, by far the worse. Situated as it was, in the middle of heathland with only Small Hanger and Broomage (or Brimage to the locals) its nearest neighbours, the site adopted the name of Hemerdon Clay Works, after the estate land on which it sat. The landlord being the same as that of Small Hanger, the Woollcombe's of Hemerdon House.

Sky tip above Nicholls' (Stockers') pit.

Nicholls' pit.

201

Concrete mica runs.

Nicholls' mica dam.

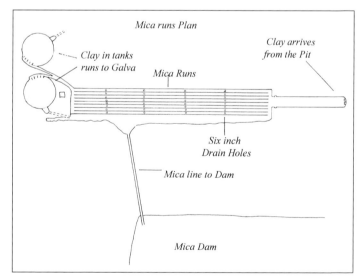

Nicholls' mica and clay separating system.

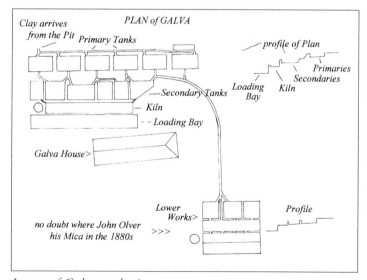

Layout of Galva production system.

After twenty years, before John died in 1897, his son John Junior took over the running of Hemerdon. By this time the pit was below adit level and employing a cornish pump, linked to a steam engine, to pull the clay stream out of the pit and deliver it to the adit. But by 1908 the pit had become so deep that the pump could no longer cope, causing for the first time a major problem to production and the family's future in the industry. The dilemma could be seen coming from a long way off and all concerned knew that to keep production on track would be a very steep financial hill to climb. After much deliberation, the family felt that the only option was to invite someone to buy into the company, and that someone was the West of England China Clay Co. of St Austell. The company, run by Medland Stocker, bought one half share in Nicholls & Co, and thus gained a foothold in the industry on Dartmoor. The Stocker family had wanted clay interest on the moor for several years, starting with Edward Medland's father. He lost out to the Martins in bidding for the Lee Moor complex when Lord Morley was wanting rid of it. Like the Stockers, a majority of the Lee Moor people were from Cornwall and knew of the Stockers' wish to enjoy a share of the Devon clay profits. When they did eventually get a foot in, it was only natural for the gossip to go around that Stockers had got in at Hemerdon and so their name stuck to the pit.

Following the transaction, larger suction gas engines were installed along with of course, the necessary gas production plant. It was at about this time that the strake system of washing was done away with and hose monitors introduced to the pit. The water was gravity fed from a source up on the moorland surface. Also altered, was the system of mica separation; concrete runs were built above the pit along with mica lagoons. Positioned near the clay-discharge end of the runs were two round clay tanks where the material was allowed to sufficiently de-water before its one-and-a--half mile pipeline flow down to Galva, just a few hundred yards above Hemerdon Village where much larger settling tanks awaited its arrival. Here also was the drying complex of Nicholls & Co. It consisted of two pan drie. The largest, with its six primary and six secondary tanks, was situated to the rear of Galva House. The smaller kiln, along with its three primary tanks and one elongated secondary that stretched the full length of the kiln, was situated in the grounds in front of the house. Both the kiln chimneys, although partially clothed in ivy, still stand, the lower stack is cracked for some of its length. Other than that they are both in remarkably good condition.

At the time of writing, the owners of Galva, Mr and Mrs Pummell, tell me they intend to renovate the lower stack and remove the ivy from both. Very little can be seen of the kilns, but at the lower one it is possible to peep through the cast-iron doors of the furnace and into its partially collapsed interior. The better tanks to see are those of the higher part of the complex where, down inside the primary tanks, can be seen the pin hole de-watering system, along with the valves and their much ruinous opening and closing mechanisms that delivered the partially settled clay into the secondary tanks. These, unlike the primary's, that are

One of the chimneys at Galva.

Primary tank showing pin hole drainage system, clay slurry delivery valve and access steps.

One of the lower furnace doors.

uniform in size and shape, are irregular in fashion. To view this upper area is a back-aching, nettle-stinging and bramble-scratching experience, for all is cloaked closely in low lying vegetation, under a canopy of rhododendron, hazel and elder. It must be noted this is private land and permission to see the remains must be requested.

Galva House, at one time was a terrace of three miners' cottages. These were converted into one dwelling with a large extension at the eastern end. The land, like the clay sett, was leased from the Woollcombes, and here is where the Nicholls family resided along with croquet lawn, flowerbeds, orchard, various hardwood trees, and a view looking out over Plympton and beyond. There was also, according to Mr John Silverlock (whose Great Grandfather was John Nicholls senior), two small reservoirs within the grounds, one supplying Galva House, the other through a pipeline sloping gently down through the contours to Hemerdon House for the landlord to use as he wished. These two reservoirs were apparently filled from the overflow of the settling tanks.

Eleven years after Medland Stocker bought his share on the moor, English China Clays was formed. At the same time Leonard Nicholls-Silverlock, nephew of John Nicholls Junior, was secured in his position as the manager of the Hemerdon side of the company. The pit on the moor and the settling tanks at Galva were at times not only employed for the furtherance of clay production, but were also utilised by other organisations.

The year 1929 not only brought economic depression, it also brought a long spell of dry weather and, with it, a water shortage. Plympton Rural District Council, was then the local authority and responsible for the area's water supply. With ECC benefiting financially, the council after installing a purification system at Galva, took all the water it could from the settling tanks' overflow.

During the Second World War, the Board of Trade allowed the Hemerdon Pit to stay in production, but only on a much reduced scale. By this time ECC had for eight years and more been ECLP. The concession was granted in order for the pit to supply water to the wolfram mine. Water was pumped to the mine until 1944, when it was decided that wolfram was no longer of great importance to the war effort. For carrying out of this simple operation ECLP was paid the handsome sum of £200 a week. Once the pump to the mine was turned off, the pit that began its life almost ninety years earlier by the industrial chemist from St Austell, was closed down.

Today, with the pit partially filled with water, the rambler when passing or stopping for a rest and a little refreshment may wonder if the level ever rises. The answer to the query is that it changes very little, because the water drains from the confines of the pit through the adit excavated during the early beginnings of the workings. Indications of those days can be seen to the west of the small hanger complex. Everywhere down this side of the little valley are old mica beds, and dotted here and there among the almost impenetrable gorse are

Where Nicholls' mica dam was situated.

Part of the pumping system.

pockets of mica spills. The mica pond that held the material from the runs is not to be seen anymore, it has been devoured by today's mobile plant and in its place is a prospecting hole in the ground the size of a football pitch.

Still to be seen is a part of the system used to gravity feed water from a source on the moorland surface to the hose monitor in the pit. The pipeline running down into the pit is still in situ, along with its valves and reducing section that disappears into a bed of silt. To the right of this feature, are the timbers and heavy cast-iron work of the clay stream suction pump, and above, half hidden among the gorse, is the concrete base for the pump's gas engine that pulled the clay stream out of the pit. This system was put in place in 1928 under the direction of Mr John Silverlock, the equipment that Mr Stocker's money had installed had deteriorated to the extent that it was necessary to re-equip a new suction gas engine complete with its twelve-ton flywheel. The engine was connected by a huge belt to a DC dynamo, the current supplying a large centrifugal pump in the pit and also a motor to drive the sand-winding equipment that took the material up to the conical heap standing there today. This heap is only a shadow of what it once was. At one time it was the tallest pile on the moor. One reason for its diminished proportions, is a contract signed in the early 1930s to supply sand for the development of the Plymouth Hoe foreshore and Tinside Pool.

Besides the moorland Plym and its tributaries, there have been other areas on Dartmoor where china clay has been searched for and prospected. Environmentalist and preservationist in caring for the welfare of the moor, believe that the china clay companies should cease their desecration of the land they love. Stop, now, before any more damage is done! But if they only thought what might have been, it would send almighty shivers down their spines.

Imagine travelling from the north of the moor via Two Bridges and Princetown, perhaps after enjoying refreshments in one of the town's hostelries. The way from here is towards Yelverton, but instead of finding more outstanding beauty after crossing the cattle grid, a blinding white sea of china clay pits and waste heaps confronts the traveller. This scenario could well have been reality, if the material had been found there in any quality and quantity, creating a wildernes from all the magnificence in view there today.

❖ ❖ ❖

CW2 stone.

After John Dickens had come and gone, and William Phillips had settled down at Lee Moor, a George Stone Baron, of Plymouth, thought he would try his hand at prospecting for the white stuff. On 29 September 1835, the indenture was signed and the area Sir Ralph Lopes allowed him to 'Dig, Work, Mine and search for Clay usually known in the County of Cornwall by the name of China Clay.' was 'upon all those parts of the wastelands usually called the common of Walkhampton within the Manor and Parish of Walkhampton.' The boundary of this sett was huge, it stretched from Little Kings Tor along the southern side of the Plymouth–Dartmoor Tramway until nearly into Princtown, to a Duchy/Walkhampton boundary stone. It then turned right and across the top of Meavy Head to the Princetown/Plymouth road to another D/W Stone. From here it followed the right hand side of the road for almost two and half miles, until the twelve mile stone from Plymouth was reached. From this point it ran in a direct line to near the hedge of a field called Furze Park, an acreage of Wattown Farm, where a bound stone inscribed C1W was set up. From this stone, the perimeter of the huge sett ran around the outer hedges of Routrundle, Babyland, Stocking Town, Withill, Criptor, Yestor, Davytown and Huckentor to the boundary stone we see today marked C2W and, finally, back to Little Kings Tor.

Also annexed to the Sett was another section of land lying to the north of the Tramway. Triangular in shape, it was bounded by three stones numerically inscribed C3W, C4W and C5W. The only thing to become of these great expectations, was the comparatively small scars on the landscape at a place called Binda, no more than an exploratory clay sett just outside Princetown, north of the railway track. According to its sale notice of 1874, it was about one square mile in extent and comprised of a fine bed of clay. The adventurers had driven two levels into the hillside, one of about seventy fathoms the other twice the length at hundred and forty. They had also excavated a cross cut of twenty five fathoms. The advert also boasted of the lower and longer of the levels locating clay at ten fathoms deep, with anticipation of adding another six to that.

On the same announcement for sale, was the Leedon Clay Sett, extending over one hundred and fifty acres, already referred to in the chapter on tinners. The clay-bearing land lies to the east of Yellowmead Down, on the lower slopes of Leedon Hill. The wording on the sale notice stated that 'an adit level of about two hundred fathoms has been driven through hard rock into clay, now proved to be of good quality, and the stope for working about ten fathoms. There are also large deposits of fire clay and valuable tin loads driven some thirty three fathoms, the Tin is held on lease for twenty-one years from the 24th of June 1874.' The clay deposit was also leased for twenty-one years, but from a couple of months earlier in March. Also included on the sale notice was Yennadon Iron Mine.

Adit entrance at Outcombe.

It was towards the end of 1871 when a Mr Woodley of Halshanger, above Ashburton, was in negotiations to lease land for china clay prospecting to a Mr Richards of St Austell. Richards had already investigated beneath the topsoil of certain areas of the Common, and was returning in the New Year to make further trials. Keeping a close eye on the situation was the ball clay company of Watts, Blake & Bearne, not so far away in Newton Abbot. The, then young, company didn't wait too long for the Cornishman to make up his mind as to whether he was returning to his exploratory delvings or not. They must have been discussing the idea of searching the Common for themselves for sometime, and they certainly didn't let a lot of grass grow under their industrious feet, for just into the New Year, on 19 January, Mr Woodley opened a letter from WBB, detailing their thoughts for the use of the heathland on the hill above his farm:

Dear Sir

Halshanger China Clay Lands

We have the pleasure to submit the following proposals for working the above.

A twelve Months Licence for search to be granted to us & then if we find Suitable Clay with water to work the same, a 12 years lease to be granted to us (if we request it before the expiration of the Twelve Months) at a rent of £100 per Annum, such rent to cover all matters, including Water & Water Courses, and the ground for Washing, Pumping, Purifying, Drying and Storing Clay.

The Lease to be determinable by us at the end of any year, if we find it desirable to cease to work the Clay, you to afford us every possible facility for obtaining the Water necessary for

Washing & otherwise washing, the Clay & are holding you harmless of Litigation, should any request from the diversion by us of any Stream of Water.

Hoping the foregoing will meet your wishes in all respects.
We remain dear Sir
Yours Faithfully
WBB.
J Woodley Esquire
Halshanger
Ashburton

Very little evidence can be seen now of any exploratory work on Halshanger Common, but on the moor above Shipley Bridge evidence cannot be missed.

On the 4 August 1871 Henry Hill, a mining agent, signed an indenture 'to have full and free Liberty, Licence, Power and Authority to do all Acts necessary or Convenient for searching for and working the Veins and Beds of China Clay.'

Mr Hill lived at Brent Moor House, the ample dwelling that once stood a short distance upstream from Shipley Bridge. The China Clay land was licenced to him from the Prince of Wales, the Duke of Cornwall. It lay on the farthest extremities of Harford and Ugborough Moors. The sett was bounded by the following limits: on the north by a straight line drawn from the point where Red Lake falls into the Erme, to Western Whittaborough otherwise Petre's Cross, on the east by a straight line drawn from Western Whittaborough otherwise Petre's Cross, to Three Barrows from Three Barrows, the line of the boundary went west in a straight line to the Erme, then followed the left bank back to Red Lake Foot.

According to William Crossing, Mr Hill was the proprietor of the Brent Moor Clay Works. Hill knew that someone had worked and found little of value at Knatta Barrow, so he chose to search for his material near the head of the Bala Brook, today shown on the Ordnance Survey Map as Pete's Pit. Sadly, within the twelve-month licence period, the adventurer knew that success in finding a valuable deposit at his chosen spot was not to be.

Yet, waiting in the wings and eagerly ready to take over the sett, was none other than Watts, Blake & Bearne. They, after a search signed a lease for twenty-one years. On this indenture were the full titles of 'his Royal Highness Albert Edward Prince of Wales, Duke of Saxony, Duke of Cornwall and Rothesay, Earl of Chester Carrick and Dublin, Baron of Renfrew, Lord of the Isles and Great Steward of Scotland.' The site WBB opted for was Left Lake, the feature passed today without a great deal of attention paid to it by the passer-by on their way along the so-called Puffing Billy Track to Red Lake.

Although there is no mention of it in his Book, Mr Worth, Richard Handsford that is, was engaged in 1907 by one Charles Cottier a Plymouth Solicitor, to search for china clay. Unlike the Martins, Olvers and, Sellecks, Mr Cottier was a city gent and had nothing to do with clay of any description, but what he did know was, that money could be made from it. With the Plym deposits taken up and other sites having proved to be commercially unsuccessful, Mr Worth being a Dartmoor antiquarian, knew the moors like the back of his hand, and being a mineralogist and a geologist, there was hope that he would find a suitable sett.

The deposit he found to his liking lay on the lower south-western slopes of Green Hill, just a few hundred yards north of the mire at Red Lake Head. The beginnings of the enterprise were slow in materialising; huge amounts of money had to be found even for the project to get off the ground. The site was farther out into the moor than any other china clay sett and was made even more distant by choosing Cantrell, near Bittaford, for its drying kilns and sheds, although this made sense with the Great Western Railway running close by. This is where the initial high financial outlay came into the equation. The distance between extracting and drying was eight miles, gradually climbing up through the contours of extremely open moorland. Mr Worth, being a civil engineer, was given the job of surveying and laying the railway, but the line began on the 750 feet contour, 300 feet and more above the kilns. This climb or drop, was negotiated by the means of an incline employing winding

Red Lake's flooded pit.

gear, similar to that on the Lee Moor Tramway. As well as the track, Mr Worth also surveyed and laid the pipeline that carried the china clay in liquid suspension from its origins back to Cantrell. Sadly, any success for the company was short lived, in twenty two years of striving effort, a great deal of money had been lost and so it was that, in 1932, Red Lake and the line to Cantrell went quiet, when all production came to an end.

Another place outside Plym country where china clay was searched for, was Broadall Lake, the little stream that runs down off the moor and through the beautiful woods of Hawns and Dendles, now one of nature's protected sanctuaries where waterfalls cascade into crystal clear water. A note in 1877 to Samuel Skidmore, the Captain at Headon China Clay Works from his employers Watts, Blake & Bearne confirms this. It said among other things, 'please get a set of triangles made at once, the purpose going to Broadall on Friday next and we hope to bring the boring tools with us.' The writer went on to request a large canvas for the men's shelter while boring, and stated that Samuel's son should superintend the work.

Hawns and Dendle Wood. Now a nature reserve.

Watts, Blake and Bearne's endeavours to locate a decent and lasting deposit of china clay, must have brought them to the Cornwood area in 1872. The first hint of their arrival, is in a letter written to Admiral Parker of Delamore, dated 1 May 1873, reminding him of correspondence between them in November 1872, referring to searching for clay on Brimage (Broomage) Waste. A letter to Admiral Parker a few days later reads 'We have received your favour & agree to the preliminary terms upon which you express yourself ready to allow us to search for clay, with a view to granting us a Lease of the same if we desire it. Enclosed is our cheque for £10 which you can please cash & retain the money as security for the proper filling in by us of the pits that we may sink.

Mr C.D. Blake must have been extremely confident of success, for on the ninth of May, he wrote to John Phillips of Aller: 'I got your private note so long after it was written that I thought I might defer replying to it until my return home which happened quite recently...'. After some personal remarks concerning everyday life, it was back to business , with C.D. asking John if he had in stock, 'tiles such as those used by China Clay Merchants in their Kilns'.

From thereon, the Brimage or Broomage explorations matured into working stopes and have spread right across the head of the Piall Brook on to Headon Down, into what is known today as the Headon China Clay Works, the flagship of WBB's china clay concerns.

WBB was formed in1860 when Mr W.J. Watts leased ball clay-bearing land on his estate to his son W.J. Watts Junior and his two partners C.D. Blake and Lewis Bearne, although the trio did not trade under their combined names until the following year. While young W.J. nurtured production, C.D. Blake, whose father, Edward, was a ball clay producer and had dabbled in china clay at Small Hanger, looked after the marketing, leaving Lewis Bearne, who having worked in banking, took care of the young company's finance.

W.J. senior obviously knew what he was doing, knowing already the qualities of his own son. He would not have wanted him to fall flat on his face so soon after being released from the family's apron strings for the first time. He must have vetted thoroughly the abilities of young Blake and Bearn for the combination to work so well together, so well in fact that it was not long before other members of the Watts and Bearne families jumped on the flourishing bandwagon, including senior Watts himself. In its infancy the company, as well as mining for ball clay, also bought and sold ochre, coal and of course china clay.

There is a letter among WBB archives referring to talks, in the same year that they first arrived at Headon, of the company joining forces with John Olver and opening a works together. According to John Olver's business card they must surely have done so, yet the two companies did not always see eye to eye before WBB established themselves as china clay producers. They regularly purchased material from Olvers, but letters of some transactions from WBB were more akin to notes of instructions rather than letters of request, one written on 18 March 1873 reads:

Dear Sir
Please say by return, if you can let us have 5 tons of D.X. china Clay, early next week.
    Yours WBB.

What may have fostered this frosty approach from WBB can be discerned in a disgruntled letter to John Olver accusing him of not caring if he supplied them with clay or not, saying he did when it pleased him to do so. Yet relations between Chas Blake (as he liked to address himself) and John Olver were always courteous, warm and friendly. Although C.D. was a businessman he was also very caring and compassionate, and always displayed this nature in his correspondence.

With the year running into 1874 the firm had found themselves a workforce and had engaged Samuel Skidmore as the Works Captain. All the men would have been vetted and taken on by him, some even lodged with him and his wife at Quick Cottage, the little abode beside the bridge of the same name on the old Cornwood to Cadover Bridge road. Now the road as been redirected to Cadover, via Beatland Corner, and Quick Cottage has been pulled down, sparing it from further indignity.

Where some of Samuel's men slept isn't perhaps known, but in March 1875 Admiral Parker complained of the number of lodgers Mr Skidmore had in that tiny place. He wrote to the directors saying that the house was overcrowded, 'Nothing against Skidmore himself, I find him to be the most agreeable chap'.

The company's first search for china clay in the Plym valley was on grazing land associated with Dunstone Farm. The fields, not there any more, were on the other side of the road from the farm gate. It was February, one of the coldest months of the year, especially on Shaugh Moor, and things were not going to their liking. This encouraged the sending of a letter to Sir Massey Lopes' land agent, Mr C.L.Radcliff:

Dear Sir
We have your favour of the 23rd just. On that day we visited the Loads in question, we have already bored 64 holes to a considerable depth & at great expense we have found two or three small pockets of Clay, but not one large Bed of it. Before relinquishing the search we have thought it best to bore three or four additional holes, after doing which we shall have pleasure writing to you again.
 Yours Faithfully
 Watts Blake Bearne & Co
 PS
Are you in a position to offer us any other Clay Lands, Are there not indications of Clay in the Sheeps Tor ditrict. Can you grant the Clay in the enclosed lands near to opposite the Meavy Sett, we consider that Sir Massey's fields there are somewhat entangled with fields belonging to other people but perhaps we could manage to work the Clay.
 WBB & Co

After receiving a reply from Mr Radcliff, WBB Repeated its request to try for clay at Brisworthy. They wrote:

Dear Sir
We have your favour of yesterday, we referred to Brisworthy the name of which we did not recollect when writing the postscript to our last letter. We note what you say about 'Dunstone' but cannot confirm your opinion – for we bored three & found merely a superficial covering of Clay 2 or 3 feet thick with a body of yellowish sand (worthless) below. Kindly consider about 'Brisworthy' in connection with the PS to our last letter.
 Yours Truly
 Watts Blake Bearne & Co

In the end WBB did not get their wish and the fields of Brisworthy were spared the touch of the boring tools. The Meavy sett, in the first letter referred to, is the now water filled-pits on Wigford Down just above Cadover Bridge. This sett was first leased to a James Evans who came up from the Cornish clay country to work. The indenture dated 23 March 1866, informs us that he was allowed to dig:

all that portion of Wigford Down in the Parish of Meavy in the said County of Devon. On the

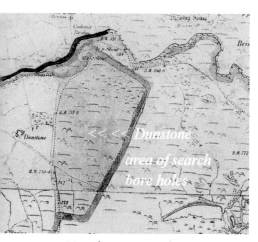

Map showing area of Dunstone.

North side of the river Cad (Plym) and adjoining the Parish road on each side North of Cadworthy Bridge set and described in the ground plan there of endorsed on these presents and tinted Pink together with the right of using such portions of West Down in the Parish of Shaugh nearest to Shaugh Bridge, for the purpose of making Catch Pits for Filtering and Purifying the water used in the manufacture of Clay and also for the purpose of Drying Houses and other Buildings necessary for the purpose of carrying on the Clay Works.

Two years after their request to search for clay among the Brisworthy fields was turned down, WBB were back on Shaugh Moor with their boring mechanisms. But, they were not the first to try their hand there; that claim belongs to Mr Spencer Rogers, he was there forty years before them in 1837. The agreement was made on 27 October, between him and Sir Ralph Lopes. Spencer, according to the minute of agreement was from a place called Watlands in Staffordshire. The agreement recorded:

Sir Ralph Lopes grants permission and Licence to the said Spencer Rogers for the space of Five Months from this day to dig search and try for all and every the Clay usually called or known in the County of Cornwall by the name of China Clay and for all other Clay, Clay stone and other Potters materials to be found in under and throughout all that part of the open Common or Waste lands belonging to and Parcel of the Manor of Shaugh Prior within the Parish of Shaugh in the said County of Devon which is usually distinguished by the name of Shaugh Lake – and if at the expiration of the said Five Months or at an earlier period the said Spencer Rogers Shall be so satisfied with the results of the search and trial as to be desirous of obtaining a regular Sett or Grant for digging such Clay and other Potters Materials for a term of Twenty One Years the said Sir Ralph Lopes will be ready to execute such Sett or Grant to the said Spencer Rogers...

But if Spencer was not satisfied and wanted to get out, he had to fill in and restore the ground to the level of the surrounding surface.

WBB returned to Shaugh Moor on 13 of September 1879 and have been there ever since. Before they arrived with the tools of the trade, they were looking at the gradual failure and eventual demise of James' Evans efforts on Wigford Down, with a hope of taking over the drying kilns at Shaugh Bridge where Wigford's Clay ran to be processed. This was in the era when the industry was going through hard times. On 14 January of the same year, Samuel Skidmore at Headon received a letter from the frugal C.D. Blake, instructing him to make his way to Shaugh Bridge, to observe, investigate and generally weigh up the situation:

...get a sample of the old and new Meavy clay and learn what quantity of wet and dry clay remaining at Shaugh Bridge. Take length & width of the Dries there & learn what quantity the

sheds will hold, confer with Captain Evans for our future guidance as to the advantage or disad-
vantage of having to land the clay upon the kiln from such a great height above. I explained to
you that if we cannot get Meavy Drys it will perhaps suit us to put up a small Dry on Shaugh
Sett near Cadover Bridge to prove the Shaugh Clay at a less cost than putting up a dry (with
intermediate launders) at Shaugh Bridge and the Cadover Dry would (if the cartage were not
heavy) come useful for sending Clay up Country by Rail.

Ascertain whether for certain you can bring on the Black Lake stream by gravitation to wash
the lower bed of clay on Shaugh. We would like to prove the clay without taking Martin's water
and paying for it, we can get it afterwards if we want it.

Don't spend a penny that can be advantageously saved, we cannot afford to spend a shilling
superfluously. It is considered that half the Cornish Clay Works are losing money and if we become
compelled (as we may be) to sell at Cornish prices, we shall lose a great deal of money unless we
can prepare the clay for a less price per ton than it is costing us now including the interest on the
large sum that we have expended. The times are very bad, we have reduced wages here, can they
be reduced at Headon. They are reduced all over the Country except at Headon.

No matter how hard the times were, the development of Shaugh Lake went ahead, with
Samuel Skidmore's son John being made the captain of the works. Although happy with
what they were processing in their new pit, they were still hankering after Brisworthy. In
1888, Dunstone was again being investigated and their attention had spread across the Plym
to Wigford Down. On 25 May the company complained to Maristow that neither were as
'promising for Clay as Brisworthy, we regret that you are unwilling to let us make a trial
there.'

Just over twelve months later, on 22 June, C.D. Blake wrote to John Skidmore saying that
he had spent a good part of Thursday last, with Sir Massey Lopes, and it now looked almost
certain that they will be working the clay at Wigford. He went on to say:

I think you had better select a couple of suitable men & at once set to work to examine the Level
(Adit) to see what will have to be done to it & ascertain what timber will be required. As we
shall not require the Level for sand, don't you think we had better clear the Level as cheaply as
possible, and use the least possible amount of timber & then lay in iron pipes at once. Much of the
cost of pipes would be spent in making it a well-timbered Level & then it would be a nobbled affair
which would perhaps not last long. Of course if the lower end of the Level is in hard solid rock it
might not be necessary to pipe that part nor timber it.

Almost a month later on 20 July, Mr Blake, in another letter, is making suggestions as to
how he thinks the level could be made safe and workable for the clays run to Shaugh Bridge,

without spending too much money on the project. He also says he will meet John and his father, Samuel, on site within the very near future. He went on to suggest that the pair could obviously think of ideas of their own.

By the September of the same year, the pit on Wigford Down began to come alive again, with eight men toiling away there. This number gradually increased to twenty-three. However, scanning through WBB pay records of the time, it appears very much as if the works shared its manpower with Shaugh Lake. It could well have been that Mr Blake asked for time to clean up the pit before placing his signature on the indenture, for the document wasn't signed until 10 October.

A few years later, with the Wigford works up and running, John Skidmore began to suffer with his health and the problem was allegedly beginning to affect his ability to carry out his duties in a proper manner. In the late days of January 1896 he was accused by the directors, via his father, of liking a tipple too many and was starting to fail his responsibilities. John, not afraid to have his say, put pen to paper in defence of himself:

Dear Sirs
Referring to two letters which my father has received from you anent myself.
The state of my health during the past twelve months has been much more serious than I have ever mentioned to anyone. – it is nothing but a naturally buoyant hopeful temperament that has kept me going at all – the influenza I had some two years ago left me with a very troublesome Liver complaint & shattered nerves – during the past year I have been to a great extent the victim of insomnia – sometimes I get no sleep for three or four nights in succession – I have been very strongly advised to give over all work & go away for a change & take a long rest – but there are two things which has kept me from asking for a holiday – one is that my dear old father has been in bad health for a very long time & consequently would not be able to give the works here the attention they deserve & require – beside it would be bad for you to have two managers sick at the same time – the other is that a man with a big family like I have cant afford to rest whilst there is any go left in him. The shakiness of my writing which you speak of is due to a nervous derangement & not to drink as you seem to think – after a fast walk or excitement of any kind my hand shakes so that I cant write at all - & have to take a dose of brandy to steady my nerves before I am able to hold the pen – my Doctor very carefully examined me last Sunday & he says I am toning up & am in a fair way to recovery – I should never have told you this – but would have pegged along till I either got well or dropped in my work. But I cant bear your distrust – imputation of drunkenness. Seven years ago next month I like an idiot got drunk but since that I have never been worse for drink – I am not a tippler I go along for months together & never touch a drop of any kind of intoxicant & then perhaps for a month or two I may take a glass of ale when I feel inclined – you may trust me to do any business that I am capable of doing without sending my father along with

me to see that I keep sober – you say that my appearance indicate that I drink a good deel – as well as my manner & talk – if such is the case I want to say right here that this complex indicator & not John Skidmore is wrong – you ask if my wife & family tipple – if any one else had asked the question they would have got a very different answer than you will get. My wife has been a total abstainer for at least 15 years & my children don't know the taste of drink – so that instead of being a nest of topers we are excepting the writer disciples off the pump. Nevertheless if you prefer that I abstain totally I am willing to do so.

    Yours Obediently
    John Skidmore

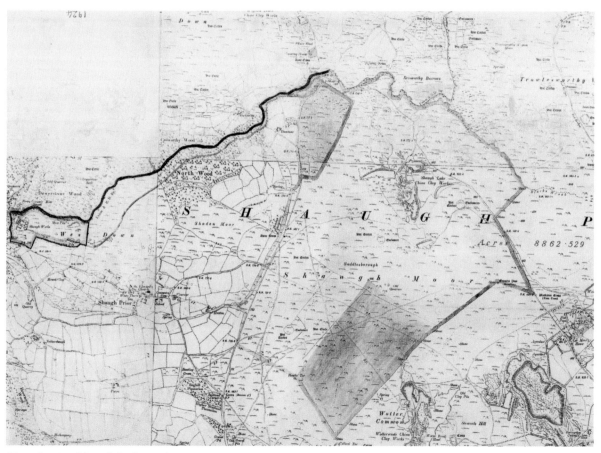

Map showing Shaugh Lake working area.

The captain of his works was effectively the manager. He was responsible for the whole works, that is to say the whole of the land within the bounds of the sett, which in the case of Shaugh Lake ran from about two hundred yards below Cadover Bridge, up the River Plym to the Black-Brook. Following the stream until reaching the Shaugh/Lee Moor bound stone set in the foot of the left bank, from there it went up across the moor and after passing another stone, recumbent and mostly covered in moorland vegetation, it carried on to the next set in the turf beside the Cornwood/Cadover road and like the two before it etched with the S/L, from this stone the boundary ran to Blackaton Cross. It then almost turned back on itself till reaching Emmit's Post another S/L stone this time set on top of a prehistoric cairn. The way then was to Collard Tor. From this jumble of rocks the line led on to Hawk's Tor before running down over the waste to where it met the first field of Huxton Farm that edges the Beatland Corner to Cadover Bridge road. Here it turned right and followed the field hedges all the way to the Plym where it began.

In today's world it seems that sometimes we accept vandalism as part and parcel of our culture and instantly believe that such things did not happen in days gone by. Yet two of the boundary marks just mentioned in the perambulation of Shaugh Lake Sett, were at one time vandalised. John Skidmore reported that someone had recently attempted to overthrow Blackaton Cross and had succeeded in upsetting the S/L stone further down the road.

Within the sett, the captain was responsible for all around him; his men, the pit where the appropriate materials had to be washed, mica runs and mica ponds, drying kilns and storage sheds at Shaugh Bridge, and the pipeline system that carried the liquid clay there. He was also responsible for ordering supplies, carting and railway trucks that took the finished product to the customer. One of the most important items he was responsible for was water, for without it, production would instantly cease.

Water storage ponds were, and still are, invaluable to a clay sett. The construction of one particular pond, served John Skidmore with a a puzzle that mystified him. Whilst excavating the key for the pond the workmen came across a hole full of water and no amount of head-scratching could give John any logical idea as to what it was, other than a large hole. When he wrote in his report that day, he endeavoured to explain.

Blackaton Cross.

It is the most remarkable thing to find a Hole, Hollow or Cavern in such kind of ground as forms the New Pond, it has the appearance of an ordinary level, it is full of water excepting about 6 feet of the mouth of it. As it goes onwards judging from a test I have made by pushing a staff several feet into the water the hole or cavity has a considerable downward dip, it is very much below the level of our pond so that there is no chance of unwatering & exploring it, how the hole got there I am sure I cant tell, it may be one of natures curious freaks, but it is more likely to be part of the old mans workings. There are Cromlechs, Mounds, Crosses & things of this order plentifully scat-

tered around here, which is supposed to mark certain epochs in our Country's history – perhaps the people who then lived & raised these mounds & carved the crosses & built the cromlechs, may also be responsible for this puzzling hole in the pond, the dust of their once active bodies may rest in this hole, or it may be the place of hidden treasure once belonging to these people.

In his next report concerning the apparent phenomenon, John says:

There are no indications whatever of the Cavern having been arched, the ground is firm, it is what miners call Growter, very much like granite in its formation but not sufficiently hard to be called stone, Just the kind of thing that often borders clay. Dipping the place dry may mean a big job or vice versa. I have kept my eye on the hole just to see if the water recedes – but it keeps about to the same mark. Of course I would like to see the bottom of it & perhaps if we get say a weeks dry weather the water may go back in the hole & give one a chance of getting farther into it & forming better ideas of what it really is.

The hole the hollow, cavern or level, whatever, was more than likely the earlier explorations of Spencer Rogers. The next time John's pen touched on the subject of the pond, was when he replied to the directors about its progress just before taking in its first flow of water.

Very often the Captain at Shaugh Lake had problems with keeping the water levels of his water storage ponds to the height that the everyday washing of clay required. Rainfall was, and still is of course, of the utmost importance; not only did it precipitate on the clay setts catchment area and help to fill the ponds, but also swelled the River Plym from where a supply of water also came. This source was frequently interrupted in its flow to Shaugh Lake, by Martin Brothers of Lee Moor, into whose reservoir the leat of water from the Plym initially ran. Every time the flow to Shaugh Lake was stemmed, the captain had to tramp up to Lee Moor with the aim of turning his quota back in. During the summer of 1906 the problem had got so bad, that John wrote to inform his directors, hoping that the weight of their influence would put the situation straight once and for all. The letter he sent off read:

Dear Sir
I am very sorry to inform you that Martin Bros has again shut off the water to your Shaugh Works. Some 10 or 12 years ago I met Mr T. Martin, Mr Merson & Captn Bray at Lee Moor Pond in regard to Shaugh Works Water Supply - & I think that it was then arranged that you

were to have a certain supply that was not to be tampered with. I think Sir Massey Lopes sent Mr Merson specially to settle the Water question – perhaps you have a record of this arrangement. I believe about this you complained to Sir Massey Lopes about your Water Supply & he tackled Mr Martin about it.

It seems that no matter how many times John turned his quota of water towards Shaugh Lake, it would not be long before he had to do it all over again. A month after the last affair, Mr Martin is found to be really digging his heels in, leaving John to report to his directors, to once more include the absence of water from Lee Moor. He begins by saying,

I had a long chat with Captn Bray yesterday afternoon re Water – he says Mr Martin has instructed him that no water must be sent our way until their supply exceeds their demands – he admits that there is really no scarcity of Water – but that their works are growing so much that in the future they will require all & more Water Summertime than their present source can supply. So there you have the whole thing in a nut-shell as it were – Mr Martin will repudiate your claim for Water in Summertime unless you put the screw on him through Sir Massey Lopes & I feel confident that if you appeal to him he will see that you have an ample & sure supply – if the works were mine I would at once appeal to Sir Massey. If Mr Martin is not stopped he will pinch all the Water in the district – it is time for someone to tackle him. The overflow of the big Lee Moor Pond is going into other Ponds below – Mr Martin has received no provocation from your employs they never meddle with the Water Supply...

Just two days later John wrote:

I have been to Maristow today & have seen Mr Fenton in regard to your Water Supply from Lee Moor, he says he has seen the agreement that was entered into by the late Lord Morley & Sir Massey Lopes – 14 or 15 years ago - & his impression is that you were to have all the Water you require from that time forward & the Lee Moor people to have the remainder – he is going to look up the affair - & will write to Captn Bray today requesting him to turn on our full supply of Water immediately. I hope to be in a position in a day or two to advise you that the Water is again coming along all right.

The agreement John was referring to, was in fact made thirteen years earlier, on 30 August 1893 between the Right Honourable Sir Massey Lopes and Thomas Martin of Treverbyn Plympton, the Metropolitan Life Assurance Society, Joseph Travers Smith of Throgmorton Avenue London, and the Right Honourable Albert Edmund Earl of Morley. An extract from the Lease reads:

During the continuance of the term granted by the said indenture of the First of February One Thousand Eight Hundred and Eighty Nine to supply to the said Sir Massey Lopes or other the owner or owners for the time being of the Clay Works in the Parish of Shaugh formally part of the settled Estate of the said Sir Massey Lopes and his and their tenants of the said Shaugh Works from the Pond at Lee Moor Clay Works in accordance with the covenant in that behalf contained on the part of the said Earl of Morley in the said indenture of the Twenty Ninth Day of August One Thousand Eight Hundred and Ninety Three a corresponding quantity of Water to that which has hitherto been supplied to the said Clay Works at Shaugh namely not less than such a quantity of Water as will flow through a Hatch Thirteen and a half inches wide placed in the Shaugh Works Leat raised One Inch and a Half with a head of Water of at least Six Inches at the back of such Hatch.

Provided that in the event of the supply of Water to the Pond for the use of the Lee Moor Clay Works being Diminished by reason of exceptional drought the supply to the said Clay Works shall be correspondingly diminished.

And it is hereby agreed and declared that during the continuance of the said term granted by the said Indenture of the First of February One Thousand Eight Hundred and Eighty Nine the yearly rent of Twenty Five Pounds payable by the Lessor under the said Indenture of the Twenty Ninth day of August One Thousand Eight Hundred and Ninety Three so long as the said Water shall be supplied shall be payable to and received by the said Thomas Martin.

Seven years later, drought, and Mr Martin, were causing the Shaugh Lake captain to fret. He complained to the Board that the long spell of dry weather was beginning to have disastrous effects on clay washing and there had been no water at all to haul sand for nearly two weeks. John also complained that Martins had been up to their tricks again by turning off quite three-quarters of Shaugh Lake supply. Now with his dander up, John strode off again to Maristow to get Mr Fenton involved once more, from whom a letter arrived on Mr Martin's doormat telling him to put the matter right and he would be there at Lee Moor Pond to see it was done. John and Mr Fenton arrived there and met Captain Bray who was ordered to turn in two-thirds of Shaugh Lakes supply immediately, but as he did so, he complained that he thought it unfair whilst the dry weather lasted, but Mr Fenton would have no nonsense and watched until the demanded quota flowed free.

The captain's job was certainly a full one; at one time he was in a quandary as to what to do about boring on a piece of land who no one knew for sure to whom it belonged. It was apparently claimed by Sir Massey Lopes and Mr Strode. It did not seem to matter who owned the acreage, John was sure it was included in the WBB lease and had been boring there on and off for many months. He wrote to his directors with fighting talk saying that, if the land belonged to Mr Strode, he should put his fist up and fight for it, and prove that it was his.

In the meantime, John is a little concerned about the results of his borings, not being able to be kept away from prying eyes. People went there purposefully to watch him and his men at work and, whilst there, could see the nature of the material brought up from the depths of the bore. Even Mr Selleck of Dartmoor China Clays whose land it bordered, spent time there nearly every day watching proceedings.

After some thought on the matter of the land's ownership, John set about investigating who it really belonged to. He spent time seeking out tenants who paid rent to either claimant, to try and get an answer to the problem. He already knew that the Martins rented shooting rights over Shaugh Moor but not the parcel of land in question. His answer came when he bumped into Sir Massy Lopes' retired gamekeeper who assured him that the land belonged to the Strodes of Newnham. After all the uncertainty of whose land it was, there was not enough quality clay there worth bothering about.

With all the trials and tribulations the works' captains faced, it seems that when it came to their value to the company, they were thought very little of, especially by one particular director. This was confirmed in the director's disrespectful and belittling words to John in the New Year of 1919. When replying to John and his two foremen's request for a pay rise (one of the men was John's son, Howard, the other his nephew, Samuel), the letter read:

We duly received your letter & letters from Samuel & Howard dated the 25th inst. We have given the matter our careful consideration and we shall be pleased to pay your salaries in future as follows, Yourself £3.15s.0d, your Son & Nephew £3.0s.0d each which we hope will be satisfactory to the proper proportion of this advance may be made retrospective from October last and the rest from the 1st Jan.

We think it right to remind you that these three salaries in the ordinary way, would be divided by two, because there being only two small works one Foreman Manager at each would be quite sufficient. We are nevertheless pleased to pay the salaries as above in view of our long pleasant business relations with the family of Skidmores. We would also remind you that in regard to two comparatively insignificant little China Clay Works, the work of Management is a bagatelle a plaything compared with work done by manual labourers.

With regard to the delay in coming to this decision, for which we are sorry, we would remind you that Messrs Martin Bros, inform us that they had not advanced the salaries of their Foremen nearly so much as we are now proposing to advance yours and we would like also to point out that these little China Clay Works have up to the present time, proved un-remunerative to us, not from any fault of your Management.

We shall be glad to receive a line from you saying if you are satisfied with our proposals and also one from Samuel & one from Howard to the same effect.

In another letter, one director displays his feelings to another concerning the contents of the Skidmore letters. It can only be guessed at that the words were from the more caring Mr C.D. Blake:

The tone of the Skidmore's letters is rather more truculent than I like, but I think we ought to forgive them for seeing that their patience has been 'sorely tried' it is not surprising that they are dissatisfied and unhappy.

I would like to pay Samuel & Howard Skidmore £3 per week, even if that that is rather more than they are asking for and if it is less than they are asking for I would like to pay them the additional sum. I have long been living on only two meals a day and would gladly relinquish one of them rather than let Samuel & Howard Skidmore suffer want or be rendered unhappy in consequence in any injustice on our part.

As regards to John Skidmore I am not surprised at any value set by him on his own service, for he has long suffered from megalomania, but I like him nevertheless and he possesses a good deal of ability, therefore I would like to satisfy any reasonable request by him for an increase of salary. In view of Samuel & Howard increase, I think John's should be increased to the same proportion or even a little more if he pressed for it.

About nine years before the little episode of wage negotiations were settled, Wigford Works had again become redundant. The twenty-one year lease was spent and WBB felt it was not worth renewing. But having updated the works at Shaugh Bridge in 1893 whilst working the Wigford Sett, they had the convenience of it transferred in 1901 on to the new twenty-one year Lease of Shaugh Lake.

What remains of the system can be seen shrouded in bramble, fern and young trees of various kinds. Concrete pillars, looking oddly out of place, sit among the labyrinth of round pits, square pits and water channels as if waiting for the modern age to arrive. They were erected in the late 1950s to carry a press deck for compressing liquid clay into a solid state, but the development never fully materialised on account of a place at Shaugh Lake being preferred at the very last moment. The press system was not going to be operated by mechanical compression but by gravity, with the clay flowing down from a concrete tank built specially for the operation situated higher up in the woods on West Down.

On the other side of the Plym, right in the V of the confluence where the Plym and the Meavy converge, where all the seasons are equal in beauty, where people picnic, play and wander at leisure, are the shadowy ruins of an old iron mine. What remains to be seen today, after being abandoned and left to the mischievous hand of man and the ravaging moorland elements for well over one hundred years is quite surprising.

On today's maps, it is merely marked 'Mine Disused', on earlier ones the words Ferro-Ceramic

Pipeline to Shaugh Bridge.

Inspection tank in North Wood.

Concrete tank in the wood on West Down.

Grassed-over mica dam in the wood.

Disused launder above round primary tank.

A slurry feeding tunnel from the primary tank.

Wooden pin-hole system.

Furnaces of the kiln.

Steps to the kiln and tanks.

Iron mine adit beside the Meavy.

The ironworks wheel pit.

Mine was attached to it. But in its working days, it was Brogdon, named after the man who initiated its beginnings. The term 'ceramic' here derives from the fact that, whilst extracting the iron ore, it was necessary to delve cave-like to follow the lodes through a huge amount of foreign material in order to gain access to the iron ore. This over-burden was in places soft and growan-like, similar to kaolinisation, and mostly stained red with iron oxides. As one can see there are no waste heaps here, for this material became a valuable by-product, being utilised by the management and made into building bricks. It was because of the mine's dual-production, that the term 'ferro-ceramic' was attached to it after its demise.

Today for the interested or inquisitive to ponder over, the two walls of the brick kiln remain. This structure was about 55 yards long over 9 feet wide, and in one place, where a quite splendid hawthorn tree now grows, the walling on both sides is still about six foot high. Here the well-constructed stonework of the rebates that carried the brick-baking floor can still be seen.

Inside the ironworks brick kiln.

There is no mention of the kiln in a letter written in 1874 by Thomas Gregory to C.L. Radcliff, the Massey Lopes land agent at the time, yet its clearly drawn on an Ordnance Survey map printed ten years later in 1884. Thomas, a mining engineer, had been asked to look over the mine with a view to reopening it. The letter opened by saying: 'Agreeable with your instructions of the 10th, I have inspected this Mine and for my assistance took with me one of the Miners from our Iron Mine.' Thomas found that in places the ore had been, as he put it, taken away, but in other places where it was thought that iron could be found, he said they broke very good ore, which appeared to be going down in a satisfactory manner towards D. on the plan. He went on to say:

> *To work this Ore in an economical & Mine like way, it will be necessary either to drive up the South Adit at E' (this would have been the adit near the building clearly marked 'Smithy' on the old map), 'or put up a Water Wheel with pumping gear attached and clear up the old Adit at B. In this way the Mine can be kept drained very cheaply, and the Ore raised to the surface. The line of the old or former Water Course to the Mine over Shaugh Down from the Cad (Plym) can be traced & which I presume is available for such purposes as may be required at the Mine.*

Ruins of the blacksmith's shop.

The adit at B is just a few yards up the Meavy from the ruins of the kiln. The roots of an oak tree now entangle the mouth of this adit like the tentacles of an octopus around its prey. A lot of children come to play at this beauty spot so, for safety reasons, a grill has been placed across the entrance barring any access.

To place a little more belief in the mind of Mr Radcliff, that the mine was worth reopening, Thomas Gregory wrote:

I am assured by old Miners who worked here many years since, that the Mine was in good Ore at the bottom of the shaft B but the then enormous price paid for carriage of the Ore together with the low price of the same, was the principal cause of suspension at that time & not for the want of Ore.

Thomas went on to tell, that trial pits to the south of the workings whilst the mine was in operation were not, in his opinion, sunk to the required depth to prove the existence of the Lode and it is very possible they are not even on the main line of the lode. The mine must have been assessed at some earlier date, for Thomas finished his letter by saying:

I cannot for a moment entertain an opinion that the Ore is exhausted & the Mine worked out. Deeper sinkings are required, therefore the Shaft should be sunk and open new levels at D see plan, or resume the South deep Adit at E – possibly the erection of Water Wheel at A will be found the cheapest & quickest mode to develop the Mine in length & depth, where I have no doubt the lodes will be found of Equal value which will yield a large & profitable output of Ore for a long time to come
    I am Sir
    Your Obedient Servant
    Thomas Gregory.

Among a few other features of interest to see in relation to the mine are the two shafts marked on the old map of 1884, now either collapsed or filled in. Both can be found quite easily by climbing up on to the higher ground above the two adits. On the slopes of the depression above the adit beside the Meavy, can be found growan the material mentioned earlier. The likes of this material, that is here stained red with iron oxide, along with quartz and perhaps with a little added mica, purchased cheaply from the china clay works on the other side of the Plym, could well have gone into the kiln for making bricks; after all the conglomeration holds the same substances that William Phillips used at Lee Moor.

Near the remains of the kiln, as one approaches it from the wooden footbridge over the Plym, there is the substantial remains of a wheel pit. Running away from it, is its tail race, the feature that returned the wheel water back into the Plym from where it came from, curving around what could well have been three oddly-shaped settling tanks.

In 1928 the pit on Wigford Down came awake again, when the Selleck family of Dartmoor China Clay Co. decided to see if anything there was worth working. A great deal of money would have to be spent to get it up and running; the drying facilities at Shaugh Bridge were no longer available to the works, pumping and drying systems would have to be installed. To help in their quest they looked around for someone to join them in the venture, and that someone was a Mr Alfred Clough, a manufacturer of china and earthenware of the St Louis Works in Longton, Staffordshire.

This man must surely have liked what the Sellecks were offering for he soon leapt on to the china clay band wagon and formed the Brisworthy China Clay Company Ltd, with his family having the largest slice of the cake. Alongside him, sitting on the board, was Ashley Clough his son, C.B.H. Selleck and C. Selleck. Real ambition, total conviction, was the road to follow for this team. Mr Clough actually purchased the sett and bought land on Brisworthy side of the road where mica dams were built. Although a lot of enterprise was put into it, the venture soured within just a few years, no doubt brought on by the 1930s recession that put a lot of companies through a rough time and collapsed others. On 30 July 1935 the sett was offered to WBB by letter to the Chairman,

BRISWORTHY CHINA CLAY Co Ltd
PRODUCERS OF FINE CHINA CLAY

Directors	*Registered office:*
C.B.H.Selleck. Managing Director	*SHAUGH*
A.E.Clough	*CORNWOOD*
A.J.Clough	*S.DEVON*

The Chairman.
Messrs Watts Blake Bearn & Co
Newton Abbot Devon.

Dear Sir
We are desirous of selling the above Company, which comprises of a Lease and small works at Wigford Down once worked by your Company
We shall be glad to know it you are interested in this or alternatively in the purchase of the whole property known as Brisworthy which includes an extensive bed of clay on the opposite side of the road to Wigford Down

Yours Sincerely
For and on behalf of
The Brisworthy China Clay Co Ltd.
A.E.Clough. Director Secretary.

A letter went back to Mr Clough telling him that Mr W.J.V. Watts was away, but in order that he may deal with the matter on his return, WBB requested further particulars of the Wigford Down and Brisworthy properties, including the area, length of lease and the value, which they set upon the undertaking as sellers.

The answer to the request arrived in Mr Watts' in-tray two days later, on 3 August. It read:

> *...as requested in yours of the first inst, I am enclosing fuller particulars of the above Company. From the Lease dated June 1933 you will see that the Company hold 125 Acres (Wigford Down) with the option of working the Clay on Brisworthy (coloured blue on the map) This for a period of Seven Years renewable for Two more terms of Seven Years. As Debenture holder and Governing Shareholder I consider the Assets of the Company – the Lease small works, book debts of £250 and the goodwill to be worth £2000.*
>
> *Enclosed is a map of the property belonging to the writers father, Mr Alfred Clough of Longton, Staffs, from whom the Company Lease the Clay Land. I am authorised to ask for offers for this property, in case the buyers of the Company wish to own the land instead of renting it. This property is outlined blue and pink on the map and shaded in pencil. The fields shaded in ink belong to Mr Northmoor of Gratton, but have no bearing on Clay workings. There is also approx 9 acres of land by the railway at Leighbeer, near Goodameavy, with ways for laying a pipe track thither. This is ideally suited for a large works.*
>
> *There is an abundant supply of water carried in a leat from Legis Mires, for which Mr Massey Lopes charges a rental of £50 P.A.*
>
> *All this yields a yearly rental of £198 – 11s – 0p extra to the Clay rent and I think Mr Cough would consider £11000 to buy this.*
>
> *If this is of interest to you I shall be pleased to meet you at Brisworthy and give you more details.*
>
> *Yours Sincerely.*
> *Ashley Clough.*

Lack of a reply from Mr Watts was causing Mr Clough some concern; he was beginning to get a little impatient, sending two letters, one on 5 September, the other on the 11th. The first asked if WBB were interested in the offer made, the second requested the return of the lease map if they were not. On the same day that the second letter arrived, Mr Watts had returned to his office and by return of post, offered his regrets at not being available to answer the letters sent to him. He went on to say, that family bereavements had filled his time and he was ready for business again. He informed Mr Clough that the lease and map of Brisworthy were enclosed and gave the opinion that the figures mentioned concerning the value of the property for sale were too high. Although WBB had in the past wanted to delve under the soil of the Brisworthy fields, negotiations went no further and the matter was allowed to fade.

A gent who did take up the challenge, was one Edgar Jost, he inherited an established production system of a monitor (hose) washing method, two small presses and a diesel-fired static cylindrical drier. Introduced into this odd contraption were the clay slabs from the presses. After being cut into quarters, the slabs were placed by hand on shelves inside the large steel cylinder. Once loaded, a flame was directed through the slabs until the moisture content of the clay was low enough. The works was never a big concern, at most the manpower amounted to no more than nine, with four or five more men brought in when burden had to be removed.

For the duration of the Second World War, Mrs Jost took care of the works, until her officer husband came home again. Arthur Vanstone, 'Hardy' to all those who know him well, remembers Mr Jost as being a true gentleman, and Mrs Dunn (née Vincent) of Brisworthy Farm, tells of when, as a young girl, she would, on the half year, stroll over to the works to pay her father's rent. After receiving the money and signing the appropriate books, Mr Jost always gave her half-a-crown for sweets.

Arthur Vanstone who lived with his parents just a stone's throw away down at Cadworthy Farm, went to work at Brisworthy Clays more-or-less on leaving school in 1944 and stayed until the place closed in 1969. Arthur remembers seeing the bore-hole scars of Mr Clough's explorations whilst assisting drilling in the Brisworthy fields close to the works. He recalls that there was some very good clay found there, and would have no doubt suited the needs of any clay producer.

It is ironic what life brings along or, is thrown spitefully into your path. The Josts, who had two children, a boy and a girl, were developing the business with expectations of the son taking it on in the future. He was already a young man studying mining, when further education in the field took him to Australia. Whilst there one day, assisting surveying, the team was caught out in a storm and the young man of just 21 was struck by lightning and killed. Arthur, who told me the story, could not say for sure whether the tragedy was the reason behind the sale of the works to ECLP.

An ex-soldier who was an extraordinary success in the industry, was Mr Claude Pike. While still serving in the army, the young Captain on account of family business connections, was invited on to the Board of WBB. On his release, after hostilities were over, he became a full-time director, and, in less than twenty years, he was the Company's Chairman, succeeding W.J.V. Watts who retired.

Claude Pike's father was a Westcountryman from Belstone, the tiny village situated in the very northern edge of Dartmoor, not far as the crow flies from Okehampton. He was an engineer by trade and moved about the country working on various enterprises owned by C.D. Blake. Eventually the travelling ceased and he settled in the Yorkshire town of Castleford to run one of his employer's potteries. This is where Claude Pike's boyhood school years were spent, and his early academic work earned him a place at Cambridge University, where he studied Law. After gaining an MA and LL.M. he qualified to become a Lawyer. Along the way the Castleford Pottery fell into the hands of the Pike family and Claude became a director; also to join the Board was W.J.V. Watts the man who later invited Claude to the Board of WBB.

It is ironic that C.D. were also the initials of Mr Blake, a man who had the same passion, the same vigour in his quest to succeed, as had C.D. Pike. He was a businessman to be held in high esteem. Not only was he the backbone of WBB's early years, he also personally owned potteries in Castleford, Stoke-on-Trent, Bristol, and closer to home at Bovey Tracey. C.D. Pike's achievements with WBB earned him the OBE and, under his leadership, the Company won the Queen's Award for technical innovation in underground mining and, another, for its considerable exports. Added to that list, was a Countryside Award for recreating the landscape once quarrying was spent.

It can be said that the vast majority of the work that won these awards were earned within the area of ball clay production in the Bovey Basin, but his efforts put into the production of china clay on Dartmoor was the same. The clay works had to keep up with the times or be swallowed alive, like the fate of other companies on the moor.

But, with modernisation, out went the captain of the sett, the man who knew his works inside out and in came a manager, an under-manager and the so called section-manager, who relied heavily on the main man under him. He was the man who was never going to be promoted because of his local knowledge; the man who could have made an excellent captain. One such man was Leonard Vincent who lived for the clay works, ate and slept the industry. This Man (spelt with a capital M) was far too valuable to move upwards and out of the day-to-day running of the works. Often his ideas were not his by the time they reached those who paid his weekly wage, but became someone's just a little further up the promotional ladder. Yet he often put forward ideas that gave an advantage to production. He may not have been too articulate or wanted to wear a tie, yet he was liked and respected by those who worked with him.

Although Leonard and Claude Pike came back from the war and began their WBB careers about the same time, both were WBB men through and through. Whereas Leonard remained near the bottom of the ladder of importance, as far as his position in the company stood, he nevertheless watched the progress of his contemporary with total admiration and spoke of him as if he was a friend who occasionally dropped in for tea.

Unfortunately in 1983, Leonard, along with a group of other men of round about the same age, were asked to take early retirement. It was during a slump in the industry. Even with just one year to go before retirement, it hurt Leonard to have to go, but rather than seeing younger men go down the road to the dole queue, he agreed to finish and to stay at home in the Counting House above Cadover Bridge with his beloved Tryphena.

The following year Claude Pike stepped down as Managing Director, allowing his son, John, to take over the mantle, but another two years went by before he made vacant the Chairmanship. By the time he retired as a director, within that span of fifty years, the man had created an international company of the first order, with a series of mergers and acquisitions of overseas competitors, WBB became the world's leading ball clay producer, and was valued on the Stock Market at over £100 million, but, being at the mercy of the Stock Market speculator, the Company was open to losing control of its own steering wheel.

On Friday 28 June 1996, WBB held an official ceremony at their Park House headquarters to celebrate its re-dedication after the completion of its refurbishment. The result, the Chief Executive said, 'is a building of which we can all be proud – which stands ready to take WBB through into the next Millennium – and I thank Mr Claude Pike for agreeing to re-dedicate Park House as our group headquarters. In recognition of all he has done for our business, we have re-named the former Park House Board Room in his honour.' The Chief Executive went on to say 'Mr Pike's portrait now hangs proudly in the room overseeing our meetings and perhaps making sure that we lose none of the important fundamental values of WBB. Next time you are here in Park House, take a few minutes to have a look round and appreciate the new surroundings and working conditions – and I think you'll agree with me that we now have a building to match our aspirations for continued strong development in the future.'

Less than three years later, on 19 January 1999, it was announced that SCR Sibelco, a Belgian company, who already held 54% of WBB shares, would be making a formal bid to buy the remaining shares. On 1 October 2001 came the merger of two long-established organisations – namely Watts Blake Bearne with Sibelco Minerals and Chemicals. Park House that was supposed to have taken WBB through into the next Millennium, only just made it, for it now stands empty, the Board Room quiet with sadly no portrait of C.D. on the wall looking over any proceedings. So much for those supposedly sincere words spoken only three years before.

Mr Claude Drew Pike OBE, passed away on 2 October 2002 at the age of 87 following a short illness. His portrait was taken down off the wall of WBB Board Room and given to John, his son. It now hangs on the wall at Dunderdale Lawn his Newton Abbot home.

Claude Pike's era took China Clay production along the modern road with advanced systems and methods of achieving the end product. Of course along with this came the new way of China Clay extraction. Gone are the strakes, and the hand-held monitor. In is the water jet worked by hydraulics, that can be employed manually or automatically. Gone are the hand shovels and stone forks loading small trucks on rails. These days huge mobile plant aid extraction, taking off over-burden and ripping and pushing forward the clay to be

Taking off burden with today's machinery.

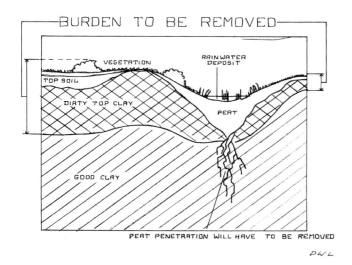

BURDEN TO BE REMOVED

VEGETATION

RAINWATER
DEPOSIT

TOP SOIL

DIRTY TOP CLAY

PEAT

GOOD CLAY

PEAT PENETRATION WILL HAVE TO BE REMOVED

DWL

Burden to be removed

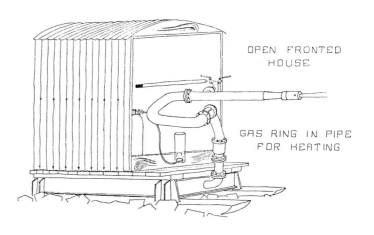

OPEN FRONTED
HOUSE

GAS RING IN PIPE
FOR HEATING

Obsolete hand-operated hose (monitor).

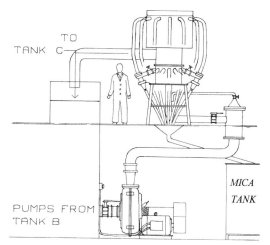

Hydro-cyclone separating system.

Modern hose house.

House seating and controls.

Clay slurry pump house. Bucket wheel on the skyline.

Bucket wheel that takes the sand out of the slurry.

Shaugh Lake mica dam and delivery pipeline.

washed. Huge pumps, bucket wheels and conveyor belts take the resulting contents of the clay stream out of the pit and on to where it is separated into its component parts to be refined. The clay stream is now put through hydro-cyclones that throw the clay, still in liquid suspension, into the settling tanks, whilst the mica is sent along the pipe track to the mica dams. Water from the settling tanks and dams is allowed to overflow, to be pumped back into the production line again.

Problems in production, whether electrical or mechanical, can be put right by repair, but geological or weather conditions are a different matter. These cause problems that can not be put right with a spanner or nut and bolt, a screwdriver or, a piece of wire. Weather, with its rain, ice and snow can ruin production for days, and geologically the various seams in the pit can spoil production when its unwanted contents get into the clay stream. These seams cost thousands of pounds to be removed. Sometimes, along with over-burden, waste material can aid the building of a mica dam, but more times than not this unwanted and troublesome material is discarded on to a waste heap.

Iced all over.

234

Environmental issues are of course of the utmost importance, and so are the operations of mining, wherever they may be. The spoil, the hole in the ground, and the waste heap, unsightly? Well it depends on what one determines unacceptable to the mind or the eye. For what the eye sees is what the mind interprets it to see. Like the impressionist artist, he or she paints or sculpts what their mind wants the end result to be. It is then left to the viewer to determine whether it satisfies or not. Opinions differ, they allow us the freedom of choice, whether in the mind or spoken. We say what we think, what is acceptable to some may be totally and utterly unacceptable to others. What the brain must always do is accept and appreciate the opposite thought. There are those people, adult or child, male or female, who may walk a few yards along the same street or country lane, at the same time, yet one will return to tell a story about what was there, while the other may say they had seen nothing. The latter individual's eyes were open but the mind did not take in what was there to be seen.

Industry very often does not have the privilege of choice. Whether raw materials are in the sea or in the ground, that is where they have to be prospected and delved out. Here I am talking about china clay on Dartmoor, on the fringe of the National Park. Gone are the undressed sky tips (except one), that let off their clouds of blinding dust when the wind blew. These are now controlled by safety regulations, dressed with top soil and seeded with grass and, in places, planted with shrubs and trees. Gone are the days when effluent was allowed to drift aimlessly into streams and rivers. We know a lot of regulations have been forced upon the industry to clean up their act, but the methods and enthusiasm in the way they have gone about it, should, I think, be respected.

The industry will argue that they have never courted controversy, but that controversy has come to them from those who have not agreed with their colonising parts of the moor. Here one must remember that it was at first the landed gentry who gave the industry the licence to work the land, even people as high up the ladder as the Prince of Wales. Even the man who wrote the following words: 'I commend Dartmoor to the regard and protection of all who desire to preserve the unspoilt and ancient land, old when the hut dwellers built their homes, now older but unchanged,' condoned the progress of china clay extraction. This was none other than R.H. Worth, the man who searched for and found china clay at Red Lake on the Erme, for one Charles Cottier.

In 1951 Devon County Council allowed ECLP to industrialise an enormous area of land, with planning permission to work for clay right up the Shell Top and Penn Beacon. It meant another one thousand acres being eaten out of the moor. This was done knowing that in only a few months Dartmoor was going to be designated a National Park. The Dartmoor Preservation Association were incensed that no one had the slightest chance of stating their opposition to such an enormous allocation of land. The situation prompted urgent action and right away a letter was written to Parliament and the Minister concerned asking for a Public

Inquiry into the principle of the planning application. As a result of the request, there was a local inquiry into the whole affair. Even more daunting was the fact that the china clay company also applied to have the opportunity to search for clay right up to the forest boundary, taking in another five square miles.

The first inquiry, to have taken place at Plympton St Mary R.D.C. offices, was, much to the disappointment of the DPA, postponed at the request of the clay company.

The DPA, in drawing up their plan of attack, decided that much of the area under dispute should be exlcuded from their primary concern as it had no planning permission on it. They also thought that their worries for Shaugh Moor, Wotter Common, Blackalder Tor, and Headon Down, should not be brought into the argument, as they were already despoiled. By now the DPA had strong allies standing alongside them in their determination to fight, including the National Park Commission, the Council for the Preservation of Rural England, the Ramblers Association and the Cornwall River Board (who were concerned with the threat of river pollution).

Seven long years were to go by before the matter was settled. With five days of wrangling at the enquiry the DPA were pleasantly surprised with more than a partial victory in their hands. Their argument had stemmed the flow of extraction into the 1557-foot hill peaked by Shell Top, and stopped it on the 950-foot contour.

1961 brought more fretting for the DPA when the Cholwich Town prehistoric stone row and circle was being threatened by china clay workings. ECLP wanted, or needed, to place a waste heap on the site. The stone row and circle was, of course, a Scheduled Monument. Samuel Row described it in his *Perambulation of Dartmoor*, published in 1848, as:

...this venerable monument of antiquity has been lamentably despoiled within the last few years, but the line can still be traced to the extent of upwards of seven hundred feet. The stones are placed erect, at intervals of from three to six feet; at the northern extremity is a sacred circle of five yards in diameter, formed of six stones. The line nearly north and south; the highest stone is about six feet. A much larger stone was removed a short time since; this is described as having been twelve feet high, and was therefore probably a Menhir, similar to others on the moor.

In 1912 William Crossing says 'in a field called Great Hill, is a fine single stone row, over 230 yards in length, with the remains of a circle at the N.E end. In a wall on the slope above is a large stone that may once have served as a Menhir.' Forty years later Mr Worth counts the same amount of stones in the Circle 'which is 18ft internal diameter. The row which is 700ft long although imperfect in places, is a well-marked row, and some of the stones are larger than ordinary.' The Menhir above the Monument, spoken of by Rowe and Crossing, would have by the time Mr Worth put pen to paper, disappeared as the Cholwich Town pit grew wider.

Like the menhir, the row and circle were not spared, sacrificed when the Ministry of Works waved goodbye to compulsory preservation and allowed ECLP to do what they felt they had to do. Archaeologists were permitted to examine the site before its burial and they found more than three dozen debris-filled sockets in the ground where other stones in the row would have originally stood, no doubt pulled out to occupy other uses. Another intriguing find, through pollen analysis, was that the stones were set up in an oak wood clearing, where before the monument's construction, some sort of cereal was grown.

The DPA wrote of what they saw as a disaster:

We have lost this battle, the power and influence of big business rendered the case for saving the Stone Row a virtually hopeless one from the start. The Minister refused even to hold a Public Inquiry; he came down in favour of the Clay Company's application to destroy the Stone Row on the basis of an extraordinary one-sided argument, most ludicrously set out in his decision letter (where nobody could refute them) so the Stone Row and Circle – scheduled Ancient Monument – will be obliterated under a mountainous heap of clay spoil, which the Clay Company could have sited harmlessly on the lower ground had they chosen to accept some additional cost and effort. The Company is a fabulously wealthy concern, with Directors in high places. It would have been a pleasant gesture, and in the long run a wise one, if as a slight return for all the wealth it obtains from Dartmoor, this very powerful Company had decided to spare the Stone Row.

Spoil heap that swallowed the stone row.

A foot note to the DPA wording reads: 'The professional archaeologists are frail reeds in a case like this. One of them advised the Ministry and County Council that the obliteration of the stone row need not be opposed, provided an accurate record was made of it first! No wonder Sir Richard Livingstone often said that specialists are like safety matches: they will only strike on their own box.'

Another casualty of waste tipping was an enclosure surrounding five hut circles. The site lay on Shaugh Moor beside the old Cadover-to-Cornwood road this time the culprits, with permission, were Watts Blake Bearne.

Like in life, mishaps occur at any time and anywhere, some with nigh-on calamitous consequences. An earlier and much smaller Cholwich Town waste heap, not so long after the Aberfan disaster, slipped down across the fields eventually stopping short of the ancient house and farm of Cholwich Town.

One Christmas whilst WBB's works were quiet at Shaugh Lake, the mica dam overlooking Cadover Bridge, broke out, all for the sake of one hand not knowing what the other was doing. The man on stand-by duty, came on to the works to pump out the pit after a heavy downpour, not knowing that certain doors in the production line had been left open for maintenance work to be carried out during the holiday shut down. Once the pit pump was started the water by-passed the usual production line when it reached the open doors, eventually finding its way to the mica dam. When the water met the top of the dam wall, it seeped out over, gradually eating the wall away until a mass of soup-like mica cascaded down over and across the public highway trapping a woman in her little Morris Minor, before pouring into the Plym.

A little more devastating was when Portworthy Dam went out in the late 1960s; a calamity waiting to happen. The overflow was where the problem lay, a design that was not, with hindsight, man enough for the task it was employed to do. It was successful for quite some time, but the more material that arrived, the higher and heavier the dam got. Increased pressure on the culvert and overflow's re-enforced concrete trap system, caused the huge mass to push its way through. Millions of tons of grey mica slurry met the water of the Tory Brook. Now, with the two flows coupled together, the volume crashed down through the beautiful tree-clad Newnham Park taking along with it anything in its path. The torrent bloated the usually gently-flowing brook into a slurping, slopping snake-like river that spread its width as it poured its contents on to low lying fields. Mr Tom Willcocks, just one of the few that remembers the incident, tells of how it flooded parts of Colebrook and, in particular his hardware shop and outbuildings.

Sometimes blunders can be quite frightful, but thankfully for Watts Blake Bearne they are of rare occurrence. In 1999 a local archaeologist told of a fine ox-bow lake on the course of the Plym above Cadover Bridge. His findings can be seen in a booklet concerning the preservation of certain parts of the moor where WBB and ECC International had the right to work for china clay. Yet all with the little lake is not well for it was despoiled, and not naturally through the river finding its own way down the valley, but by a huge machine, a D8 traxcavator. Allegedly, a junior manager of WBB, in the course of conversation with a River Board man of little status within that organisation, together agreed to use the D8 to straighten the course of the river. Heated disapproval followed, heads were shaken in disbelief, and voices raised in frustration more than anything, except for the rage vented on the junior by his manager who was given a severe dressing down. The consequences of this foolish fiasco was that the flow then filled the fish-loving pools further downstream with sand and rubble and anything else the river pulls along with it. The only good to come from it is that sand martins now excavates the machine-made bank for their nest.

Fishing lake that was a clay pit.

Model boat pond that was a clay pit.

No matter how much the China Clay Industry on Dartmoor is disliked by the protesting preservationist and environmentalist, its presence will leave a mark forever. Like everything man has touched on the moor, the artefacts we see all around us are the signature of man's labour. Menhirs, stone rows, circles, kisvaens, cairns, barrows, hut circles and enclosures, all from prehistory, still stand to remind us of man's times on the moor. Crosses, inscribed stones of all sorts, clapper bridges, artificial rabbit burrows, vermin traps, gate post, sheep leaps and sheep creeps, dried leats and running leats, smelting houses, stamping houses with their associated mould stones, mortar stones and caches. There are granite tram lines, granite sleepers, apple crushers and apple presses and all shapes and sizes of granite troughs. All remain with us to tell the story of our past, and so will the china clay industry leave something for our minds to ponder over and recall that it was once here and gave employment to thousands over the years.

Already the scars of its past are part of the landscape we enjoy for our leisure activities. The old railway track to Red Lake is there, where the walker and cyclist finds it almost effortless to view the inner character of the moor, where the everyday rush of urban life can for a while be forgotten. Just off the road above Cadover Bridge, on Wigford Down, are the disused china clay pits which now give pleasure to the angler and model-boat enthusiast. The pipeline track that runs down through the woods on higher slopes of West Down, allows a wonderful stroll that provides fabulous views. Once down at Shaugh Bridge are the fascinating remnants of old workings. Many of these remains are now being preserved for our future, to ponder over and enjoy.

After many years of fretting over whether they would or wouldn't, the year 2001 placed a broad smile on the face of the environmentalists, for that was the year when WBB Minerals and Emerys relinquished planning permission within the Dartmoor National Park. Shaugh Moor and the Blackabrook Valley were safe at last from desecration, Shaugh Moor is saved from being buried in waste and the Blackabrook safe from, as propaganda put it, a Super Quarry, 400-feet deep. As it turned out WBB's borings in this valley found very little to encourage further capital expenditure on the site. No one in this confrontation won the war, although there are those who would say they did. Indeed, while this book was being written Imerys have been excavating the area of the old Hemerdon China Clay Works.

With their fifty-year permissions to excavate almost up, the clay companies decided to jointly employ an independent consultant to undertake an environmental assessment of the areas concerned. With the conclusions reached, they were soon acted upon. In this day and age it was the sensible thing to do. Unlike in earlier years, when the companies supposedly rode roughshod over anything or, anyone, in the way, this situation was handled with diplomacy. The companies could well have prolonged the agony for much longer if they chose to be awkward. They could have even taken their case to the Secretary of State, for a Public Inquiry, just to keep the protesters hanging on. Millions of pounds may well have been claimed for loss of revenue if permissions were refused. It seems quite clear to the level-headed, and to someone not interested in scoring points, that common sense eventually won the day, not for any one person, group, society or association, but for the National Park.